# Measure and Value

## *The Sociological Review* Monographs

Since 1958, *The Sociological Review* has established a tradition of publishing one or two Monographs a year on issues of general sociological interest. The Monograph is an edited book length collection of research papers which is published and distributed in association with Wiley-Blackwell. We are keen to receive innovative collections of work in sociology and related disciplines with a particular emphasis on exploring empirical materials and theoretical frameworks which are currently under-developed.

If you wish to discuss ideas for a Monograph then please contact the Monographs Editor, Chris Shilling, School of Social Policy, Sociology and Social Research, Cornwallis North East, University of Kent, Canterbury, Kent CT2 7NF, C.Shilling@kent.ac.uk

Our latest Monographs include:

Norbert Elias and Figurational Research: Processual Thinking in Sociology (edited by Norman Gabriel and Stephen Mennell)
Sociological Routes and Political Roots (edited by Michaela Benson and Rolland Munro)
Nature, Society and Environmental Crisis (edited by Bob Carter and Nickie Charles)
Space Travel & Culture: From Apollo to Space Tourism (edited by David Bell and Martin Parker)
Un/Knowing Bodies (edited by Joanna Latimer and Michael Schillmeier)
Remembering Elites (edited by Mike Savage and Karel Williams)
Market Devices (edited by Michel Callon, Yuval Millo and Fabian Muniesa)
Embodying Sociology: Retrospect, Progress and Prospects (edited by Chris Shilling)
Sports Mega-Events: Social Scientific Analyses of a Global Phenomenon (edited by John Horne and Wolfram Manzenreiter)
Against Automobility (edited by Steffen Böhm, Campbell Jones, Chris Land and Matthew Paterson)
A New Sociology of Work (edited by Lynne Pettinger, Jane Parry, Rebecca Taylor and Miriam Glucksmann)
Contemporary Organization Theory (edited by Campbell Jones and Rolland Munro)
Feminism after Bourdieu (edited by Lisa Adkins and Beverley Skeggs)
After Habermas: New Perspectives on the Public Sphere (edited by Nick Crossley and John Michael Roberts)

Other Monographs have been published on consumption; museums; culture and computing; death; gender and bureaucracy; sport plus many other areas. For further information on Monograph Series, please visit: http://www.wiley.com/WileyCDA/Section/id-324292.html

# Measure and Value

edited by Lisa Adkins and Celia Lury

Wiley-Blackwell/The Sociological Review

Editorial organisation © 2012 The Editorial Board of the Sociological Review
Chapters © 2012 by the chapter author

BLACKWELL PUBLISHING
350 Main Street, Malden, MA 02148–5020, USA
9600 Garsington Road, Oxford OX4 2DQ, UK
550 Swanston Street, Carlton, Victoria 3053, Australia

All rights reserved. No part of this publication may be reproduced, stored in a retrieval system, or transmitted, in any form or by any means, electronic, mechanical, photocopying, recording or otherwise, except as permitted by the UK Copyright, Designs, and Patents Act 1988, without the prior permission of the publisher.

Designations used by companies to distinguish their products are often claimed as trademarks. All brand names and product names used in this book are trade names, service marks, trademarks, or registered trademarks of their respective owners. The publisher is not associated with any product or vendor mentioned in this book.

This publication is designed to provide accurate and authoritative information in regard to the subject matter covered. It is sold on the understanding that the publisher is not engaged in rendering professional services. If professional advice or other expert assistance is required, the services of a competent professional should be sought.

First published in 2012 by Blackwell Publishing Ltd

*Library of Congress Cataloging-in-Publication Data*

Measure and value / edited by Lisa Adkins and Celia Lury. – 1st ed.
  p. cm. – (Sociological review monographs ; 8)
  Includes bibliographical references and index.
  ISBN 978-1-4443-3958-1 (pbk.)
 1. Social sciences–Methodology.  2. Social sciences–Research–Evaluation.  I. Adkins, Lisa, 1966–  II. Lury, Celia.
  H61.M4825 2012
  300.72–dc23
                                              2012012469

A catalogue record for this title is available from the British Library

Set by Toppan Best-set Premedia Limited

Printed and bound in the United Kingdom

by Page Brothers, Norwich

The publisher's policy is to use permanent paper from mills that operate a sustainable forestry policy, and which has been manufactured from pulp processed using acid-free and elementary chlorine-free practices. Furthermore, the publisher ensures that the text paper and cover board used have met acceptable environmental accreditation standards.

# Contents

Series editor's introduction  
Chris Shilling  1

Introduction: special measures  
Lisa Adkins and Celia Lury  5

A flank movement in the understanding of valuation  
Fabian Muniesa  24

General Sentiment: how value and affect converge in the information economy  
Adam Arvidsson  39

The changing lives of measures and values: from centre stage in the fading 'disciplinary' society to pervasive background instrument in the emergent 'control' society  
Helen Verran  60

Transactional politics  
Evelyn Ruppert and Mike Savage  73

Dirty data: longitudinal classification systems  
Emma Uprichard  93

The economy of social data: exploring research ethics as device  
Ana Gross  113

Measuring the value of sociology? Some notes on performative metricization in the contemporary academy  
Aidan Kelly and Roger Burrows  130

Measure, value and the current crises of sociology  
Nicholas Gane  151

Notes on contributors  174

Index  177

# Series editor's introduction

## Chris Shilling

This is the first of two *Sociological Review Monographs* to focus on methods and values; issues that played a central role in the writings of the founding figures of the discipline and have come increasingly to preoccupy a subject suffering in recent years from a pronounced loss of confidence. If our present concern with methods and values can be associated with what Mike Savage and Roger Burrows (2007) have referred to as a 'crisis of empirical sociology', the classical sociological interrogation of these issues, in stark contrast, was bound up with the bold establishment of sociology as a distinctive science possessed of its own identity. This journey from disciplinary confidence to crisis sets the scene for the important task that Lisa Adkins and Celia Lury have taken on in bringing together this set of original papers that address some of the central dilemmas facing the discipline today.

The classical sociological focus on *methods* was necessary for a discipline seeking to go beyond and liberate itself entirely from philosophical models of *homo clausus* preoccupied with how individuals could 'reach out' from their enclosed minds to gain knowledge of the world beyond them (Elias, 1978). In this context, the discipline was confronted with the need to adopt and develop techniques that would generate reliable interpretive as well as statistical and comparative data. This step was vital if sociologists were to transcend controversies surrounding the possibility of acquiring knowledge, and concentrate their energies instead on the analysis of research findings. It was a step also commensurate with the wider public acceptance of a discipline dedicated to the possibility of cumulative progress.

The classical sociological concern with *values* was just as necessary if the discipline was to explore a modern Western world in which norms associated with the consolidation of social orders in traditional societies seemed no longer to 'fit' the rationalized, differentiated nature of the new secular industrial era. In this context, it is not surprising that, in addition to guiding the accumulation of theoretically informed knowledge of social existence, one core feature of sociology would turn out to be a sustained search for alternative sources of meaning and significance that could inform individual actions *and* provide a basis for understanding collectivities. Having embarked upon this search for individually, interactionally and collectively created norms, it did not take a great visionary leap to recognize that sociology was itself involved in the instantiation, or at least the consecration, of value (Turner and Maryanski, 1988).

In dealing with matters of method and value, moreover, the founders of sociology recognized that these were *interrelated* phenomena. This was evident in how Weber (1949), following his engagement with the writings of Rickert, discussed the problems generated by the value-bound researcher, value-relevant topics of research and the possibility of value-neutral methods of research (Bruun, 2001). It seemed, at the very least, that the most basic conditions associated with measuring social entities and gathering data on social actions, institutions and trends was bound up with attributions of significance effected by the researcher. This was evident not only in Weber's own deliberations on the empathetic demands associated with *verstehen*, a method that validated the existence of the interiority of social subjects, but also in its valorization across sociological analyses. It was manifest, for example, in disciplinary concerns with the ethics of the metropolitan personality, the pre-contractual bases of social contract, and the challenges associated with seeking to illuminate and explain (without performing a reductive analytical violence upon) elementary human beliefs and practices through the employment of methodologically generic 'social facts'.

Traditional methods such as those derived from the Weberian and Durkheimian traditions of research were enormously successful in helping to consolidate a new academic discipline that was oriented toward establishing and interrogating the valued sphere of 'the social'. As the discipline developed, however, its methods came under increased scrutiny over such issues as the distinctions it posited between facts and values, the objective and the subjective, the researcher and researched, and whether the methodological frameworks sociology constructed effected an ethnocentric distortion of the subjects of their investigation. Influential critical publications such as C. Wright Mills' 1959 *The Sociological Imagination* and Alvin Gouldner's 1970 *The Coming Crisis of Western Sociology* highlighted further something of what was at stake in the relationship between the methods and values of sociological research, insisting that the discipline was bound inextricably to the values of social classes and groups and needed to acknowledge its implication in power relations.

During the latter decades of the twentieth century, traditional sociological approaches to these issues confronted an even more fundamental challenge from writings influenced by postmodern and poststructuralist philosophies that heralded 'the end of society' and called into question the validity of *any* set of methods or values based upon conceptions of normatively integrated collectivities or subjects. As the century closed, the more constructive of these critical interventions wrestled with the consequences of how methodological purchase could be gained during an age in which the proliferation of information meant there was no 'outside' to the flows of data in which we were ensconced (eg Urry, 1999; Lash, 2002).

Sociology may rarely have been short of intra-disciplinary announcements of crisis, but the cumulative impact of these developments generated a sense among many that what may have seemed in retrospect to be a period of relatively 'normal' social science was coming to an end (Kuhn, 1962). Focusing on the loss of confidence in its own identity, together with the huge profusion of data from a period Thrift (2005) refers to as 'knowing capitalism', Savage and Burrows (2007, 2009) captured the spirit of this insecurity in pointing to 'a world in which commercial forces predominate; a world in which we, as sociologists, are losing whatever jurisdiction we once had over the study of the "social" as the generation, mobilization and analysis of social data become ubiquitous' (Savage and Burrows, 2009: 763).

This latest *Sociological Review Monograph* addresses core features of the present crisis in method and value. Individual papers explore the threat that transactional data poses to the expertise of sociologists, the capacity of apparently benign and 'proper' ethics procedures to alienate data from subjects, the harvesting of such alienated data for commercial and political purposes, and the tendency for sociology to replicate what C. Wright Mills referred to as the dualism between abstract empiricism and grand theory. These papers also, in many instances, seek to go beyond the discipline's current problems through fascinating analyses that demonstrate the validity of Lisa Adkin's and Celia Lury's editorial argument that 'questions of measure and value should not be confined to the sociological past'.

The editors' introduction to this volume highlights the many important contributions made by the analyses that follow, but without pre-empting their explication of these valuable analyses I want to mention two themes that reoccur throughout this volume and signify its significance to contemporary debates in and beyond the discipline. The first concerns the diverse ways in which measuring is itself a performative technique that creates values of various sorts. In the contemporary era marked by a major assault on public sector services, for example, modes of assessment ascribe values to institutions that can result in their restructuring. Methods are political. The second concerns the very fate of sociology as a subject. While the collection and analysis of vast data sets may indeed be eroding the lines between sociologists and other professions, this can be seen as expansion of sociological consciousness and an acceleration of that 'double hermeneutic' analysed by Giddens (1984) as much as it can be viewed as a threat to the sociological profession. If this broader consciousness is focused upon measurement, moreover, perhaps this reinforces the historic importance of the discipline as the provider of *theoretical* sensitivities and sensibilities. At a time when funding bodies responsible for postgraduate training in the social sciences in the UK and also beyond are seeking to promote increasing levels of methods training, perhaps there is an equally strong case for re-stating the far wider founding ambitions of the discipline. We should perhaps be wary that the current focus on methods does not turn into 'methodolatry'; the debilitating pursuit of ever more 'sophisticated' techniques of data collection or manipulation at the expense of sociological ideas, theories and imagination (see the concerns expressed by Weber, 1949; Mills, 1959; Gouldner, 1965).

The *Sociological Review Monograph* series consists of collections of refereed papers and could not continue without the goodwill, advice and guidance of members of the Board of the Sociological Review, and of those anonymous referees who assess and report on each of the papers submitted for these special editions. I would like to thank all of those involved in this process, especially Liz McFall, Rolland Munro, Denis Gleeson, and also the editors of *Measure and Value* for having produced such a stimulating and interesting volume.

# References

Bruun, H.H., (2001), 'Weber on Rickert: from value relation to ideal type', *Max Weber Studies*, 1(2): 138–160.
Elias, N., (1978), *What Is Sociology?* London: Hutchinson.
Giddens, A., (1984), *The Constitution of Society*, Oxford: Polity.
Gouldner, A., (1965), Enter Plato, New York: Basic Books.
Gouldner, A., (1970), *The Coming Crisis of Western Sociology*, New York: Basic Books.
Kuhn, T., (1962), *The Structure of Scientific Revolutions*, Chicago: University of Chicago Press.
Lash, S., (2002), *Critique of Information*, London: Sage/TCS.
Mills, C.W., (1959), *The Sociological Imagination*, Oxford: Oxford University Press.
Savage, M. and Burrows, R., (2007), 'The coming crisis of empirical sociology', *Sociology*, 41(5): 885–899.
Savage, M. and Burrows, R., (2009), 'Some further reflections on the coming crisis of empirical sociology', *Sociology*, 43(4): 765–775.
Thrift, N., (2005), *Knowing Capitalism*, London: Sage/TCS.
Turner, J. and Maryanski, A., (1988), 'Is "neofunctionalism" really functional?', *Sociological Theory*, 6: 110–121.
Urry, J., (1999), *Sociology beyond Societies*, London: Routledge.
Weber, M., (1949), The Methodology of the Social Sciences, (translated by E.A. Shils and H.A. Finch), Glencoe, Illinois: Free Press.

# Introduction: special measures[1]

## Lisa Adkins and Celia Lury

Issues of measure and value and the relations between the two have inhabited the heartland of sociology since its inception. This continues to be the case even as many commentaries on the current state of the discipline position sociology as occupying a space beyond such concerns. Thus, while many of the texts now recognized as constituting the sociological canon wrestled with questions of how and if sociology could be defined by its abilities to measure, record and document aspects of the social, and of how and if such measurements might be entangled with values, much contemporary sociological commentary appears to foreclose these questions by proposing that the organization of the contemporary world is beyond both social facts and social meaning (Law, 2004; Law and Urry, 2004).[2] But it is the contention of this Special Issue that questions of measure and value should not and cannot be assigned to the sociological past. This is so not least because while the contemporary world may not be organized and ordered via a separation of reality and representation, facts and values, the concrete and the abstract, and is not straightforwardly amenable to either the methods of positivism or constructionism, it is also one in which there is a proliferation of information, data, calculative and other research instruments, measurements and valuations.

The explosion in the production and circulation of information and data, including its archiving and manipulation, and the role of search engines, data mining systems, sensing systems, logging software and tracking and tagging devices has been noted by a number of writers (see, for example, Terranova, 2004; Thrift, 2008), but of particular significance for sociology is that much of this data is described as 'social' data, sometimes but not only produced in social media. In short, there is an ongoing expansion of the social by way of techniques of mediation, measurement and valuation. Commercial organizations, for example, now routinely produce customer and user profiles by assembling information on tastes, preferences, 'likes', ratings and lifestyles, which in turn are manipulated with powerful research tools for a range of purposes. Indeed, armed with such data, commercial organizations – rather than sociologists – are now held by some to be at the cutting edge of social analysis, defining, for

© 2012 The Authors. Editorial organisation © 2012 The Editorial Board of the Sociological Review. Published by Wiley-Blackwell Publishing Ltd, 9600 Garsington Road, Oxford OX4 2DQ, UK and 350 Main Street, Malden, MA 02148, USA

example, the most significant (and sometimes surprising) social measures for explanatory purposes (Burrows and Gane, 2006). For some observers these developments spell a potentially bleak future for sociology. Savage and Burrows (2009), for example, have argued that such developments are contributing to a potential crisis for the discipline, in part because they challenge sociology's claim to jurisdiction in the production and analysis of social data.

However, just as significant as any challenge to the professional expertise of the sociologist, are the implications of the properties and characteristics of such data for sociological practice. Neither inert in character nor contained or containable in any straightforward sense, data increasingly feeds back on itself in informational systems with unexpected results: it moves, flows, leaks, overflows and circulates beyond the systems and events in which it originates. As Matthew Fuller (2009) suggests, in digital cultures, data has an afterlife. Transactions such as sales, user subscriptions and memberships, for example, routinely generate by-products (an information surplus) that cannot be contained by the original coordinates of the transaction. Indeed such surpluses are routinely harvested and put to work in new ways, including in novel forms of value creation. In short, rather than being inert or dead, in the contemporary world data is brought into existence as active or 'alive'.

At the same time, as Adrian Mackenzie (2010) notes, contemporary shifts in data aggregation practices are disturbing established boundaries between commercial, scientific, technological and regulatory domains of expertise. He describes, for example,

> the proliferation of databases and software for managing clinical trials of pharmaceuticals, connecting medical records and biomedical research databases. [At present] clinical drug trials superimpose the procedures of regulatory approval processes, the logic of global pharmaceutical enterprises conducting international drug trials, the demands of clinical practice, the recruitment and organisation of cohorts of patients, the biopolitical statistics of epidemiology, as well as the organisation of high-throughput genomics research across institutional and commercial settings (Mackenzie, 2010: 3).

But as Mackenzie also notes, this is likely to change in the near future as Google, Microsoft and Oracle enter the domain of health care as the problem of aggregating scattered sources of personal health, information and medical records, as well as enrolling patients and patient groups in clinical trials of treatments and drugs is redefined as a major business opportunity.

Yet while such developments are undoubtedly significant, we propose that they should not necessarily be understood in terms of the removal of expertise from the professional sociologist. Instead, we suggest, they pose a series of compelling questions and problems for the discipline concerning the changing place of both measures and values in the contemporary world. If, for example, the work of measures is not merely to index or to represent, what else might measures and measuring do? How might the perceived multiplication of orders of worth (Stark, 2009) be linked to the contemporary proliferation of experimental measures? The contributions to this volume provide some answers to this question, by both reaching back into the discipline's history and pointing forward to new possibilities.

In the first contribution, Fabian Muniesa outlines a pragmatist attitude to value, or more precisely to valuation. With reference to the work of John Dewey, Muniesa takes issue with, on the one hand, what he terms a sociological understanding of value, which posits that value is a property that something has by virtue of how people consider it, and on the other, the view that value is a property that an object has as a result of its own condition, or is attached to it via its relation to other things. Such understandings, as Dewey observed, collapse the question of value into the 'modern "objective-subjective" bipolar scheme', positing value as either subjective or objective: as either a matter of reality or of representation. Yet in its focus on activity, process and practice in regard to both reality and ideas, a pragmatist take on value cuts through the subjective-objective controversy, and proposes instead a view of value as a practical action – as valuation, an activity that 'considers reality while provoking it'.

The adequacy and significance of a pragmatist view on value, Muniesa suggests, can be identified through the example of financial valuation. The recent global financial crisis serves as an important case in point. While often discussed in terms of bad or incorrect estimations of financial value, or as about the breakdown of a deluded system of beliefs and opinions, Muniesa argues these interpretations downplay the practical character of valuation at issue in the crisis. Both before and throughout the crisis, Muniesa maintains, financial valuation was neither objective nor subjective but a practical activity, and moreover an activity that was openly performative in character. At times this was a matter of turning things into objects of valuation, and at others about turning persons into subjects of valuation, but it was 'above all quite an activity'. Indeed Muniesa reflects that it is not just the recent financial crisis in which the pragmatist character of valuation as an activity is laid bare, but also in pedagogical materials focused on the valuation of corporate assets and securities. Such materials, Muniesa makes clear, emerged in roughly the same historical period as that in which the pragmatic philosophical discussion on the 'problem of values' was taking place: just as philosophical pragmatists stressed valuation as a practice, these materials grappled with valuation as an activity. Thus the Harvard case method of instruction in business administration shares a number of ideas with the North American pragmatist tradition, particularly in as much as this method aimed to teach not how to think but how to act.

But such pedagogical materials do more than show the connections between pragmatic philosophy and the emerging practices of financial valuation, for they also show how in processes of valuation the distance between values and their measures collapses. Specifically these materials show how, in the emerging practices of valuation, processes of measurement both ordered enterprises in a manner that made them amenable to valuation, and created value, notably by enabling the capitalization of businesses, through that very process. Financial valuation did not seek to devise finely tuned devices to map or measure features of businesses in relation to external measures of value, and nor did they seek to interpret or give an opinion on the value of a business. Instead, in the operation of the activity of valuation the appraisal of the characteristics of something in terms of its value and the setting of that thing for the purpose of making it valuable merge together, and 'become two aspects of the same act'. It is in the *practices* of valuation then that measures and values merge, or rather become two aspects of the same phenomenon.

In Muniesa's account then, valuation as a practice links up measures and values in a seriously consequential way, not least because the value obtained in the valuation of finance is capitalization. In his interrogation of Dewey's 'flank movement', Muniesa thus not only compels us to think of value as an activity rather than a thing, but also shows how this activity is itself a source of (economic) value. Moreover, in his claim that Dewey's 'flank movement' has particular relevance for today's financialized reality, Muniesa implies that a pragmatic stance towards both measure and value is both useful and necessary for understanding and engaging with the contemporary world.

Following Muniesa, Adam Arvidsson explores the activity of valuation in relation to practices of branding, focusing specifically on the emergence in the contemporary economy of techniques for the measurement of what he calls General Sentiment. Such a development, he suggests, enables a stabilization or becoming objective of affective value. To support this claim he puts forward a historical account of the rise and decline of labour time as the principal measure of productivity in capitalist economies, pointing to the importance of a range of technical, accounting and managerial processes for the internalization and subdivision of productive processes by firms. Such processes, he suggests, provided the basis for the creation of standardized productivity in such a way that contracted labour time could become its measure. The legitimacy and efficacy of such historical measures is being undermined, however, Arvidsson argues, by a number of contemporary developments including, notably, the socialization of production, and the increasing strategic importance attached to so-called 'intangible assets' including innovation, flexibility and branding. As he notes, the production of such assets often occurs outside the formal boundaries and control of single organizations and sometimes, as in the case of branding, builds on the activity of non-salaried actors such as consumers and the public at large. Furthermore, the creation of value in this way typically employs resources, such as communicative and social skills, the value-creating potential of which are poorly related to the quanta of time in which they are employed.

While such developments do not mean that measures of labour time have by any means 'disappeared' or 'no longer count', they are, so Arvidsson claims, increasingly being supplemented by alternative measures of value, including metrics of consumer affect. Exploring the proliferation of such metrics, he asks 'what does it mean for affect to become public and assessable?' and answers that it means that it can be represented independently of the specific idea to which it is linked. Such a possibility arises, he believes, in the context of the remediation of affect brought about by the restructuring of the public sphere associated with the rise of consumer culture. Here Arvidsson draws on the ideas of Gabriel Tarde relating to 'mental communion', and also the development of new measurement devices that are able to create a new general equivalent against which specific manifestations of affect can be evaluated regardless of the concrete ideas or representations to which they are tied. This is what he calls General Sentiment. Here then, as in the practices described by Muniesa, the appraisal of the characteristics of something – in this case brand equity, in terms of its value and the setting of that thing for the purpose of making it valuable, merge together and, to repeat Muniesa's revealing phrase, 'become two aspects of the same act'.

There are a number of other points that might also be drawn out from Arvidsson's contribution that have a relevance for the volume as a whole: the intensive force of numbers that is captured in measures of sentiment; changes in the distribution and media of metrological methods and related shifts in authority; the opportunities afforded for methodological innovation of large data sets; and – the point with which he concludes – the importance of whether and how the new large data sets that are now being created can be deployed in ways that can be rendered ethical, in the sense of being open to public, political deliberation, even as the nature and organization of the public is being reconstituted. And here, we would want to note that a number of other sociological commentators on measurement and value have focused precisely on this issue in the past. So, for example, Desorisières shows how the administrative production of statistics has, from its very origins, been forced to combine 'the norms of the scientific world with those of the modern, rational state, which are centred on the general interest and efficiency' (1998: 8). As he argues, 'creating a political space involves and makes possible the creation of a space of common measurement, within which things may be compared, because the categories and encoding procedures are identical' (1998: 9).

Helen Verran's contribution to this Special Issue directly addresses these matters, with specific attention to the uses of number in relation to processes of political deliberation. In her contribution, Verran describes a shift in policy eras; a shift that is linked to the emergence of science as a service industry, and the growth of a market in scientific expertise. This shift, she suggests, is fundamental to the move from a disciplinary to a control society. To instantiate this shift she compares two policy interventions, separated by only a few years, in regard to the rehabilitation of the Snowy River in Victoria, Australia. In the first policy era, measure and value are brought together in the numbering practices of professionals, that is in the practices of scientists, technicians, sociologists and others. The latter carry out this work usually invisibly, but diligently and rigorously, in the epistemologically accountable ways with which natural and social scientists are familiar, that is, through scientific trials that can be assessed in terms of validity, reliability and representativeness. In the second era, however, the trials are organized differently; the implications of this shift, so Verran argues, is apparent in the different ways in which numbers are rendered (ac)countable.

In the first era, Verran argues, measures and values are brought together through their linkage in numbers that are established as indices of actual and projected river flow. As she notes, the capacity of such numerical indices to extend beyond the here and now in which they are initially secured, requires work to be put in, work on the part of the river, government and scientists. This work is what Latour (2000) describes as the scientific work of 'extension in time', that is, the work of ensuring the adequacy and verifiability of the calibration of metrological tools, and their traceability inside and – crucially – outside particular trials. It is described by Desorisières in relation to the specific case of statistics in terms of a costly investment – of technical and social forms – of objectifying, of 'making things hold' (1998: 9). Verran herself observes that even if such work is put in, things to do with the here and now are 'always floating off [as rivers do] in one way or another, leaving policy, implementation, and evaluation in a shambles'. However, there is a sense in which, for Verran, the possibility of a 'shambles' does not – and should not – undermine the epistemological principles at work in the first era she describes.

In relation to the second era, though, she is more concerned. In the particular case she discusses, the scientific trials deployed involve the use of 'a physical model'; specifically, a model of the river-reach in a huge sound box in the grounds of a nearby university, what was described as a 'mobile' river-bed. Importantly the model could be visited by 'members of the community', who could watch the flow of water under various simulated conditions, indeed who could become experimenters themselves. They could simulate a flood and see what would happen to the surrounding environment, a representation of their own locality. The results from these modelling exercises were 'workshopped' with scientists from the biological sciences and lists of requirements assembled. Groups of children and local volunteers were formed to plant and tend the natural habitat; feedback from local meetings was incorporated; and policy recommendations were provided. For Verran, the trial involves the use of numbers created as indices in relation to a set of values that were specifically created to be traded; values in *potentia*, as she puts it, to be bought and sold 'in the environmental interventions services market' (see also Thrift, 2008).

The major problem Verran identifies in such practices is that the numbers are created as ephemeral products, designs for intervention; to be purchased, not as indices, but as symbols. Such symbols, she says, will not endure, since 'no institution is going to put resources into maintaining [them]'. Rather, she argues, they will inevitably come to be separated from their constitutive materialities, and, as a consequence, cannot provide an enduring foundation for policy. In short, the (social) scientific validity of trials in this second era is undermined for Verran as a consequence of the fact that its measures and values are not provided with 'extension in time'; they do not objectify or make things that hold.

One question we, as editors, want to pose, however, is whether and how the endurance of (social) scientific measurement, value and participation described by Verran as characteristic of the second era can be provided in new ways? It is a question we think it is important to ask since, as well as dangers, there are opportunities for sociology in this period of experimentation with measurement and value, including those that Verran identifies herself. These include the opportunity for: new kinds of interdisciplinary work; the development and support of indices (and symbols) that relate to people-place-things; new kinds of engagement with different kinds of publics and users in the doing of knowledge; and the use of a wider range of criteria, including perhaps relevance and efficacy, alongside accuracy and validity. Perhaps, in short, there is something to be gained for sociology from a period in which there is an explicit and knowing politicization of measurement and valuation?

This question returns us to the issue of a possible politics or ethics of measurement, an issue raised not only by Arvidsson but also by Evelyn Ruppert and Mike Savage. In their contribution to this volume, focused on the case of the 2009 British MPs' expenses scandal, Ruppert and Savage directly consider the question of whether and how transactional data has the potential to provide the basis for a politics (and also, although more indirectly, consider what kind of politics might support – or make durable – the analysis of transactional data). The case on which they focus is one in which one form of political accountability, that of the scrutiny of the expenses claimed by MPs by a public body, namely the parliamentary Fees Office and the Department of Finance and Administration's Green Book, was found wanting, and was uncovered as such by investigative journalists. But while Ruppert and Savage recognize that the ensuing scandal could be represented as a classic instance of a political exposé, in which journalists 'represent' the interests of the public, they focus instead on the way in which the case opens up an alternative: the potential for public engagement.

As Ruppert and Savage note, the initial form in which this information was made public, that is, as a leak, made use of the 'traditional muckraking journalistic model' in which the activities of 'scurrilous individuals' are exposed. But rather than accepting this description of the process of publicization, Ruppert and Savage develop an alternative account by drawing our attention to some unusual features of this process, including, notably, the requirement by those who leaked the information that data relating to the whole population of MPs be made public, rather than only that relating to a few individuals. It is this insistence, Ruppert and Savage propose, that opened up the possibility for what they call a transactional politics. Such a politics has a number of features in their description. On the one hand, transactional data enables the interpreter to focus on activities or practices rather than elicited attitudes and views. Through this reorientation, they suggest, the distinction between what is deemed private and what is held to be public is being reconfigured (for further consideration of this issue see Gross below). But more than this, for Ruppert and Savage, the digital data at the heart of this case affords new analytical possibilities insofar as it can be deployed not only to examine standardized aggregate properties of the population in question, but also to explore the specificities of the activities of the individuals in a variety of relations to each other.

Here, Ruppert and Savage identify the importance of the use of relational visualizations to enable such forms of analysis. Indeed, they propose that in the emerging transactional politics of which this is but one example, forms of knowledge based on textual and numerical manipulation will come to acquire a new significance as visualizations enable individualized and discrete measurements to be highlighted. In the use of such visualizations, they suggest, the interpreter can be given the capacity to move from individuals to aggregates and back again. Such techniques are different from standard social scientific forms of measurement that deal with pre-given categories and statistical means and averages, and rely upon practices of representation and representativeness that are neither required nor significant in relation to complete data-sets such as that of MPs' expenses. Since it is the individual and not a group or category, or the one person in relation to an average, that is made visible it is, Ruppert and Savage suggest, becoming possible for individuals to constitute their own categories, that is, to become 'a thing that scales' (Holbraad and Pedersen, 2009).

Of course, the kinds of claims to knowledge that might be produced in such a dynamic and open-ended politics of measurement raises questions and concerns, including the issues of endurance identified as fundamental by Verran: that is, by what means, if neither by (state-) scientific extension in (space-)time nor by market competitiveness, will the categories and values of this emerging social scientific politics of measurement be shared and sustained? What or where are the new ontological forms that will support this emerging politics of measurement? Here it is worth observing that Ruppert and Savage suggest that it may be possible for the labour involved in the analysis of such data to be carried out by amateurs as well as professionals, volunteers as well as paid analysts. Indeed, they hypothesize that the possibility of a new politics of measurement may be linked to the formation of constituencies of informational gatekeepers, organizers and interpreters who may be only loosely or not at all attached to formal organizations and companies. This is a way, they suggest, that such a politics has the potential to engage publics at an ontological level rather than simply eliciting their opinion in a politics of representation (see also Latour and Weibel, 2005; and Marres, 2007). It is also, we suggest, a way in which such transactional (real-time) data may come to acquire its own, specific, forms of social and technical endurance. Whether this will really be the case is, of course, an empirical question, to which it is probably too soon to give an answer, but is nevertheless important given the contemporary transformations in the public sphere. As Desorisières points out in relation to statistics,

> The construction of a statistical system cannot be separated from the construction of equivalence spaces that guarantee the consistency and permanence, both political and cognitive, of those objects intended to provide a reference for debates. The space of representativeness of statistical descriptions is only made possible by a space of common mental representations borne by a common language, marked mainly by the state and by law. (1998: 324)

Conversely, as he also says, the space of (post-)representativeness is important if 'one wishes to study whatever makes a sphere both possible and impossible' (1998: 325).

It may be, of course, that the contrast emerging here between an old and new politics of measurement is too sharply drawn, for the data analysis that underpins what Verran describes as the first era was never clean, but always dirty, as the chapter by Emma Uprichard makes clear. That is, the categories of social scientific analysis have always had an ontological complexity and instability. Uprichard begins by noting that longitudinal data analysis has a long history: over three centuries. However, in the last decade it has acquired a growing currency in large part because of the increase in public access to large-scale longitudinal surveys and the fact that longitudinal techniques have become more available in standard quantitative software packages. She further notes that in the pursuit of identifying trajectories in such quantitative research, classifications are typically tracked over time. However, as she is at pains to point out, most classifications change both in absolute terms – in that some disappear whilst others are created – and in their meaning. In other words, the work of extension in time of social scientific analysis has never been straightforward. There is a need therefore, she argues, to rethink how longitudinal quantitative research might explore both the qualitative changes to classification systems as well as the quantitative changes within each classification.

By drawing on the changing classifications of local food retail outlets in the city of York (UK) since the 1950s as an illustrative example, Uprichard presents an alternative way of graphing longitudinal quantitative data, so providing a description of both types of change over time. In so doing, she argues for the increased use of 'dirty data' in longitudinal quantitative analysis, by which she means data that has not been cleansed of classificatory change, since such data allows for both qualitative *and* quantitative changes to and within classification systems to be explored. Such a proposal challenges existing assumptions about the quality and type of data used in social scientific quantitative research and how change in the social world is measured in general by providing a new way in which the triple aims of such research – what has changed, how that thing has changed, and why that thing has changed the way it has – are brought together. This is, as she puts it, where the money is: 'Predicting changes and continuities to classifications – not to variables, but to polythetic types of cases – is what the global commercial enterprises, such as the large supermarket chains, insurance and credit card agencies, etc. are now doing with our quantitative data'. The point she makes to justify the need to address this issue is fundamental: namely that quantitative (and qualitative) data are always and necessarily manifestations of the processes involved in describing a changing object of study; data do not exist in a vacuum independent of our knowledge any more than the objects they describe. Such a recognition is certainly not new and this is why we do not want to draw a clear line of distinction between old and new politics of measurement, but we do want to suggest that it is only recently that these more-than-representational qualities of measurement are being mobilized in the social sciences (Thrift, 2000, 2008; Lorimer, 2005), or to put it more bluntly, that social scientists have become interested in getting their hands dirty.

Ana Gross suggests something similar as she considers the increasing association of economic value with entities and qualities previously disassociated from practices of valuation. The emergence of economies of vitality, that is, the harvesting of value from the qualities and capacities of life and living processes is one well-documented instance of this process (see, for example, Rose, 2006; Cooper, 2008). Thus Melinda Cooper (2008) documents how innovation and creativity in the bio and life sciences from the early 1980s onwards moved biological processes, or 'life itself', and capital accumulation closer together, a movement that, she argues, is thoroughly entangled in the project of neoliberalism. In her contribution Gross draws upon and extends this body of work, by insisting that the creation of value out of the qualities or capacities of living entities is not specific to the bio-sciences. Such value creation is also characteristic of the practices of social scientists, Gross claims, especially the practices of social scientists conducting empirical research with human subjects. Her point is that social scientific practices are implicated in a set of complex processes whereby the vital emissions of human subjects, including utterances, actions, opinions and interactions, are increasingly rendered economic.

To examine this process Gross describes the emergence of devices of social science ethics, especially those which relate to the regulation of contemporary sociological practice in the United Kingdom. Within this domain Gross pays particular attention to informed consent and anonymization principles, which she posits as participating in economic value creation in both social scientific and commercial research. Such devices do so, Gross claims, since they contribute to a conversion of vital emissions into data which is disentangled or abstracted from the human agency to which it makes reference, a process which in turn enables the circulation of vital emissions in regimes 'where they can be made commensurable . . . and rendered of economic value'. Informed consent devices, for example, frame social research transactions in market terms, specifically as consensual or freely chosen exchanges.

Yet while in market transactions the parties involved are recognized as already holding property rights over what is being exchanged, 'research or data subjects do not, strictly speaking, hold property rights over their personal data'. In this respect, Gross maintains, informed consent renders legitimate what would otherwise be an illegitimate detachment and transfer of what is normatively framed as the personal or the private into value regimes. In short, informed consent is a device that unleashes the economic potentiality of the private. Devices of anonymization also unleash such economic potential, and do so by erasing previous attachments and facilitating new appropriations of vital emissions, particularly in as much as they aid in the process of making such emissions more thing-like and hence amenable to ownership. To support this argument, Gross documents how devices of anonymization, devices which are usually understood as rendering research ethical, transform vital emissions from being singular and incommensurable, that is as attached to activities denoting personhood, to data that is equivalent, comparable, measurable and tradable. In short, anonymization devices frame vital emissions as thing-like and hence as amenable to manipulation, crucially including the creation of aggregates.

In her examination of ethics devices, and in particular in understanding such devices as economic, Gross therefore questions the idea that social science data is an unmediated expression and function of human agency, and argues instead that ethics devices equip human agency with the properties of autonomy and privacy 'so as to enable the extraction and manipulation of data'. Her contribution asks us to consider how the techniques and devices associated with social science measures are not only participating in the creation of an omnipresence of value and implicated in the folding of society into economy, but also how such techniques also enable and distribute particular forms of agency. More than this, and in a context of the potential crisis of sociology outlined by Savage and Burrows (2009), and especially the threat posed to sociology by the expansion of commercial social research, Gross's analysis alerts us to the fact that any such crisis should not be pitched as one in which social science research does not (or should not) participate in economic value creation, and nor as one which can be countered with recourse to more relevant methods (and less still by recourse to frameworks of ethical regulation). Instead, Gross's analysis alerts us to the fact that the shifts at issue in this so-called crisis involve an emergent political economy of social data, a political economy which demands that attention is focused not simply on the proliferation of social data, but also on 'devices which serve to articulate particular forms of property and value'. Moreover, Gross's analysis underscores the significance of asking just how social science may make knowledge claims in the context of the new politics of measure.

Yet social scientists are only just beginning to engage with this emergent political economy of data including the politics of measurement attached to it. This is so not least perhaps because, as academics, we feel that we are being experimented on, rather than with, as the case of the UK's Research Assessment Exercise (RAE) discussed by Kelly and Burrows illustrates. Locating the RAE as part of the increasing metricization of academic life, Kelly and Burrows lay out a detailed case study of the way in which the discipline of sociology has participated in the various attempts that have been made to measure the value of academic research in the UK. They focus in particular on the most recent exercise whose results were reported in 2008. Such an analysis they make clear is important not only because such evaluations are used to inform state funding allocation decisions in the UK, but also because the institutional arrangements and processes at issue in this exercise, and especially the relationship between measure and value that such arrangements enact, are fast becoming internationalized. And this is so even when state-sponsored measurement of research quality is not yet being used to determine the allocation of resources (notably in the case of the United States). More specifically, while state-sponsored exercises have measured and ranked research performance via a range of devices to distribute funding in the UK, commercial providers of data 'merely' rank research performance to indicate the supposed global standing of institutions and disciplines within them.

The key argument presented by Kelly and Burrows concerns the performative powers of such exercises. Thus, just as the processes of valuation Muniesa describes turn both things and persons into objects and subjects of valuation, so too do the devices and instruments associated with the Research Assessment Exercise. This latter is evidenced in how in the UK academic and organizational practices have been 'incrementally recalibrated in relation to the RAE'. Specifically, the mundane practices and processes of academic life (for example, recruitment, reviews, audits, restructures) are now lived through not only the exercises themselves, but also in 'institutional imaginings of what the future might bring'. Scenario planning for possible RAE[3] outcomes is, for example, now a routine feature of academic life in the UK. Kelly and Burrows demonstrate exactly how hard-wired this recalibration of academic and organizational practices is via a consideration of how a range of shadow metrics may be used to predict or mimic the outcomes of the latest research exercise assessment for sociology. More specifically they show how a relatively simple three-variable linear regression model – where the variables are size of submission, income from UK research councils per capita, and the percentage of articles published in the top quartile of the highest quality journals – may be used to produce a very similar ranking to that produced in the 2008 exercise. This finding is significant particularly in as much as a more qualitative process of informed peer review produced the 2008 rankings.

In establishing this 'agreement' between the long and complex deliberations between the peer review panel and the predictions of a three-variable linear regression model, Kelly and Burrows are, however, not suggesting that panels are a simple means of reproducing already established intellectual hierarchies. Instead, their aim is to raise a series of questions regarding the measuring of value, or as Muniesa would put it, valuation. One of these questions concerns the recursive implication of the complex qualitative and quantitative data assemblages (including impact ratings, journal rankings and citation scores) at issue in measuring the value of academic disciplines, while another concerns the performative powers of valuation in regard to mundane academic practice. As Kelly and Burrows put it 'although we sometimes comfort ourselves that . . . judgements of the value of our work . . . made by our peers still provides the basis for our position in the academic "league table", in actuality these judgements almost perfectly mirror a set of quite basic underlying statistical drivers of "quality".'

It is not only then that the more-than representational qualities of measurement raise a range of challenges for sociological practice, but that sociologists themselves are the objects and subjects of – and implicated in – such measures and measurements. Kelly and Burrows speculate that the entanglement of sociologists in such measures may be linked to the crisis being felt in the discipline. In his contribution Nicholas Gane asks us to consider the terms of any such crisis differently. Taking the challenge faced by sociology as a consequence of the explosion in the generation, mobilization and analysis of social data by commercial organizations, Gane suggests that the latter demands that sociologists must revisit the question of the promise of the discipline. This is the case not least because the threat posed by commercial sociology to the discipline is more than one of scale and powerful resources, but also one which questions the value and relevance of quantitative sociologies that centre on the production of data through techniques of measurement. Yet while Savage and Burrows (2009) locate such developments as potentially disastrous for sociology and for quantitative sociology in particular, Gane locates them more ambivalently, and does so by reference to the work of C. Wright Mills. Specifically, Gane observes that aspects of these developments are anticipated in *The Sociological Imagination* (1959), and especially in Mills' critique of the sociology of his day. Sixty years ago Mills argued that the discipline was caught between, on the one hand, a parochial empiricism concerned primarily with questions of method, and on the other, grand theory concerned with highly disembedded, abstract concepts. The former, Mills argued, confused what is to be studied with methods for its study and hence lost its grip on the problems of the empirical world, while the latter fetishized its concepts to the extent that theory outran any specific empirical problem.

Gane maintains that this double impasse of theory and method remains with us today. On the one hand, contemporary social theory is dominated by what he terms, following Ulrich Beck, a zombie canon, where rather than re-forged or invented anew, sociological concepts are drawn ready-made from the writings of a select body of thinkers. Just as the social theory of Mills' day fetishized the concept, so too does the sociology of the present. The latter 'blocks rather than exercises the sociological imagination because it starts with a meta-concept or process that is then stamped on every aspect of the so-called "empirical" worlds under study'. And just as Mills' grand theory is evident in the contemporary discipline, so too is an institutionally engrained parochial empiricism. Thus, in much quantitative (but also some qualitative) sociological research, ready-made methods and procedures take precedence over the specific qualities of the empirical world, to the extent that method determines the problems to be studied. The outcome is that many 'urgent and pressing events of our times barely feature within mainstream sociology'.

Indeed, Gane suggests, the continued operation of empiricism has contributed to an aversion to the analysis of events within the discipline. Such an event-adverse sociology, Gane notes, can never meet the criteria of adequacy set out by Mills, namely that of an imaginative discipline whose methods do not precede empirical problems but are determined by and unfold with them. Crucially, and understood in this Millsian light, the current crisis of measure faced by contemporary (and especially quantitative) sociology is therefore not necessarily constituted via the rise of external, resource-rich, commercial competition in the generation, analysis and mobilization of social data. Instead the crisis, such as it is, relates to deep-seated and institutionally engrained practices within the discipline, whereby the production of data through techniques of measurement is procedurally rather than empirically led, a practice which contributes to the production of data and measures which have little traction or relevance in the contemporary world.

In addition to allowing the current crisis of measure to be understood as both long-term and relating to factors internal to the discipline, analysing this crisis via the work of Mills also enables Gane to raise some suggestions for the reanimation of the sociological imagination. The zombie canon, for example, might be displaced via a renewed theoretical imagination; a renewal that Gane argues requires inventive conceptual work addressing the pressing empirical demands of the day. As such, a process of conceptual invention will necessarily also involve a renewed and reworked empirical sociology. For just as sociological methods should emerge out of, and in connection to, the complexities of the empirical world, Gane insists, so too should concepts. Thus, rather than static or abstract devices, concepts should be alive, open and on the move. Such a renewal moreover does not only involve conceptual invention, but a confrontation with a range of complex questions. These include questions regarding the value of measurement, and the value of a sociology that is not necessarily implicated in quantitative forms of measurement. Addressing such questions, Gane maintains, is vital if the promise of sociology is to be reignited.

So then, how could we not conclude this introduction by reflecting on the kinds of experimentation with value that we are witnessing. First, let us make it clear that we do not want to imply that we are seeing an unprecedented proliferation of modalities of measurement. As Jane Guyer (2004) among many others has argued, the expansion of capitalism did indeed involve struggles to impose commensuration and calculation of the ideal modernist type, that is, professionalized statistical skills, the use of standardized criteria, and the role of banks and other state-regulated institutions as the custodians and integrators of relevant transactional memories (Hart, 2001). However, it also witnessed the growth of a parallel architecture of disjuncture, including the building of dissonant and dynamic value scales, in which the terms of difference are accepted as partial transformations and indices of each other, with repertories of value always under re-creation. Nevertheless, we do want to suggest that a set of inter-related transformations is occurring in which linkages between value scales are being renegotiated, in ways that enable a multiplication of conversions, and that such transformations are fundamental to the current flowering of multiple orders of worth (Stark, 2009), as well as affording new kinds of intensive and extensive geographical and temporal reach for exchange. Such transformations, we suggest, are supported by the emergence of what we have already called spaces of more-than-representation (Rheinberger, 1997; Thrift, 2008; Lorimer, 2005). Our proposal is that sociologists should at least attempt to describe the specificity of such spaces, if not perhaps also themselves engage in the practices they make possible. This is so not least because of the opportunities such transformations provide for sociology to re-imagine itself.

So let us say a little about these more-than-representational spaces. The notion draws most evidently on Nigel Thrift's (2008) use of the term post-representation to capture the significance of practices in their more-than-human, more-than-textual, multi-sensory, happening actuality, but it also references not only Desorisières's attention to the 'space of representativeness' that has been fundamental in the history of statistics but also the sociologist of science Hans-Jörg Rheinberger's emphasis on the importance of a 'space of representation' for the doing of science (1997). At a very simple level, the recent emphasis on the post-representational has challenged the assumption of the importance of the symbolic over and above the responsive and the rhetorical dimensions of representation, and in doing so has complicated the terms of the politics and values of representativeness. Desorisières argues for the importance of analysing the place of statistical information in the public sphere in terms of a network 'of stabilized connections, of routinized equivalences, and words to describe them. It forms a language: that is, a discernible set of bonds that make things hold.... It is precisely this language that provides the reference points and the common meaning in relation to which the actors [of the public sphere] can qualify and express their reactions' (1998: 333). What Rheinberger adds to this helpful linking of measurement and value to the public is a framework for understanding experimental research systems in terms of the workings of 'co-ordinates of signification', rather than language alone. This is a way in which the agency of the operation of material traces or graphemes – symbols, indices and icons – can be acknowledged in experimental systems. In other words, Rheinberger's insistence upon the significance of the material-semiotic organization of a space of post- or more-than-representation is important for us since it provides a basis for exploring the social-scientific capacities of contemporary experiments in measurement and value in ways which do not presume the terms of representativeness or public debate.

The first and most obvious characteristic of such spaces that we can observe, identified by all our contributors, is that the values of the 'what' and the measurement of the 'how' are co-produced in such spaces; that is, not only is the 'what' that is measured a product of 'how' it is measured, but also the 'how' of measurement is a response to the 'what'. Such spaces are therefore not only performative. They do not simply involve a movement from the 'what' to the 'how', but are spaces in which (and to draw once more on Muniesa) the distance between the 'what' and the 'how' collapses. Second, we observe that in many cases the indexical and the symbolic are being combined in new ways in such spaces. Let us say a little more about this. A number of writers, from a range of different disciplines, have proposed that the importance of symbolic culture across societies arises because symbols allow humans to ignore most of a vast web of word-object and object-object indexical associations by using the shortcut of symbol-symbol relations to make and mark a specific associative path. Symbols, in this view, are powerful because of their virtual character, because they are shared, and because – in systems such as language – they are exterior to the individual human mind (Lenoir, 2008).

They are also powerful because they are central to the liveliness of culture as a result of their capacity to introduce movement through their use in metaphors.

The capacities of indices and icons have historically been limited in their capacity to move, or make movement, to enable inventiveness as Roy Wagner (1986) would say, by their dependence upon perception by individual minds, and their positional situatedness. But, as we and our contributors show, the ability of the indexical to enable (social) relations is being vastly extended through the development of diverse, iterative and automatic information processing systems, supported by memory systems with the capacity to support, extend and make intelligible indices outside the individual mind. So, for example, Parisi (forthcoming) describes the way in which the computation of urban data contributes to what she calls an algorithmic mode of planning defined by an extended apparatus of prediction, able not only to establish the condition of the present through the retrieval of past data but also to change these conditions according to data variations immediately retrieved from the environment. As she says, this cybernetic logic of control opens its mechanisms of value and measure to non-quantifiable conditions so as to capture qualitative changes before their emergence. This transformation, we suggest, is one of the sources for what Helga Nowotny (2002) calls the expansion of the present, a term that she suggests is characteristic of the post-environmental phase that we have entered today, but that we describe as the bringing into visibility of value latency across a range of domains of social life. That the terms of this expansion are contested is evident in the contributions to this volume, and is what is necessarily at issue for sociology, not least since this value latency emerges as inextricably tied to the social, however that is defined.

To say more about this emerging indexical or transactional politics then, let us focus for a moment on the example of changes in number and numbering. The remarkable capacities of numbers, as Verran describes them, are two-fold: they participate in processes of ordering and in representing that order as value. This dual role of number – ordering and valuing – is conflated in many routine everyday and scientific uses of number, in which both the order and value of numbers is given by the relation afforded by a fixed (external) measure, a metric, or unit of quantity, of magnitude. In such uses, numbers as symbols have relied upon numbers as indices in a particular kind of way, as apparently neutral, external markers of order and value in one. As Badiou puts it, 'What counts – in the sense of what is valued – is that which is counted' (2008: 2). In many contemporary uses of number, however, including in some of the examples described in this volume, ordering and valuing are being brought together without reference to an external measure, but rather by – or in – relations in which the performative capacities of number to order and value are combined in different ways. In this process, as our other contributors make plain, new kinds of liveliness are being introduced into culture. The implications of this liveliness for sociology are as yet unclear.

Indeed, as Ruppert and Savage suggest, the implications for sociological analysis of data-sets that have no 'outside' to which they might make reference are only beginning to be explored (see also Rogers, 2010). As noted above, such data resists being treated as a collection of numerically measured facts (or stand-ins for facts) that require working on to be brought to life by analysis. On the contrary, as lively and vibrant, constantly in movement, such data calls the distinction between data and analysis into doubt. Specifically, such data does not comprise a set of abstractions that attempt to model, represent or index aspects of an external or more real reality. Instead, and because such data concerns whole populations and is often continuously updated in real time, its properties render the demand that social data (meaningfully) represent or (quantitatively) index 'reality' beside the point. Indeed, in place of such demands, Ruppert and Savage identify the capacity, for relations to be established between an individualized entity and the population of which it is part, specifically for the individual to become its own category. One of the things that is interesting to us about this and of particular significance for sociology is that such spaces open up the possibility that 'quantitative' techniques can address the 'qualitative' dimensions of social and cultural life. Whether and how numbers can indeed capture qualitative values is the subject of much contemporary debate, including a number of the chapters included here: what we are pointing to is the importance of understanding the changing relation between icons, indices and symbols in spaces of more-than-representation for an appreciation of what is at stake in contemporary experiments with measure and value.

A further point concerns the general rather than universal nature of the experiments described by our contributors. As briefly noted above, Latour (2000) has proposed that the capacity of epistemic things (problems, measures, standards, facts, hypotheses) to endure (their extension in time) is relative to the circumscribed and well-defined spatio-temporal envelope of their network of production. What is interesting to us, however, for a sociology in the making is that in many of the measuring practices described here there is no aspiration to the spatio-temporal universalism of always and everywhere. Rather, the relative existence of epistemic things between never-nowhere and always-everywhere is not simply acknowledged, but reflexively operated in. So, for example, in many of the contributions to this volume, measures are not understood as external spatio-temporal coordinates of signification, that may be reproduced without modification elsewhere, but are participants in dynamic surfaces of coordinatization (Adkins and Lury, 2009).

In such coordinatized surfaces of more-than-representation, measures produce individualized objects or entities in terms of the properties of superimposition, dynamism and multiple relationality, the capacity to affect and be affected, rather than those previously characteristic of objects, such as those of substance, magnitude and externality. Such entities thus not only have the capacity to move in extensive time and space, but also to display singular values of individualized intensity: that they are self-reflexively general rather than universal in their making is what makes them lively.

For this reason, the question of participation, or the engagement of the public becomes crucial. Indeed, the nature and characteristics of partiality – of the taking part, or participation – or partisanship (Latour and Weibel, 2005; Rogers and Marres, 2002) rather than representativeness may thus come to be a crucial judgement of entities in relation to the use of measures in such spaces. In relation to partiality rather than representativeness, the dynamic composition of social scientific objects or entities in generalized (and generalizable) time-spaces becomes available for sociological analysis, in ways which make visible the ontological as well as epistemological commitments that are required for their specific endurance.

Reviewing these developments then, we suggest that in post- or more-than-representational spaces, experiments in measurement and value are helping to bring into existence an expansion of the social in terms of an apparent omnipresence of value that is linked to changing relations between the quantitative and the qualitative, the extensive and the intensive, representativeness and partiality. As we and our contributors are only too aware, this expansion of the social also raises questions about how to assess the validity, adequacy and efficacy of measurement in such spaces. It is thus both because of the opportunities and dangers that such developments pose that sociology must continue to put questions of measurement and value, of quantity and quality, of subjectivity and objectivity, at the heart of the discipline.

## Notes

1 According to the Crown Prosecution Service, 'special measures' are available to assist vulnerable and intimidated witnesses to give their best evidence in criminal proceedings. The special measures apply to prosecution and defence witnesses, but not the defendant. Special measures are available to defence witnesses in the youth court. It is also a status applied by Ofsted and Estyn, the schools inspection agencies, to schools in England and Wales, respectively, when it considers that they fail to supply an acceptable level of education and appear to lack the leadership capacity necessary to secure improvements.

2 It is worth noting that it is not only in the sociological canon that a wrestling with issues of measure and value is at play, but also in contemporary social theory. Thus in the latter we paradigmatically encounter attempts to overcome the schism between a sociological positivism and a sociology of meaning and interpretation, between on the one hand facts and their measurement and on the other values constituted in meaning systems. Indeed such an overcoming – often by a form of synthesis – has been routinely located as the key criteria of adequacy for contemporary social theory. Given the centrality of these issues of measure and value in both classical and contemporary social theory it is therefore striking that more recent social theory appears to have put such issues to one side.

3 Or REF, Research Excellence Framework, as it has been renamed.

## References

Adkins, L. and Lury, C., (2009), 'What is the empirical?' *The European Journal of Social Theory*, 12(1): 5–20.
Badiou, A., (2008), *Number and Numbers*, Cambridge: Polity Press.
Burrows, R. and Gane, N., (2006), 'Geodemographics, software and class', *Sociology*, 40(5): 793–812.
Cooper, M., (2008), *Life as Surplus: Biotechnology and Capitalism in the Neoliberal Era*, Seattle and London: University of Washington Press.

Desorisières, A., (1998), *The Politics of Large Numbers: A History of Statistical Reasoning*, translated by C. Naish, Cambridge, MA: Harvard University Press.
Fuller, M., (2009), 'Active data and its afterlives', available at: http://www.spc.org/fuller/texts/active-data-and-its-afterlives/ (accessed 6 June 2009).
Guyer, J., (2004), *Marginal Gains: Monetary Transactions in Atlantic Africa*, Chicago: University of Chicago Press.
Hart, K., (2001), *Money in an Unequal World: Keith Hart and his Memory Bank*, New York and London: Texere.
Holbraad, M. and Pedersen, M.A., (2009), 'Planet M: the intense abstraction of Marilyn Strathern', *Anthropological Theory*, 9(4): 371–394.
Latour, B., (2000), 'On the partial existence of existing and nonexisting objects', in L. Daston (ed.), *Biographies of Scientific Objects*, Chicago: University of Chicago Press.
Latour, B. and Weibel, P., (2005), *Making Things Public: Atmospheres of Democracy*, Cambridge, MA: MIT Press.
Law, J., (2004), *After Method: Mess in Social Science*, London: Routledge.
Law, J. and Urry, J., (2004), 'Enacting the social', *Economy and Society*, 33(3): 390–410.
Lenoir, T., (2008), 'Foreword: Machinic bodies, ghosts and para-selves: confronting the singularity with Brian Rotman', in B. Rotman, *Becoming beside Ourselves: The Alphabet, Ghosts and Distributed Being*, Durham, NC: Duke University Press.
Lorimer, H., (2005), 'Cultural geography: the busyness of being "more-than-representational"', *Progress in Human Geography*, 29(1): 83–94.
Mackenzie, A., (2010), 'More parts than elements: how databases multiply', available at: http://www.lancs.ac.uk/staff/mackenza/papers/mackenzie_database-multiples-sept2010.pdf (accessed 23 April 2011).
Marres, N., (2007), 'The issues deserve more credit: pragmatist contributions to the study of public involvement in controversy', *Social Studies of Science*, 37(5): 759–780.
Mills, C. Wright, (1959), *The Sociological Imagination*, Harmondsworth: Penguin.
Nowotny, H., (2002), 'Vergangene Zukunft: Ein Blick zurück auf die 'Grenzen des Wachstums'. In *Impulse geben – Wissen stiften*. 40 Jahre VolkswagenStiftung, VolkswagenStiftung: Göttingen.
Parisi, L., (forthcoming), 'The labyrinth of the continuum: topological control and mereotopologies of abstraction', in C. Lury, L. Parisi and T. Terranova (eds), *Topological Culture*, Special Issue, *Theory, Culture and Society*.
Rheinberger, H.-J., (1997), *Toward a History of Epistemic Things: Synthesizing Proteins in the Test-Tube*, Stanford, CA: Stanford University Press.
Rogers, R., (2010), 'Internet research: the question of method', *Journal of Information Technology and Politics*, 7(2–3): 241–260.
Rogers, R. and Marres, N., (2002), 'French scandals on the web, and on the streets: stretching the limits of reported reality', *Asian Journal of Social Science*, 30(2): 339–353.
Rose, N., (2006), *The Politics of Life Itself: Biomedicine, Power and Subjectivity in the Twenty First Century*, Princeton, NJ: Princeton University Press.
Savage, M. and Burrows, R., (2009), 'The coming crisis of empirical sociology', *Sociology*, 43(4): 762–772.
Stark, D., (2009), *The Sense of Dissonance: Accounts of Worth in Economic Life*, Princeton, NJ: Princeton University Press.
Terranova, T., (2004), *Network Culture: Politics for the Information Age*, London: Pluto.
Thrift, N., (2000), 'Non-representational theory', in R.J. Johnston, D. Gregory, G. Pratt and M. Watts (eds), *The Dictionary of Human Geography*, Oxford: Blackwell.
Thrift, N., (2008), *Non-Representational Theory: Space, Politics, Affect*, London: Routledge.
Wagner, R., (1986), *Symbols that Stand for Themselves*, Chicago: Chicago University Press.

# A flank movement in the understanding of valuation

## Fabian Muniesa

**Abstract:** The sociological understanding of valuation often starts with an idea of value as something that something has by virtue of how people consider it (that is, it is socially constructed, a convention, a social representation, a projection). At some point, however, analysis also often draws a contrast between this sort of appraisal and some other type of value that the thing may have as a result of its own condition (what it costs, how it is made, with what kind of labour, money and materials, what it is worth in relation to objective standards and fundamental metrics). Dissatisfaction with this binary approach has been expressed in various quarters, but the pragmatist contribution of John Dewey provides a particularly useful resource with which to engage with the subject. This article reviews some aspects of this dissatisfaction, with a focus on the pragmatist idea of valuation considered as an action. I discuss this idea in relation to financial valuation, referring in particular to early pedagogical materials on corporation finance elaborated in the context of the professionalization of business administration. Finally I elaborate on the usefulness of a pragmatist stance in the understanding of financial valuation today.

**Keywords:** valuation, pragmatism, corporation finance

## Introduction

Defending a pragmatist attitude in the study of value requires replacing the very notion of value with the notion of valuation.[1] In what follows I briefly discuss some aspects of John Dewey's call to do just this and contrast it with the notion of valuation put forward, in the same period, in corporation finance and business education, focusing in particular on the teachings of Arthur Stone Dewing at Harvard University. The aim in drawing this contrast is to help refine a contemporary pragmatist approach to valuation: that is, one that makes the distance between value and its measure collapse in an analytically constructive manner. I conclude with some reflections on the historical opportunity offered by what I call, after Dewey, a 'flank movement' for the contemporary understanding of valuation.

© 2012 The Author. Editorial organisation © 2012 The Editorial Board of the Sociological Review. Published by Wiley-Blackwell Publishing Ltd, 9600 Garsington Road, Oxford OX4 2DQ, UK and 350 Main Street, Malden, MA 02148, USA

## Pragmatism and the problem of value

In 1913, *The Journal of Philosophy, Psychology and Scientific Methods* (later to become simply *The Journal of Philosophy*) and, to a lesser extent, *The Philosophical Review*, initiated in their pages, at the request of the Executive Committee of the American Philosophical Association, a very interesting discussion thread on 'the problem of values' (Spaulding, 1913). One initial formulation of the problem goes like this: '[i]s Value (1) something which is ultimate and which attaches itself to "things" independently of consciousness, or of an organic being with desires and aversions, or (2) is it a characteristic which a thing gets by its relation to the consciousness of an organic being, or to an organic being with desires and aversions?' (McGilvary *et al.*, 1913: 168). One first, almost immediate, reaction to this formulation of the problem is by John Dewey: '[t]he formulation seems unnecessarily tied up with the idealistic-realistic controversy. I recognize that this complication has the advantage of preserving continuity in the discussions from year to year; yet it is possible that the questions at issue might, in the present juncture, be dealt with in the end more effectively if approached by a flank movement' (Dewey, 1913: 268–269). As would be made clear in further published exchanges on the problem, Dewey's 'flank movement' consists in a shift in subject matter from value (or values) to valuation, considered explicitly as an action.[2] Dewey writes for instance that

> [s]peaking literally, there *are* no such things as values. . . . There are things, all sorts of things, having the unique, the experienced, but undefinable, quality of value. Values in the plural, or value in the singular, is merely a convenient abbreviation for an object, event, situation, *res*, possessing the quality. Calling the thing a value is like calling the ball struck in baseball, a hit or a foul". (Dewey, 1923: 617, emphasis in the original)

Emphasis on the activity, process or practice of valuation rather than on value as something in itself was critical in Dewey's attempts at pulling the debate away from what he called the 'idealistic-realistic controversy'. Considered in the terms of the modern 'objective–subjective' bipolar scheme, the controversy quite fades away: to say of something that it is 'done' subjectively or objectively is less mutually exclusive than to say that it 'is' subjective or objective. Observed through the more classical angle of the philosophical debate on the reality of ideas, the controversy also dissolves to some extent: if reality is action and ideas are acts too (a fair summary of the pragmatist standpoint), then there is not a great deal in quarrelling about the difference.

After having observed that 'a value, in short, means a *consideration*, and a consideration does not mean merely an existence, but an existence having a certain claim upon the judgement to be formed' (Dewey, 1915a: 516, emphasis in the original), Dewey writes that

> the conclusion is not that value is subjective, but that it is practical. The situation in which judgement of value is required is not mental, much less fanciful. It is existential, but it exists *as* something whose good or value resides (first) in something to be

attained in action and (secondly) whose value both as an idea and as existence depends upon judgement on what to do. Value is 'objective,' but it is such in an active or practical situation, not apart from it. To deny the possibility of such a view, is to reduce the objectivity of every tool and machine to the physical ingredients that compose it, and to treat a distinctive 'plow' character as merely subjective. (Dewey, 1915a: 516, emphasis in the original)

Here, as in many other places in the discussion, Dewey rejects the bifurcation of value in favour of an understanding of valuation as some sort of performance.

But Dewey's 'flank movement' was difficult to establish, demanding in terms of its own clarification, and repeatedly confronted by dualism, not only in philosophical discussion but also, perhaps more fatally, in ordinary ways of talking. As he puts it in one of his more elaborate efforts of elucidation (his *Theory of Valuation*):

> [W]hen attention is confined to the usage of the verb 'to value', we find that common speech exhibits a double usage. For a glance at the dictionary will show that in ordinary speech the words 'valuing' and 'valuation' are verbally employed to designate both *prizing*, in the sense of holding precious, dear (and various other nearly equivalent activities, like honouring, regarding highly) and *appraising* in the sense of *putting a value upon, assigning* value to. This is an activity of rating, an act that involves comparison, as is explicit, for example, in appraisals in money terms of goods and services. The double meaning is significant because there is implicit in it one of the basic issues regarding valuation. For in *prizing*, emphasis falls upon something having definite *personal* reference, which, like all activities of distinctively personal reference, has an aspectual quality called emotional. Valuation as *appraisal*, however, is primarily concerned with a relational property of objects so that an intellectual aspect is uppermost of the same general sort that is found in '*estimate*' as distinguished from the personal-emotional word '*esteem.*' That the same verb is employed in both senses suggests the problem of upon which schools are divided in the present time. Which of the two references is basic in its implications? Are the two activities separate or are they complementary? In connection with etymological history, it is suggestive (though, of course, in no way conclusive) that 'praise,' 'prize,' and 'price' are all derived from the same Latin word; that 'appreciate' and 'appraise' were once used interchangeably; and that 'dear' is still used as equivalent both to 'precious' and to 'costly' in monetary price. (Dewey, 1939: 5–6, emphasis in the original)

Value can be understood as something that something has by virtue of how people consider it (how they personally like it, in particular), but also as something that something has as a result of its own condition and of its relation to other things (for instance, in relation to work or to money, or to any sort of standard metric). Valuation, in turn, refers to something that happens to something, and this happening can be a matter of consideration or of relation, or both at the same time. In this sense, the idea of valuation may be tackled in the same way in which the notion of signification is elaborated in pragmatism – that is, as an action.[3] It is interesting to note in this respect that, parallel to the discussion on valuation, John Dewey was also defending the theory of signification of Charles Sanders Peirce (Dewey, 1946). At that time, the 1940s, the pragmatist theory of signs had suffered from Charles W. Morris's influential interpretation of the 'pragmatic', supposedly based on Peirce (Morris, 1938). Morris famously introduced the 'interpreter' (that is, the person who, quite subjectively indeed, makes sense of a sign) as a key feature of the process of semiosis (Peirce's word for the action of the sign) and called 'pragmatic' (as opposed to 'syntactical' and 'semantic') the relation of signs to 'interpreters'. But, as Dewey suggests, 'one has only to read Peirce to see that Morris's account effectually splits apart the very subject-matters with which Peirce labors in order to provide an integrated solution' (Dewey, 1946: 87). He adds:

> The misinterpretation in question consists in converting *Interpretant*, as used by Peirce, into a personal user or interpreter. To Peirce, 'interpreter,' if he used the word, would mean *that which interprets*, thereby giving meaning to a linguistic sign. I do not believe it is possible to exaggerate the scorn with which Peirce would treat the notion that *what* interprets a given linguistic sign can be left to the whim or caprice of those who happen to use it. (Dewey, 1946: 87, emphasis in the original)[4]

## Financial valuation and the pedagogy of business

Did Dewey's 'flank movement' succeed? His call for a pragmatist approach to the study of valuation certainly resonates with more recent social-scientific vocabularies in economic sociology, in organization studies and the anthropology of economic exchange.[5] But the 'realist-idealist' syndrome sneaks into social-scientific discussions on value often enough to suggest that the fulfilment of the pragmatist ambition is still in question. Value as socially constructed, as a convention, as a collective representation, as a projection, a speculation or a point of view, cohabits with value as a problem of metrics in accounts of material conditions. The recent financial crisis provides an interesting test for this continuing cohabitation of positions. Some commentators propose that financial value was badly estimated and that incorrect valuation practices were followed, whereas others claim that the crisis is a consequence of a self-sustaining, delusive system of beliefs and opinions breaking down. The fact that valuation is a costly and irregular activity that brings value about (it is, very literally, a construction)[6] does not go unnoticed, but is neglected in favour of an exacerbation of the differences between what is objective and what is subjective. Yet, before and throughout the crisis, financial valuation was neither subjective nor objective: it was practical, and while this practice was sometimes a matter of turning things into objects of valuation, and at other times about turning persons into subjects of valuation, it was indeed and above all quite an activity.

Take, for instance, the notion of 'valuation' as it is used in financial professional practice. It means precisely that: to account for value (to 'consider' it), but in an active and practical manner, in which value is precisely formed for the purpose of business. The notion is meant to be openly performative. Valuation practitioners in finance may talk about valuation being smart or not, but they know, at the same time, that something (such as, for example, an asset) does not have the same value before and after it has been valued; that value depends on how valuation is done, when, by whom and for what purpose; and that to value is a highly creative process. The value of an asset is, so to say, entirely in their hands.

An interesting source for the understanding of the pragmatics of valuation in finance is the proliferation, in roughly the same period in which the philosophical discussion on 'the problem of values' was taking place, of pedagogical materials focused on business in general and on the valuation of corporate securities in particular. The distinctively North American world of which that discussion was a part was much concerned with valuation as a topic for business, capitalist enterprise and corporate finance. At the time the discussion mentioned above started (Spaulding, 1913), for instance, Walter Lippmann was getting his *Drift and Mastery* published: a book that mentions, among other topics deemed of interest to progressive opinion-makers, the development of graduate schools of business administration (Lippmann, 1914: 46–47). The Harvard Business School (that is, the Graduate School of Business Administration of Harvard University) had been founded a few years before (Copeland, 1958).[7] The professionalization of the North American businessperson was acknowledged to be a crucial issue, and valuation was considered as a (perhaps the most) relevant practical component of this businessperson's professional skills.

In Arthur Stone Dewing's *Financial Policy of Corporations*, for example, the personae required for 'the organization and establishment of the corporation as a going enterprise' were presented as follows: 'as business enterprise has become more intricate, especially when conducted under the form of the corporation, promotion has become correspondingly intricate, involving the co-operation of a specialized kind of entrepreneur ability and large amounts of capital. The former is represented by the promoter and the latter by the banker' (Dewing, 1920: 3).[8] The banker values the enterprise, in order to finance it; the promoter imagines the banker valuing the enterprise, in order to give the enterprise value. The profitable business enterprise springs from this interaction. Dewing writes that the investment banker's judgement 'is a matter of business intuition' and that he 'must feel, with extreme sensitiveness, the intangible atmosphere that surrounds every enterprise' (Dewing, 1920: 33). Valuation is about the investment banker and the entrepreneur imagining and sensing each other, simulating each other but also stimulating each other.

In further editions of his *Financial Policy of Corporations*, Dewing further clarified his take on valuation by adding new sections devoted to 'the problem of value': '[i]t may concern the business as a going enterprise; or it may concern the property employed in the business, both tangible and intangible. However phrased, further study of the financial operations of the business rests on an understanding of what we mean by the values of a business' (Dewing, 1941: 173). Dewing was not Dewey, of course, and, although he was probably convinced of the view that valuation is a 'practical' affair, he also subscribed to a psychological, individualistic ideal of valuation, compatible with a liberal, bourgeois standpoint:

> Value is subjective; it is based on individual human experience. Hence, when the individual tries to find an objective standard or criterion for his own personal values, he is confronted with endless confusion. Value changes from hour to hour; value is different according to the standards of experience and the standards of judgement. Consequently, when attempts are made to set up legal postulates to control economic value – such postulates as original cost or the cost of reproduction – nothing but uncertainty and contradiction results. In the end the test of value is pragmatic – where does the judgement of most men meet? (Dewing, 1941: 175)

One can recognize here elements of a sort of a mild pragmatism, a form of pragmatist thought in which the depth of the philosophical discovery is removed and replaced by a floppy idea of adventure in the face of uncertainty and courage after the failure of knowledge.[9] But it is nonetheless useful to observe some correspondence, some correlation between the pragmatist discussion on valuation and the progress of financial pedagogy.

These were, in any case, the kinds of things that were taught at the Harvard Business School, by Dewing and others, in the 1920s and 1930s. The Harvard Business School was also the site in which an important pedagogical device was developed in that very same period: the case method of instruction in business administration (Fraser, 1930, 1931; McNair, 1954). It would be probably going too far to say that the case method is, in essence, a pragmatist device, but it undoubtedly has some pragmatist aspects, or at least partakes of a number of ideas that connect to the North American pragmatist tradition. Dewing was again here at the forefront. As a Professor of Finance at the Harvard Business School he wrote, in defence of the case method, that education 'asks not how a man may be trained to know, but how a man may be trained to act'; that it 'deals with the oncoming new in human experience rather than with the departing old'; adding that 'power to deal with the new and power to think are pragmatically the same, even though logically the two expressions may not have the same connotation' (Dewing, 1930: xxii).[10] Note the distinct philosophical tone to his opinion of the content of educational knowledge in business: 'when one attempts to reach fixed and certain facts, not to say truths, underlying human action, one is confronted with an intricate and disordered heteronomy of happenings apparently devoid of order and causal relation. The situation is at its worst – or, perhaps, most complex – stage when we attempt to discover order and scientific precision among the events of social economics' (Dewing, 1930: xxiii). He adds:

> This increasingly complex social environment, into which the young businessman is thrown, requires resourcefulness, mental courage, confidence in the untried – in short, exactly those qualities which in the space of three centuries brought into existence a new nation and a new economic order. Πάντα ῥεῖ, and the ideal of our business education ought to be to teach young men to meet the oncoming flow of things with the courageousness and resourcefulness of their forefathers (Dewing, 1930: xxv).

There was in the past, and still is in the present, a variety of approaches to case-based pedagogy in business education, but a shared distinctive feature is an emphasis on form, process and experience. The case method of instruction in business administration is about enacting a business situation, living it almost for real, or in a very realistic fashion. But the reality of business is not considered in terms, for instance, of an empirically realistic depiction of the day-to-day life of a company. The reality of business is, rather, rendered in terms of the reality of 'mental courage', of the making of a vital, psychological and exciting act of decision in the face of uncertainty. Actual business documentation serves the purpose of realism – and source books such as Gerstenberg (1915), referred to for instance in Fraser (1930: 515), were important in the development of realism in the pedagogy of corporation finance. But the situation inside the classroom resembled business rather by means of expression, through the staging of and required participation in an act of business appraisal and decision. In his own philosophical disquisitions, Dewing had written (not, it must be said, directly about business but in connection with the notion of reality) that 'the expression of life, self-expression in its fullest sense, is for each one of us the thing above all worth while' (Dewing, 1910: 149), adding the following: 'I feel that I am real; this feeling demands self-expression' (Dewing, 1910: 168).

In the first edition of Dewing's *Financial Policy of Corporations* (1919, reprinted in 1920), the key word for valuation was "promotion" – also the central topic of the second volume (the book was initially published in five volumes, then six). In the 1934 edition, a new volume devoted entirely to 'valuation' was introduced, and transformed into a chapter in the two-volume edition of 1941 (Welk, 1935: Feller, 1941).[11] One important notion is the capitalization of earnings (or the rate of capitalization):

> The phrase, capitalization of net earnings, is frequently used both in present-day discussions of business theory and in the current literature of economics. The idea behind it is simple, but the practical application of this idea to a concrete case is difficult. Nevertheless, in spite of the practical difficulty of determining a definite and precise value for a specific business, the capitalization of earnings is the only means at our disposal for determining the value of a going business. This is because the business, as a going enterprise – a combination of organization, fixed and current capital – was designed primarily to earn profits. Its value is measured by the extent to which it conforms to this purpose. (Dewing, 1941: 182)

The usual implications in terms of capitalistic investment follow, that is, valuation is understood as the act of virtually 'buying' the business with the aim of making money:

> [u]nder our competitive system of economic values, the business is the instrument which creates the earnings, and the valuation of the business is the valuation of this instrument. It is true, too, under our competitive system, that the price which men pay for this instrument will depend on the relative certainty with which these earnings can be counted upon to continue. In other words, the rate at which a business shall

be capitalized, to obtain its value, will depend on the confidence the buyer may feel in the continuation of the earnings. (Dewing, 1941: 183)

A number of observations can be made concerning this vocabulary of valuation. The first is that value is something that is obtained, objectively, when the business enterprise is made fit for valuation and enters into such a process. It is clear by now then that the valuation of business means the financial valuation of corporate securities, and that the 'financial policy of corporations' consists precisely in getting enterprises prepared and organized for this valuation. The second is that great emphasis is put on purpose: the valuation of something is held to be best aligned with the business purpose of that thing. The situation in which the value of a business is required to be considered is thus a practical situation. The third is the correspondence established between the act of valuation and the act of purchase, which is recognized as an act of investment in the vehicle of valuation (the buying of corporate securities, the provision of credit, etc.). The interplay between the businessperson and the capitalist investor in their many forms – between the 'promoter' and the 'banker' – is visibly at the heart of the valuation process. Of course, as indicated by Dewing, this is what corporation finance is about in a capitalist system in which emphasis is put, as Polanyi (1944) would have indicated, on the production of earnings through markets for money (that is 'our competitive system of economic values'). But what is quite striking, I believe, is the openness and clarity with which Dewing translates the constructivist aspect of valuation: an operation in which both the appraisal of the characteristics of something in terms of its value and the setting of that thing for the purpose of making it valuable (a 'going enterprise', as Dewing likes to say) intermingle, and become two aspects of the same act (valuation).

Valuation is, in short, about capitalization. Estimation of return on capital becomes the key to financial valuation and, as Dewing writes, '[p]erhaps the most difficult and, so far as results are concerned, the most important point in any theory of value based on earning power, is the rate at which earnings shall be capitalized' (Dewing, 1941: 185). He adds:

> [T]he determination of this rate is at best a matter of guesswork, but guesswork supported by the evidence of prices at which businesses of various kinds are being actually valued at any one time. And this evidence from current experience with reference to the value of different enterprises can be culled out not only from the prices at which enterprises are actually sold, but also from the valuation put upon them by bankers extending credit to them and by investors who are willing to buy their bonds and stocks. In other words, such guesswork is subject to the best kind of pragmatic test, namely the evidence of actual experience. (Dewing, 1941: 186)

In the context of this discussion it is particularly interesting to read Dewing writing about a 'pragmatic test' (although the use of this expression is probably only loosely connected to a proper understanding of the pragmatist standpoint). The 'pragmatic test' (which financial valuation consists of) concerns neither emitting a personal opinion or desire about a business nor measuring a set of external features exhibited by a business, but rather the 'actual experience' of getting it bought and capitalized, that is, the conversion of a business into a ratio between income and cost (that is, the cost of capital). The quantitative transfiguration of corporate finance later to be prompted by Modigliani and Miller (1958), for example, is not far (see Nitzan and Bichler, 2009).

## The flank movement and financial capitalism

A comprehensive understanding of the performative aspects of corporation finance requires a more detailed examination than I can provide here.[12] My purpose is more limited: to make clear the meaning of Dewey's 'flank movement' in the understanding of valuation. The 'flank movement' is, I have suggested, partly recognizable as a pragmatist strategy. As was pointed out in reference to Peirce, rather than considering signs as such, a pragmatist perspective considers signification as an action. The same way of thinking applies to values: a pragmatist viewpoint shifts attention to valuation as an action. In both cases, this idea of 'as an action' should be understood in the sense of a process, a form of mediation, of something that happens in practice, something that is done to something else, and so forth; value is definitely not something that something just has. If value is something that something just has, then we need to ask: by virtue of what? In answering such a question, we might easily make use of the classic division between reality (things, the world, objects, matter, etc.) and what or whoever looks at it (mind, thought, the knowing subject, ideas, opinion, self, etc.). In doing so, we would be preserving the 'continuity' that Dewey identified in the formulation of 'the problem of values' by the Executive Committee of the American Philosophical Association (Spaulding, 1913; McGilvary *et al.*, 1913; Dewey, 1913). The 'flank movement' consists precisely in putting that continuity aside and approaching what happens in a more agnostic, empirical manner – a radical, pragmatist departure from the classical division in fact allows a tracing of the empirical origination of its two terms.

The case of valuation in corporation finance (its pedagogical unfolding in the context of the professionalization of the businessperson) is of interest, then, because it provides a compelling illustration of the adequacy of a pragmatist view on valuation. Valuation is about considering a reality while provoking it. It implies the virtual act of 'obtaining value', as is made clear in the very notion of capitalization. The valuation of corporate securities is an interpretation of the business enterprise, but, so one might say, paraphrasing the defence of Peirce's theory of signification by Dewey (1946), this does not need to lead to an idea of, say, the investment banker being an 'interpreter', emitting a view. Signification (read 'valuation') happens because what interprets the business as a valuable object is itself a relational, active process out of which something can hold as the sign (read 'the value') of something. In the case examined above, this involves a series of inter-related processes such as the description of the business as an instrument which creates earnings, the plotting of a virtual action of capital investment, the simulation of its consequences and the actual setting of the business (by the proverbial businessperson, which is itself a valuation device) as something fit for this process.

It is not claimed that Dewey has a monopoly on the 'flank movement': rather, the movement is a constant, albeit sometimes underground current in philosophy, and it has been expressed in many other ways by other people in other times. Gilles Deleuze (who claimed at many points affiliation to pragmatism in philosophy) has, for example, highlighted many particularly acute instances of the 'flank movement' in philosophical thought, including Nietzsche's philosophy of values (Deleuze, 1962), the notion of expression in Spinoza (Deleuze, 1968), and the idea of the simulacrum in stoicism (Deleuze, 1969). But Dewey's take on the problem of valuation is located in a context (the shaping of North American liberal thought, the Progressive Era, the Great War, the Roaring Twenties and the rise of Corporate America, the Wall Street Crash of 1929 and the Great Depression) for which a 'flank movement' was perhaps particularly suitable and which bears some resemblances with the situation that obtains today.

The current situation is indeed characterized to some extent – as Dewey's America was – by a crisis in the representation of value.[13] The fact that valuation is a form of performance (almost in the dramaturgical sense of the world) is exposed sometimes in a puzzling way. In ethnographic depictions of investment banking today, particular attention is paid to the importance of shareholder value or, more precisely, to the narrative unfolding and performative staging of 'shareholder value' as a massive professional shibboleth (eg Ho, 2009: 122–212). It has also been shown recently how the moral persona of the 'free investor' serves as a crucial element of the professional imaginaries that inform the work of valuation in the financial services industry (Ortiz, 2010). Furthermore, Deleuze's approach to the simulacrum has been used in anthropology to analyse the functioning of the contemporary stock market (Hertz, 2000).[14] Precautions of a pragmatist sort have also been taken in the examination of valuation techniques used in financial markets, for instance through increased attention to what valuation formulas actually do rather than to what they are meant to represent (Maurer, 2002; MacKenzie, 2006). In short, work in the anthropology of contemporary finance focuses, to a noticeable extent, on aspects of the choreographies of valuation described in the specialized literature of Arthur Stone Dewing and others, and may thus 'be dealt with in the end more effectively if approached by a flank movement' – as John Dewey would have said (Dewey, 1913: 269).

Periods of unrest in valuation often open interesting opportunities for the questioning of available theories of value and for the renewal of the intellectual repertoire, sometimes also of the political one. It would of course be entirely justifiable to interpret, for example, the intellectual move of considering capital not as a thing in itself but rather as a relation as an instance of a flank movement; it is, of course, one central but often overlooked characteristic of the move that Karl Marx undertook in the reading room of the British Museum.[15] But the oblique stance on valuation is clearer in North American pragmatism. It suited the rise of the North American businessperson and the North American financier, their professional craft, the performative aspects of their work of valuation, their adventurous philosophy and the dramaturgy of the 'going enterprise' they set out to create. Today's financial reality (today's financialized reality) is heavily indebted to the practices that were developed during that period, and consequently a contemporary pragmatist stand can perhaps further our understanding of what is going on.

# Notes

1 I am grateful to Horacio Ortiz, Talha Syed, Michel Callon, Liliana Doganova, David Stark, Celia Lury, Lisa Adkins, Helen Verran, Peter Karnøe, Margareta Bertilsson, Anders Blok, Maria Duclos Lindstrøm and two anonymous reviewers for comments and conversations in relation to this paper. The research is supported by ERC Starting Grant 263529.
2 Notable further interventions in the discussion thread include, in chronological order, Dewey (1915a, 1915b, also in 1916), Urban (1916), Perry (1917), Bush (1918), Dewey (1918), Picard (1920), Costello (1920), Dewey (1922), Picard (1922), Prall (1923), Dewey (1923), Prall (1924), Clarke (1925) and Dewey (1925a, 1925b). Dewey (1939), a landmark in the discussion, is then followed, for instance, by Rice (1943a), Dewey (1943a), Rice (1943b, 1943c), Dewey (1943b), Geiger (1944) and Dewey (1944).
3 A price, which is an instance of valuation, can very well be considered as a sign. But a pragmatist appraisal of this calls for an understanding of signification in a proper pragmatist sense – that is, as a process. For an analysis of stock prices using Charles Sanders Peirce's theory of signs, see Muniesa (2007).
4 The 'flank movement' is also at work in the following clarification: '[w]e seem to have here further evidence of the extent to which the type of logic presented by Morris and others is controlled by the epistemological heritage of a knowing subject, person, self, or what have you, set over against the world, or things, or objects, and capable of reference to the latter either directly in virtue of its own faculty (epistemological realism) or through an idea or thought as intermediary (epistemological idealism)' (Dewey, 1946: 89).
5 See for example Stark (2009), Vatin (2009), Ortiz (2005, 2010), Lury and Moor (2010), Kockelman (2006, 2010), Guyer (2009), Maurer (2006), Barrey (2006), Anzalone (2009), Muniesa (2007), Teil and Muniesa (2006), Callon, Millo and Muniesa (2007), Caliskan and Callon (2009, 2010), Doganova and Eyquem-Renault (2009), Karnøe (2010), Verran (2007) and Hoeyer (2009) for some recent contributions.
6 The idea of something being a 'construction' (or a 'social construction') is often interpreted, quite strangely and despite repeated materialist warnings (eg Latour, 1999), as being 'mental', 'ideal' or 'not quite real' (but a bridge over the river is both constructed and very real).
7 For a detailed sociological analysis of the history and purposes of business schools in the United States of America, with particular attention to the Harvard Business School, see Khurana (2007). For an examination of the lives and works of pragmatist philosophers in the context of the transformation of higher education and intellectual elites (especially in Boston and Cambridge, MA), see Menand (2001), and for a broader contextualization of the pragmatist moment in North American thought, see Purcell (1973) and Lears (2009).
8 Dewing's *Financial Policy of Corporations* was a widely read manual. For a couple of reviews of its multiple editions, see Simpson (1921), Welk (1935), Feller (1941) and Hunt (1943).
9 This is a vision of pragmatism that has been transmitted by many commentators, including for instance Rorty (1979).
10 Dewing's introduction to the case method, quoted here from Fraser (1930), is also printed for instance in Fraser (1931) and McNair (1954).

11 I use here the one-volume version (published without footnotes) of the 1941 edition.
12 The examples examined here could for instance be confronted to different ways in which economic valuation can be staged and the corresponding business realities provoked. A quite useful, coetaneous, North American contrast could be drawn for example with Veblen (1921). For a study of connections between institutionalism in economics and pragmatism in North America, see Mirowski (1987). For a historical contextualization, see Yonay (1998).
13 See Shell (1982) and Agnew (1986) for an exploration of this form of crisis in earlier contexts.
14 Ellen Hertz shows how the Deleuzian notion of the simulacrum (Deleuze, 1969), as opposed for instance to a Baudrillardesque one (Baudrillard, 1981), serves the anthropology of financial valuation in a crucial way. The notion helps countering in particular the absurd idea according to which financial value would not be real (Hertz, 2000).
15 An explicitly semiotic, relational (and hence radically pragmatist) view of capital, inspired by Marx, is what the reader can get, for example, in some parts of Deleuze and Guattari (1972, 1980; see also Guattari and Alliez, 1983).

# References

Agnew, J.-C., (1986), *Worlds Apart: The Market and the Theater in Anglo-American Thought, 1550–1750*, Cambridge: Cambridge University Press.
Anzalone, G., (2009), 'Comment transformer un produit en marchandise et lui attribuer un prix: le traitement de la viande dans la grande distribution', *Sociologie du Travail*, 51(1): 64–77.
Barrey, S., (2006), 'Formation et calcul des prix: le travail de tarification dans la grande distribution' *Sociologie du Travail*, 48(2): 142–158.
Baudrillard, J., (1981), *Simulacres et Simulation*, Paris: Galilée.
Bush, W.T., (1918), 'Value and causality', *The Journal of Philosophy, Psychology and Scientific Methods*, 15(4): 85–96.
Caliskan, K. and Callon, M., (2009), 'Economization, Part 1: Shifting attention from the economy towards processes of economization', *Economy and Society*, 38(3): 369–398.
Caliskan, K. and Callon, M., (2010), 'Economization, Part 2: A research programme for the study of markets', *Economy and Society*, 39(1): 1–32.
Callon, M., Millo, Y. and Muniesa, F. (eds), (2007), *Market Devices*, Oxford: Blackwell.
Clarke, M.E., (1925), 'Valuing and the quality of value', *The Journal of Philosophy*, 22(3): 57–75.
Copeland, M.T., (1958), *And Mark an Era: The Story of the Harvard Business School*, Boston, MA: Little, Brown and Co.
Costello, H.T., (1920), 'Professor Dewey's "Judgments of Practice"', *The Journal of Philosophy, Psychology and Scientific Methods*, 17(17): 449–455.
Deleuze, G., (1962), *Nietzsche et la Philosophie*, Paris: Presses Universitaires de France.
Deleuze, G., (1968), *Spinoza et le Problème de l'Expression*, Paris: Éditions de Minuit.
Deleuze, G., (1969), *Logique du Sens*, Paris: Éditions de Minuit.
Deleuze, G. and Guattari, F., (1972), *L'Anti-Oedipe*, Paris: Éditions de Minuit.
Deleuze, G. and Guattari, F., (1980), *Mille Plateaux*, Paris: Éditions de Minuit.
Dewey, J., (1913), 'The problem of values', *The Journal of Philosophy, Psychology and Scientific Methods*, 10(10): 268–269.
Dewey, J., (1915a), 'The logic of judgments of practise (Part I)', *The Journal of Philosophy, Psychology and Scientific Methods*, 12(19): 505–523.
Dewey, J., (1915b), 'The logic of judgments of practise (Part II)', *The Journal of Philosophy, Psychology and Scientific Methods*, 12(20): 533–543.
Dewey, J., (1916), *Essays in Experimental Logic*, Chicago: University of Chicago Press.
Dewey, J., (1918), 'The objects of valuation', *The Journal of Philosophy, Psychology and Scientific Methods*, 15(4): 253–258.
Dewey, J., (1922), 'Valuation and experimental knowledge', *The Philosophical Review*, 31(4): 325–351.

Dewey, J., (1923), 'Values, liking, and thought', *The Journal of Philosophy*, 20(23): 617–622.
Dewey, J., (1925a), 'The meaning of value', *The Journal of Philosophy*, 22(5): 126–133.
Dewey, J., (1925b), 'Value, objective reference and criticism', *The Philosophical Review*, 34(4): 313–332.
Dewey, J., (1939), *Theory of Valuation*, Chicago: University of Chicago Press.
Dewey, J., (1943a), 'Valuation judgments and immediate quality', *The Journal of Philosophy*, 40(12): 309–317.
Dewey, J., (1943b), 'Further to as valuation as judgment', *The Journal of Philosophy*, 40(20): 543–552.
Dewey, J., (1944), 'Some questions about value', *The Journal of Philosophy*, 41(17): 449–455.
Dewey, J., (1946), 'Peirce's theory of linguistic signs, thought and meaning', *The Journal of Philosophy*, 43(4): 85–95.
Dewing, A.S., (1910), *Life as Reality: A Philosophical Essay*, New York: Longmans, Green & Co.
Dewing, A.S., (1920), *The Financial Policy of Corporations, Volume II: Promotion*, New York: The Ronald Press.
Dewing, A.S., (1930), 'An introduction to the use of cases', in C.E. Fraser (ed.), *Problems in Finance*, New York: McGraw-Hill.
Dewing, A.S., (1941), *The Financial Policy of Corporations*, 4th edn, New York: Ronald Press.
Doganova, L. and Eyquem-Renault, M., (2009), 'What do business models do? Innovation devices in technology entrepreneurship', *Research Policy*, 38(10): 1559–1570.
Feller, A.H., (1941), 'Review of *The Financial Policy of Corporations* by Arthur Stone Dewing', *The Yale Law Journal*, 51(2): 359–361.
Fraser, C.E., (1930), *Problems in Finance*, 2nd edn, New York: McGraw-Hill.
Fraser, C.E. (ed.), (1931), *The Case Method of Instruction*, New York: McGraw-Hill.
Geiger, G.R., (1944), 'Can we choose between values?' *The Journal of Philosophy*, 41(11): 292–298.
Gerstenberg, C.W., (1915), *Materials for Corporation Finance*, New York: Prentice-Hall.
Guattari, F. and Alliez, E., (1983), 'Le capital en fin de compte: systèmes, structures et processus capitalistiques', *Change International*, 1: 100–106.
Guyer, J.I., (2009), 'Composites, fictions, and risk: toward an ethnography of price', in C. Hann and K. Hart (eds), *Market and Society: The Great Transformation Today*, Cambridge: Cambridge University Press.
Hertz, E., (2000), 'Stock markets as "simulacra": observation that participates', *Tsantsa*, 5: 40–50.
Ho, K., (2009), *Liquidated: An Ethnography of Wall Street*, Durham, NC: Duke University Press.
Hoeyer, K., (2009), 'Tradable body parts? How bone and recycled prosthetic devices acquire a price without forming a "market"', *BioSocieties*, 4(2–3): 239–256.
Hunt, P., (1943), 'Review of *The Financial Policy of Corporations* by Arthur Stone Dewing', *The Quarterly Journal of Economics*, 57(2): 303–313.
Karnøe, P., (2010), 'Material disruptions in electricity systems: can wind power fit in the existing electricity system?' in M. Akrich, Y. Barthe, F. Muniesa and P. Mustar (eds), *Débordements: Mélanges Offerts à Michel Callon*, Paris: Presses des Mines.
Khurana, R., (2007), *From Higher Aims to Hired Hands: The Social Transformation of American Business Schools and the Unfulfilled Promise of Management as a Profession*, Princeton, NJ: Princeton University Press.
Kockelman, P., (2006), 'A Semiotic Ontology of the Commodity', *Journal of Linguistic Anthropology*, 16(1): 76–102.
Kockelman, P., (2010), 'Value is life under an interpretation: existential commitments, instrumental reasons and disorienting metaphors', *Anthropological Theory*, 10(1–2): 149–162.
Latour, B., (1999), *Pandora's Hope: Essays on the Reality of Science Studies*, Cambridge, MA: Harvard University Press.

Lears, J., (2009), *Rebirth of a Nation: The Making of Modern America, 1877–1920*, New York: HarperCollins.
Lippmann, W., (1914), *Drift and Mastery: An Attempt to Diagnose the Current Unrest*, New York: Mitchell Kennerley.
Lury, C. and Moor, L., (2010), 'Brand valuation and topological culture', in M. Aronczyk and D. Powers (eds), *Blowing Up the Brand: Critical Perspectives on Promotional Culture*, New York: Peter Lang.
MacKenzie, D., (2006), *An Engine, Not a Camera: How Financial Models Shape Markets*, Cambridge, MA: MIT Press.
Maurer, B., (2002), 'Repressed futures: financial derivatives' theological unconscious', *Economy and Society*, 31(1): 15–36.
Maurer, B., (2006), 'The anthropology of money', *Annual Review of Anthropology*, 35: 15–36.
McGilvary, E.B., Pitkin, W.B., Overstreet, H.A. and Spaulding, E.G., (1913), 'The problem of values', *The Journal of Philosophy, Psychology and Scientific Methods*, 10(6): 168.
McNair, M.P. (ed.), (1954), *The Case Method at the Harvard Business School: Papers by Present and Past Members of the Faculty and Staff*, New York: McGraw-Hill.
Menand, L., (2001), *The Metaphysical Club: A Story of Ideas in America*, New York: Farrar, Straus and Giroux.
Mirowski, P., (1987), 'The philosophical bases of institutionalist economics', *Journal of Economic Issues*, 21(3): 1001–1038.
Modigliani, F. and Miller, M.H., (1958), 'The cost of capital, corporation finance and the theory of investment', *The American Economic Review*, 48(3): 261–297.
Morris, C.W., (1938), *Foundations of the Theory of Signs*, Chicago: University of Chicago Press.
Muniesa, F., (2007), 'Market technologies and the pragmatics of prices', *Economy and Society*, 36(3): 377–395.
Nitzan, J. and Bichler, S., (2009), *Capital as Power: A Study of Order and Creorder*, London: Routledge.
Ortiz, H., (2005), 'Évaluer, apprécier: les relations entre brokers et gérants de fonds d'investissement', *Économie Rurale*, 286–287: 56–70.
Ortiz, H., (2010), 'Value and power: some questions for a political anthropology of global finance', in R. Acosta, S. Rizvi and A. Santos (eds), *Making Sense of the Global: Anthropological Perspectives on Interconnections and Processes*, Newcastle-upon-Tyne: Cambridge Scholars Publishing.
Perry, R.B., (1917), 'Dewey and Urban on value judgments', *The Journal of Philosophy, Psychology and Scientific Methods*, 14(7): 169–181.
Picard, M., (1920), 'The psychological basis of values', *The Journal of Philosophy, Psychology and Scientific Methods*, 17(1): 11–20.
Picard, M., (1922), 'Value and worth', *The Journal of Philosophy*, 19(18): 477–489.
Polanyi, K., (1944), *The Great Transformation: The Political and Economic Origins of Our Time*, New York: Rinehart & Company.
Prall, D.W., (1923), 'In defense of a worthless theory of value', *The Journal of Philosophy*, 20(5): 128–137.
Prall, D.W., (1924), 'Value and thought-process', *The Journal of Philosophy*, 21(5): 117–125.
Purcell, E.A. Jr, (1973), *The Crisis of Democratic Theory: Scientific Naturalism and the Problem of Value*, Lexington, KY: University Press of Kentucky.
Rice, P.B., (1943a), ' "Objectivity" in value judgments', *The Journal of Philosophy*, 40(1): 5–14.
Rice, P.B., (1943b), 'Quality and value', *The Journal of Philosophy*, 40(13): 337–348.
Rice, P.B., (1943c), 'Types of value judgments', *The Journal of Philosophy*, 40(20): 533–543.
Rorty, R., (1979), *Philosophy and the Mirror of Nature*, Princeton, NJ: Princeton University Press.
Shell, M., (1982), *Money, Language, and Thought: Literary and Philosophical Economies from the Medieval to the Modern Era*, Baltimore, MD: The Johns Hopkins University Press.
Simpson, K., (1921), 'Review of *The Financial Policy of Corporations* by Arthur Stone Dewing', *Quarterly Publications of the American Statistical Association*, 17(134): 796–799.

Spaulding, E.G., (1913), 'Notes and news: the problem of values', *The Journal of Philosophy, Psychology and Scientific Methods*, 10(6): 167–168.
Stark, D., (2009), *The Sense of Dissonance: Accounts of Worth in Economic Life*, Princeton, NJ: Princeton University Press.
Teil, G. and Muniesa, F., (2006), 'Donner un prix: observations à partir d'un dispositif d'économie expérimentale', *Terrains & Travaux*, 11: 222–244.
Urban, W.M., (1916), 'Value and existence', *The Journal of Philosophy, Psychology and Scientific Methods*, 13(17): 449–465.
Vatin, F. (ed.), (2009), *Évaluer et Valoriser: Une Sociologie Économique de la Mesure*, Toulouse: Presses Universitaires du Mirail.
Verran, H., (2007), 'The telling challenge of Africa's economies', *African Studies Review*, 50(2): 163–182.
Veblen, T., (1921), *The Engineers and the Price System*, New York: B. W. Huebsch.
Welk, W.G., (1935), 'Review of *The Financial Policy of Corporations* by Arthur Stone Dewing', *Annals of the American Academy of Political and Social Science*, 180: 228–229.
Yonay, Y.P., (1998), *The Struggle over the Soul of Economics: Institutionalism and Neoclassical Economists in America between the Wars*, Princeton, NJ: Princeton University Press.

# General Sentiment: how value and affect converge in the information economy

## Adam Arvidsson

**Abstract:** The Fordist economy was marked by what David Stark calls a Parsonian Compromise in which economic value and other values were clearly separated, in theory as well as in practice. Today this is changing. Trends such as Ethical Consumerism and Corporate Social Responsibility are on the rise. More fundamentally, the economic importance of intangible assets like brands has increased. Together these developments testify to a new role for a wider range of values in determining price formation. In this paper I will argue that this trend has two principal causes. First, the socialization of production has increased the importance of affective investments in things like brands, reputation, corporate culture and efficient teamwork as sources of value. Second, a common criterion for the measurement of affective investments is forming, based on the new abstract or General Sentiment that is emerging as a new 'general equivalent' as a consequence of the present remediation of communicative relations, primarily throughout the diffusion of social media. Together these two dimensions make up the foundations for a new value logic, an 'ethical economy' that is emerging within contemporary wealth creation. After briefly summarizing the first argument, this paper will concentrate on the second, describing the emergence and features of General Sentiment as a criterion of value. The conclusion will suggest possible consequences of this development in both practical and theoretical terms.

**Keywords:** value, general intellect, affect, General Sentiment, information economy

## Introduction

'Wealth Management Group' uses the Values Tool to identify the values profile of client portfolio holdings in order to measure alignments with the value profile of clients. . . . What is of great benefit here is that relationship managers do not need to depend purely on their own judgement to identify their clients' values, but are assisted by a powerful technology. (Sales Document from small internet startup addressing a large wealth management group[1])

. . . hence exchange value must cease to be the measure of use value. (Marx, 1973 [1939]: 705)

The modern, Fordist economy was organized around what David Stark has called a 'Parsonian Pact', by means of which 'value' and 'values' were kept separate (Stark, 2009: 7).[2] For social theory, this meant that concerns about values and questions about the origins, desirability or legitimacy of preferences and motivations were considered to be outside the object domain of economics. At the same time, the question of how economic value was formed was considered beyond the reach of the disciplines like sociology and anthropology that studied 'values'. More importantly, it also applied in practice: the main criterion for the objectification and measurement of value that applied throughout the Fordist corporate economy was a notion of productive time that was considered to be devoid of any affective dimension. While there were of course alternative 'voices' within the vast corpus of modern managerial thought – including, notably, the Hawthorne Studies and the tradition of Human Relations Management that arose out of them (Roethlisberger and Dickson, 1939; cf. Rose, 1975) – the basic principle of modern cost accounting, and the Taylorist managerial system of which it was part, was the organization of productive relations so as to render them measurable in terms of standardized productivity rates. These rates paid no attention to the mess of emotions, opinions and social relations that make up the reality of concrete everyday work. This was not just a question of measurement systems abstracting from the affective dynamics of work life, but also of management philosophies actively trying to contain forms of affect within the boundaries of a pre-structured job description. As Alan Liu argues, the creation of 'abstract labor time' (to use Marx's expression) as the principal criterion of value measurement involved 'a complete system of emotional labor management that disallowed workers any "productive" emotion at all' (Liu, 2004: 94; cf. Gramsci, 1971). While such attempts at emotional governance probably never succeeded in completely purging work-life of undesired forms of affect – indeed the argument has been made that Fordist, bureaucratic organizations actually gave greater space for unstructured forms of sociality than today's post-bureaucratic organizations (du Gay, 2000) – the intention to do so was central to Fordist managerial thought.

Today it seems that this 'Parsonian Pact' is in the process of being overcome. Phenomena such as Ethical Consumerism, Corporate Social Responsibility, Fair Trade, and Socially Responsible Investment (Vogel, 2005; Stehr *et al.*, 2006) testify to a will to allow affective concerns to influence the prices of assets and consumer goods, enabling value decisions about the legitimacy and desirability of the goals that guide economic pursuits to enter the picture. Beneath these trends lies a deeper structural tendency in which so-called intangible assets and brands in particular, have become ever more important as components of the market value of companies.[3] Like many other intangible assets such as 'knowledge capital', 'reputation' or 'corporate identity' – the terminology is diverse and ill defined in this field – brands represent the pricing of a wide range of affects, such as the experience that consumers and, increasingly, other actors such as employees attribute to a brand. This might include the perception of a brand's 'fairness' or social utility, or the loyalty that it is held to inspire.

The contemporary tendency towards the fusion of 'values' and value may to some extent be driven by pressure on corporate actors as a consequence of the growing strength of a new, networked public sphere, in which consumers and other actors can find new ways to express concerns that are related to diverse orders of worth, such as environmental sustainability and social justice (Garriga and Melé, 2004). However, this article will claim that the main reason behind this development is that the corporate economy itself has opened up to the inclusion of such diverse orders of worth by means of the calculative devices that it deploys to determine value. This opening up has occurred through the rise of 'intangibles' as a new paradigm for calculating the value of assets and consumer goods. In turn, the rise of intangibles has been driven by two developments. First, a transformation of productive relations has decreased the representativeness of 'the productivity of time' as a criterion for the measurement of value. Second, there has been a development in the objectification and measurability of affect, which has enabled affect to enter into the calculative devices by means of which economic values are set.

Drawing on Gabriel Tarde among others, I will suggest that this 'becoming objective' of affect has a long history that goes back to the origins of the modern, mass-mediated public sphere. But this trend has accelerated in recent years through the proliferation of social media together with a host of new technologies including, primarily, data mining techniques such as network and sentiment analysis, that are able to represent individual affective investments as manifestations of an abstract general equivalent, what I call General Sentiment. I will suggest that these techniques, and the General Sentiment that they are able to represent, contain a new possibility for the stabilization of affective value, something that has so far been lacking in measurements of intangible value. The final section will draw out some tentative conclusions about the possible consequences of these developments for politics.

Before telling that story, however, it is necessary to give a brief description of the transformation of productive relations that have made values valuable and, consequently, such measurements desirable in the first place.

## Linking value and affect – the rise of intangibles

What is value? Classical economic and social theory has attempted to answer that question by pointing at a particular 'substance' that is held to create or determine value, whether this be 'socially necessary labor time', as for Marxists, or (marginal) individual utility as for the neoclassical school. Recent developments in economic sociology have instead pointed at the performativity of the calculating devices that are deployed either in order to measure value directly or to process the necessary information that goes into the decisions that determine the relative values of assets and consumer goods (Callon, 1998; McKenzie, 2006). It is argued that once these become successful, they are able to posit their own object of measurement as a natural 'substance' of value. In this section I will follow this lead in arguing that one important cause behind the present fusion of affect and value has been the establishment of a range of devices that measure and represent value as an expression of what are known as 'intangibles' assets, and most importantly, brands. However, I will also suggest that the success in establishing this 'intangibles paradigm' is linked to a transformation in the ways in which wealth is created. In other words, while actually operating notions of economic value may result from the performativity of calculative devices, it is difficult for those devices to establish themselves and achieve 'performative power' if they do not somehow reflect perceptions on the part of important actors or groups of actors as to the nature of the processes subject to measure and calculation.[4]

## Productivity

In the 'Fordist' economy, the prevailing measure of value was the productivity of time, and most importantly, labour time. Although this idea has a long history within economic theory, going back to 18th century economists such as Adam Smith, and before him Sir William Petty (see Linebaugh and Rediker, 2000), its institutionalization in managerial procedures and devices goes back to the managerial revolution at the turn of the last century (Chandler, 1977; Landes, 2003). This movement saw the rise of corporations and the standardization of the modern disciplines of management, marketing and, importantly accounting. The Fordist corporation was based on the principle of vertical integration, or the internalization of as many aspects of the production process as possible within a sphere of control and command. Taylorism, along with technologies such as the assembly line, allowed the subdivision of internalized productive processes into discrete units that could be supplied with specific job descriptions. In parallel, cost accounting was based on the calculation of standardized productivity rates for each such discrete subunit, and the measure of their value-added as quanta of productive time deployed. Deviations from such standardized productivity rates could be used to discipline or reward the workforce, because wages – as Fredrick Taylor himself had suggested – could be directly linked to the productivity of working time (Taylor, 1896). This meant that, at the level of the labour process, the tasks of measuring value and controlling the workforce were located in the same device: the productivity of labour as measured in relation to time.

At the level of the firm, the notion of 'productivity' served both as an object for managerial intervention, and as an explanation and legitimation of profits as well as, for shareholders, asset returns. This does not mean that labour was effectively the only source of value, as orthodox Marxists would claim, but rather that the way in which the production process was configured meant that the productivity of labour made sense as a transparent and commonly accepted way of representing processes of wealth creation, sufficient to confer legitimacy and rationality on the determination of wages and the allocation of capital.

Importantly, there were three reasons the notion of productivity could work in this way as a credible representation of the value-creating process. First because variable costs, such as labour costs, were high in relation to 'overheads' such as machine capital or patents, about 90 per cent in the 1890s; in other words labour was effectively the most important productive resource (Boer and Jeter, 1993). Second, because the internalization of the productive process meant that firms created value chiefly by deploying their own proprietary resources which could figure in their balance sheets. Third, because this internalization of the production process meant that it could be subdivided into discrete units where diverse productivity rates could be calculated. These three conditions are all less applicable today.

If the rise of the Fordist corporation constituted a managerial response to the growing complexity and socio-spatial extension of productive processes, then the impact of information and communication technology – principally the link between Computer Aided Design (CAD) and Computer Numerically Controlled (CNC) machinery – has, since the 1970s, enabled an even further extension of the levels of productive cooperation. Indeed, the present post-Fordist paradigm is marked by a socialization of productive processes outside of the factory, whether in the form of the 'Toyotist' model developed at Toyota in the late 1960s and early 1970s that combines flexible production, self-organized teams and just-in-time flows with Taylorist subdivision of tasks and the organization of production around the large factory typical of the industrial model (Morris-Suzuki, 1984); the 'Italian' model of 'industrial districts' that deploys networks of small, specialized firms (Beccattini, 1989; Piore and Sabel, 1984); or the global value chain that combines a diverse typology of firms that are, often, organized in clear hierarchies (as between first-, second- and third-tier suppliers, Fumagalli, 2007; Bertin, 1985). While Taylorist managerial practices still prevail in many parts of the economy, and are on the rise in some sectors such as fast food and certain aspects of education (Smart, 1999), the central tendency of the industrial model to concentrate as much production as possible in the factory has been inverted and replaced by a tendency to locate an ever larger share of production in productive networks that unfold outside the factory walls. Between 1985 and 2000, for example, the share of vehicle value deriving from outsourcing in the auto industry increased from 50 to 80 per cent in the case of Renault, and between 1997 and 2004 the share of (outsourced) imports to the US Auto Parts market grew from 40 per cent to 65 per cent. Today the supply chain of the automaker Hyundai involves 400 first-tier suppliers, and 2500 second-tier suppliers (Veloso and Kumar, 2002).

*The rise of intangibles*

The socialization of material production means that the ability to engage in such forms of wealth creation has been generalized. To quote management scholars Paul Adler and Charles Heckscher, 'the mysteries of effective commodity production have become common knowledge; they are now merely tickets for entry rather than the keys for winning the competition' (2006: 28). Material production has become commonplace (or 'commoditized', to use an expression popular with business writers) and its share of value-added is in decline. The strategic focus on value creation is shifting towards so-called 'intangible' assets, including the capacity for innovation, flexibility and, most importantly, branding. But the production of such assets often occurs outside the control of single organizations and sometimes, as in the case of brands, it builds on input from non-salaried actors including consumers and the public at large (Arvidsson, 2006). Furthermore, the creation of value in this way mostly employs resources, such as communicative and social skills, the value-creating potential of which are poorly related to the quanta of time in which they are employed. Instead, as Paolo Virno would argue, the creation of intangible value in the form of a corporate culture conducive to innovation or teamwork, or an attractive brand, involves 'virtuosity' in the appropriation of common knowledge, symbols, relations and competences, or General Intellect (Virno, 2004). This means that the value creation of intangible resources is less susceptible to measurement in terms of the productivity of time, and depends more on the ability to attract affective investments such as reputation, goodwill or employee motivation. While this does not mean that labour has 'disappeared' or 'no longer counts', it means that labour ever more creates value in ways that are poorly related to quanta of time. Indeed it can be argued that there is an extension of the range of social activities that now count as value-creating 'labour', including the 'labour' of consumers or that of Internet users in general (cf. Fuchs, 2010; Zwick *et al.*, 2009).

However, since the resources that are employed in the creation of intangible value, like General Intellect and communicative skills (or what Virno calls 'mass intellect') are often not proprietary, they figure badly on the balance sheets of companies. Together with a general financialization of the economy, where larger shares of corporate profit derive from financial rents, this has caused a pressing issue of growing discrepancies between the market and book value of companies (Harvey, 2010). This, in turn, has created an opening for new kinds of calculative devices that are able to account for and make good these discrepancies, not least since the rational market hypothesis of neoclassical economics (and neoliberal ideology) is losing credibility among economists, social scientists and, crucially, actual practitioners (cf. Fox, 2009).

## Brand valuation

The notion of 'intangible value' has emerged primarily as an answer to this problem of how to account for and make good widening discrepancies between market and book value. The origins of the concept can be traced to the transformation of accounting and control practices that accompanied the socialization of production in the 1980s. As outsourcing and the creation of global supply chains began to shift the strategically most important source of value away from productive time per se, to other 'assets' like capacity for innovation and flexibility, management responded by implementing measuring devices like Value Flow Analysis and Total Quality Management. These devices were aimed at measuring the productivity of the whole value chain (and not as earlier, a single unit of that chain), paying attention to novel factors like the ease of integration of the chain and the flexibility of its response to market conditions (Glover and Fitzgerald-Moore, 1999; De Angelis, 2007). In the 1980s, similar devices were developed for the control and management of knowledge work (chiefly through the pioneering work of Skandia AFS, cf. Edvinsson and Malone, 1997). Here new forms of bench-marking, such as 'balanced scorecards' measured the efficiency of employees in a wide variety of ways, including their cooperative and social skills: that is, their ability to learn from each other and extract operative skills from the General Intellect of the firm and its surroundings.

These devices were important for management and control purposes, but for value reporting purposes they tended to be subsumed under the concept of 'brand'. Again, the notion that brands could have economic value has a long prehistory. It goes back to the marketing revolution of the 1950s that began to shift managerial focus from production to sales and market demand as a source of value creation, and the parallel development of the concept of brand image as something distinct from products (Gardner and Levy, 1955). A more mobile consumer culture that created forms of demand that were more difficult to anticipate, along with the development of a global consumer culture and, with it, global brands (Levitt, 1983) put an extra premium on the additional ability to predict demand that came with brands. Along with these developments there was a growth in practices and devices, such as Customer Relations Management, that extended the scope of management to the relations that a company could entertain with consumers, and eventually other stakeholders.

While these developments have paved way for the notion that the value of assets such as flexibility and knowledge was ultimately set by consumers, the necessity of measuring the value of such relations only became acute with the financial bubble of the 1980s. The wave of mergers and acquisition that then marked the 'creative destruction' of the remains of the Fordist industrial economy called for a legitimate way to account for discrepancies between market and book value. A number of brand valuation companies rose to the challenge by identifying the variable success of brands, or the relations that a company had established with consumers, as a credible source of the difference in value (Lury and Moor, 2010). For example, while today's leading brand valuation company Interbrand was founded in 1974, under the name of Novamark, it remained a brand and design consulting company for that decade. It only took up brand valuation in 1987. As its founder John Murphy told the trade magazine *Brand Management* in 2001, there was 'a huge buying and selling of branded-goods businesses where what was essentially being bought and sold was brands. But nobody knew how to value brands' (Holdsworth, 2001). Interbrand went on to establish its leadership of the field by valuing the Pillsbury brand for the Grand Metropolitan PLC acquisition of Pillsbury Co. From the start, the Interbrand method contained three elements: first, an estimation of the strength of a brand based on its market and management; second, an estimation of the proportion of company earnings attributable to the brand; and third, a brand multiplier based on the 'quality' of the brand: a measure that built on market data as well as data on the affective relations that the brand had managed to install with consumers.[5]

Most contemporary brand valuation models maintain some version of this approach, although some simply calculate the difference between market and book value and attribute that to brand. However, the tendency has been to measure consumer affect in more and more detailed ways and to give it a more central role in the calculation of 'brand multipliers' (that is, in estimates of the share of future earnings that can be reasonably attributed to consumer attitudes and relations to the brand, as opposed to market factors like price, location or the strength of distribution channels – cf. Salinas and Ambler, 2009). For example, Young and Rubicam's *Brand Asset Valuator* centres on a calculation of consumer perceptions of brands ranked along four dimensions: 'differentiation, relevance, esteem and knowledge'. The Milward Brown *BrandZ* method creates its multiplier by estimating consumer relations to brand along a scale encompassing 'Bonding, Advantage, Performance, Presence and No Presence'.[6]

The point is that brand valuation established one of the first solid links between the public expression of affect, in the terms of the dimensions used to measure brand multipliers, and economic value, in terms of asset valuations on financial markets. In this way brand valuation constituted an emerging measure of the economic value of affect. I use the term 'emerging' because, to date, the field of brand valuation has not stabilized. In a survey from 2009 Salinas and Ambler identify 52 key operators globally, using 17 different methods. Valuations of individual brands also tend to diverge greatly: the same survey shows how the valuation of Apple, Toyota and Samsung by the market leading valuation firms Interbrand, MBO and Vivaldi differ by as much as 300 per cent. What is more, there is a growing suspicion, even among practitioners, that existing valuation methods tend to overvalue brands. While reported brand values have been continuously increasing in the last decade, underlying data such as consumer confidence in brands are on the decline (cf. Gerzema, 2008). However, a number of developments – driven by the very tendencies that made brand valuation possible in the first place – point towards a more stable measure of the economic value of affect.

## General Sentiment

General Sentiment is a technology company that produces comprehensive research products to help marketing, sales and communications executives evaluate their brand performance in the media, and assess return on investment.[7]

In the 1980s, when it first gained prominence within finance, accounting and management, the concept of brand value was a response to the desire to solve two 'mysteries': the 'mystery' of value creation in an 'emerging different model, which responds now more and more to post-industrial organizational and management criteria [that are increasingly] service-based, immaterial, low workforce rate, network shaped' (Cordazzo, 2007: 67); and the 'mystery' of growing discrepancies between market and book value. The solution to both 'mysteries' was to attribute value to measurable public expressions of affect. However, this solution was only possible because such expressions of affect had begun to become public and measurable in the first place.

What does it mean for affect to become public and measurable? It means that affect can be represented independently of the specific idea to which it is linked, that it can become visible as a distinct 'substance', so to speak. It is important to distinguish affect from idea. Gilles Deleuze does so in a masterly fashion in his lectures on Spinoza:

> the idea is a mode of thought that is defined by its representational character. This already gives us a first point of departure in distinguishing idea and affect (*affectus*) because we call affect any mode of thought that does not represent anything. So what does this mean? Take at random what anybody would call affect or feeling, a hope for example, a pain, a love, this is not representational. There is an idea of the loved thing, to be sure, there is an idea of something hoped for, but hope as such or love as such represents nothing, strictly nothing. Every mode of thought insofar as it is non-representational will be termed affect. (Deleuze, 1978: 1–2)

Seen this way, the precondition for linking economic value to affect was that affect as such, regardless of the specific idea or representation to which it was linked, was becoming public and measurable, was acquiring a tangible substance. I argue that this process – of the substantiation of affect – involves both the remediation of affect through the restructuring of the public sphere, and the development of new measurement devices that are able to create a new general equivalent, against which specific manifestations of affect can be evaluated, regardless of the concrete ideas or representations to which they are tied. I call this new 'substance' 'General Sentiment'.

## The remediation of affect

The notion that the modern, mediated public sphere is capable of transforming individual ideas into a General Will (to use Rousseau's expression) that results from rational forms of public deliberation is well established in modern social theory (cf. Habermas, 1989). There is, however, a less established, but important parallel tradition that points at the capacity of modern forms of publicity to bring forth other forms of affect.

Starting with 19th-century 'crowd psychologists' like Gustave le Bon, Hippolyte Taine and Schipio Sighele, this line of thought has its perhaps most sophisticated 'classical' expression in Gabriel Tarde. For Tarde, the becoming public of affect is strictly connected to the rise of modern consumer culture, and the new link between affect and economic value that it promoted. In his *Psychologie économique* (1902) Tarde pointed out how, with the formation of modern mass publics, the value of commodities increasingly builds on their ability to sustain forms of 'mental communion' (*communion mentale*) among members of the public. In the absence of traditional value systems, such mental communion is what sustains conventional notions of the 'truth, beauty and utility' of goods, on which, in turn, their value is ever more based. It is important to stress that for Tarde, the formation of such a mental communion precedes the formation of opinion; it is the mental communion that forms around an object, the fact that people affect each other in relation to it that sustains opinions about its utility or beauty. Indeed for Tarde the very basic elements of the social are such mental communions, in which one mind affects the other in a multiplicity of ways. That is why he kept arguing for a social psychology, against Durkheim's sociology.[8]

In Tarde's view, the production of value in consumer culture thus directly involves and includes the new and rapid forms of circulation and combinations of affect that are enabled and brought out into the open by a modern media environment and, importantly, by the new role of consumer goods as catalysts of such forms of public affect. Friedrich Kittler makes a similar point in *Discourse Networks*: rather than being experienced as something entirely interior, as in the 19th-century romantic tradition, the formation of affect and sentiment is now partially externalized, guided by the flow of public opinion and the catalytic role of celebrities and *divae* as (momentary) containers of affective investment. To put Kittler's argument in excessively blunt terms: the subject of the 1800s experienced his ideas and affects as his own, but the subject of the 1900s experienced her ideas and affects as something that she adapts from the outside world (Kittler, 1990).

For Tarde, it is the immaterial aspects of goods, their 'truth, beauty, and utility' that sustains communions of public affect. Since Tarde, cultural studies and the sociology of consumption has provided a large corpus of research that shows how the immaterial aspects of consumer goods are able to sustain subcultures, brand communities and other kinds of mental communions that are kept together by strong affective investments (Arvidsson, 2006; Maffesoli, 1995). So it would seem reasonable to suggest that the remediation of social relations that has accompanied the rise of consumer culture has effectively managed to transform the nature of affect, from something private or at least located in small interaction systems, to something that acquires an objective existence as a value creating 'substance' in the public domain. Social media have taken this process one step further.

Possibly we are in the middle of a remediation of the public sphere that is as radical as that which followed the impact of print, as social media are rapidly becoming the default application of the Internet and the 'normal' way to communicate (in the sense of transferring ideas as well as in the sense of fostering affective 'communion' with others). For example, during the first eight months of 2009 Facebook grew by 100 per cent, from 100 million to 200 million users; at the time of writing it has surpassed 500 million; twitter grew by 1440 per cent in 2008 and is presently targeting one billion users. Already today more people use social media than email (MacMillan, 2010; Rayport, 2009).

What happens when social and affective relations are remediated by social media? Social media have two central properties that are relevant to this argument. First, if, as McLuhan claimed, print fostered the cold and distant subjectivity of bourgeois culture, then social media tend to connect people to each other. As many media scholars have underlined, the result is a more interdependent, or even 'networked' subjectivity, where proximity to and close affective experiences of others become important building blocks for identity, and where other people's evaluation of one's identity (or 'brand') becomes central not only to one's sense of self-worth, but also, and increasingly, to one's objective value as a professional, networker or 'micro-celebrity' (Marwick and Boyd, 2010; Hearn, 2008). Second, social media add to the process of the becoming public of affect by introducing an aspect of objectivity. Affective relations now become tangible in a wide variety of manifestations: the links that tie a blog to its network, friends on a social media page, 'social buttons' like Facebook's 'like' button, re-tweets, or even explicit ratings of the truth, beauty or utility of a person, object or service (cf. Gerlitz and Helmond, 2010). In this sense, social media are 'phatic media' in the double sense of both fostering the formation of public affective relations through 'non-dialogic and non-informational' practices of 'keeping in touch' (Miller, 2008: 388, 395), and of enabling such manifestations of public affect to act as an objective criterion of the value of individuals and other actors. However, this becoming-objective of public affect and its becoming-effective as a criterion of value is also dependent on the development of new methods of measurement.

*Affective proximity*

Tarde's insight about the role of public affect in value creation led him to argue that economics should be rationalized through the development of instruments that are able to measure such valuable investments of public affect with greater degrees of precision (Latour, 2004). However, during most of the 20th century neither economics nor the social sciences generally have paid much attention to Tarde's call. Economics remained with a one-dimensional definition of value, and even if the social sciences have developed a rich tradition of communication research, this has, with few exceptions, been mainly directed at studying the diffusion of ideas and opinions, and not the formation of affect per se. One notable exception has been the tradition of advertising psychology, which, starting with the pioneering work of Walter Dill Scott, devoted energy to developing methods for measuring phenomena such as the suggestive power of advertisements, above and beyond their powers of rational persuasion (Arvidsson, 2003a; Beale, 1991; Chessel, 1995). This research was linked to a notion of 'suggestion' where advertising was thought to work mainly through its powers of affective attraction.

However, attention to the affective relations that advertisements were able to instil in subjects never established itself as a principle for measuring the value of advertisements or of advertising space. Instead, as radio emerged as the most important advertising channel in the 1930s, the value of advertising time was measured according to socio-demographic techniques that built on the segmentation of audiences into predetermined classes, the so-called ABCD approach (Arvidsson, 2003b; Lockley, 1950; Converse, 1987). The ABCD approach institutionalized the notion that the value of advertising space depended on the 'productivity' of its destined audience segment in transforming advertising stimuli into effective demand. In this way the value of advertising space could be calculated in terms of the attention time of a particular segment, mirroring the notion of productive time deployed in Fordist cost accounting.[9]

The notion of affect as a criterion of value would only affirm itself in the 1960s, with the establishment of methodologies for so-called psychographic, or lifestyle, segmentation. This technique built on the use of large-scale surveys that mapped consumers according to a wide range of different values that, like the AOI (Attitudes, Opinions, Interests – Wells and Tigert, 1971) and later VALS (Values, Attitudes, Lifestyles – Mitchell, 1984) went far beyond what was directly related to purchases or attitudes to consumer goods. This data were subsequently submitted to inductive multivariate analyses (or 'cluster analysis') and the resulting correlations were represented as 'lifestyles'.

The reasons behind the success of psychographics were many. The 1960s had seen a transformation of the media environment, driven by the establishment of television, that demanded new kinds of audience segmentation. The computers necessary to perform the complicated forms of data processing became affordable for mid-sized organizations like advertising agencies and market research companies. The previous decade has seen a rising popularity of qualitative audience research that supplied new and interesting kinds of information. Most importantly, however, there was a perception of a general transformation of consumer culture, and a sense that the consumer desires were being de-linked from class structures (Frank, 1997; Wells, 1974). Its methodology involved a number of important innovations. First, it pioneered the kinds of inductive statistics that have become a basis for the data-mining techniques still in use today (see below). Second, lifestyle segmentation created a picture of the market in which consumer demand was seen to be determined by a number of affective concerns that appeared as independent in relation to the position of consumers vis-à-vis their position in the industrial economy. Third, and importantly, psychographics introduced a new definition of economic value, if only in an embryonic form. As lifestyle analysis was used to determine the value of advertising space in terms of how well the value structure of a particular medium coincided with the 'lifestyle' of a targeted consumer group, it introduced, for the first time, a notion of 'value distance' or affective proximity as a measure of economic value.

In the 1970s psychographic segmentation was based on large-scale surveys. Beginning in the 1980s the proliferation of credit cards and bar codes created vast data banks that were generated 'naturally', so to speak, at the point of purchase in stores and supermarkets. This information was subjected to data-mining techniques that were essentially refined versions of the kinds of multivariate cluster analysis deployed in psychographics, to generate the kinds of information that went into Customer Relationship Management programmes, and eventually brand valuation instruments (Arvidsson, 2003b). More recently, the arrival of the Internet, and in particular of social media, has greatly expanded the range of naturally occurring data that can be submitted to such data-mining techniques and – social media in particular – has provided a wide range of data on public affect that lends itself to such statistical profiling.

The methods that have been most popular in processing social media data have been network analysis and sentiment analysis. Network analysis has been deployed within the social sciences since the 1960s, but the arrival of networked communication media has given a boost to this methodology as a wide range of meaningful large relational data-sets are now available (Barabasi, 2003; Watts, 2004). In the field of value measurement, network analysis has been used for some time by managerial scholars in computing inter- and intra- firm 'social capital', and more practically, by companies, including IBM, as a knowledge management tool, where calculations of the centrality of employees to communication flows are taken as valid measures of their economic productivity (Baker, 2009). In calculating the value of public affect the main application of network analysis has been that of identifying 'influencers', people who have a central position in relational networks and communication flows, and who are therefore 'worth more' as communication channels. Yahoo has been using this approach for a long time in order to identify 'influencers' to be used in marketing campaigns, and Facebook is developing a similar approach to enable advertising to be placed on the basis of preferences expressed in personal networks. In the growing business of applying data mining to the measurement of brand strength and return on investment (ROI) in viral marketing campaigns, network analysis is used in identifying the degree to which a certain campaign has managed to influence actors that are central to communication networks as one dimension of ROI.

A second dimension is provided by Sentiment Analysis, which is based on the automatic recognition of the affective valence of words or patterns of words used in text. The challenge consists in overcoming the ambiguity and polyvalence of natural language. This issue can be addressed by machine learning approaches where an algorithm is trained on independent data-sets (cf. Dave *et al.*, 2003; Pang and Lee, 2008; Pang *et al.*, 2002). However, such approaches have only become feasible with social media, for two reasons. First, because only these platforms supply the vast amounts of data needed to even out errors and reach reliability rates compatible with those generated by human observers. Second, because only social media provide large enough sets of training data, such as movie or product reviews, where text is linked to quantitative estimates of value (in the form of number of 'stars' or other kinds of ratings).

In practice, sentiment analysis is used to generate quantifications of the intensity of affective investments in an object. Brand valuation service such as Radian or Sysomos, for example, use sentiment analysis to determine whether a branding campaign has generated a shift in the positive or negative intensity of affect invested in the brand on the part of the public or, to use the current term, in sentiment.[10] Similarly, sentiment analysis is growing in importance as a component of information systems for financial operators and other kinds of asset valuators. The company *Streambase*, for example, generates trading recommendations on the basis of a sentiment analysis of online news. *Covalence* mines a wide range of sources on Corporate Social Responsibility and subjects them to a sentiment analysis, the output of which is presented as an indicator of the 'ethical status' of an asset.[11] Many more of these applications are emerging, in particular around twitter because it has (so far) permitted public access to its data and is rapidly becoming a fairly representative platform of Internet traffic in general.

The use of network analysis, sentiment analysis or some combination of the two is presently emerging as a new paradigm for measuring assets, communication campaigns or individuals in terms of what is increasingly talked about as their 'reputation' (Marwick *et al*., 2010). In most models, reputation is defined as some combination of three measurements: the number of times that an object is mentioned; the network centrality (or influence) of the actors mentioning it; and the affective intensity (sentiment) with which they mention it. All of these metrics measure affect independently of ideas: the ideational content of specific affective investments is removed. Instead the value of affect is defined in terms of proximity. Network analysis defines influence (or network centrality) according to a number of measures that describe their distance to other nodes in the network, or to use the increasingly influential term coined by Facebook founder Mark Zuckerberg, 'social graph' – a sociogram that depicts all relations between individuals on the site regardless of what that particular network (or social graph) is *about*. (Facebook communication is of course not *about* anything, it is a place for the formation of affective, 'phatic', relations.) Sentiment analysis defines sentiment according to two dimensions, 'valence' or the sum of the affective valence of the words occurring in a message and 'arousal' or the sum of the absolute values of the valences. Here, too, the affective valence of words is defined according to a variety of lists that report their affective charge in natural language use, independently of the ideas that they might convey, individually or in combination (see for example Bradley and Lang, 1999).

## General Equivalent

My argument is that the convergence of social media platforms and datamining techniques and methods like network and sentiment analysis are creating a common approach towards the measurement of public affect, or General Sentiment. This common approach is emergent: it has already established itself in some sectors including brand valuation and the estimation of ROI on viral marketing campaigns; it is growing as a basis for social media business models; and it is making inroads in areas such as financial asset valuation and estimations of the value of corporate social responsibility and ethics. What is more, this approach has a history that goes back to the 1970s and the impact of psychographic segmenting. In other words it has been emergent for a long time, and this emergence is undergoing a natural acceleration with social media.

This emergent common approach is built on a distinct way of objectifying affect. First, it is based on inductive statistics like cluster analysis and other forms of pattern recognition that are able to find regularities in large data sets without departing from any *a priori* presuppositions about the nature of those regularities. This means that General Sentiment is able to be represented as an emergent variable that does not appear to be caused by any other factors. Like gold for the classical economists it can be a kind of *deus ex machina*: the commodity (or in this case, the artefact) by means of which the value of all other commodities (assets or communication channels) is established.[12] Second, General Sentiment is quantified in terms of value distance or, which is the same thing, affective proximity. This was an element already present in psychographic clustering where clusters were defined according to vector distances in a multivariate space, and it is a basic presupposition in both network and sentiment analysis. The criterion of 'distance' is able to generate a measure of General Sentiment that is independent of the particular ideas and representations that might ground individual value judgements. Regardless of whether I am a Christian or a Muslim, the tweets that I produce can still be judged in terms of a universal, if temporary, scale of positivity and negativity. The same thing goes for my position in a network, or for my expression of preferences in rating systems. However, like the General Equivalent of money, and unlike the universals of modern morality, the standard of judgement does not refer to any fixed values, but only refers back to the status of the system as a whole. Positive or negative sentiment is judged according to a wordlist that is itself derived empirically from natural language use. And different such word lists are constructed as algorithms, trained on different data sets, such as movie reviews, financial data, or ratings of different kinds of consumer products (see for example O'Hare *et al.*, 2009), and network centrality is calculated in relation to the network itself. In other words: unlike modern value systems, General Sentiment has no dimension of transcendence. Instead it appears as an immanent emergent element, an effect of the intensification of communicative flows operated by emerging devices of representation and measurement

So it seems that we are acquiring a new General Equivalent – a General Sentiment – that is measured according to three dimensions: the strength of the affective charge of a message (sentiment); its influence (network centrality); and the numerical size of its occurrence. Incidentally these dimensions coincide precisely with the factors that Gabriel Tarde thought would determine the strength of the mental communions that he argued underpinned perceptions of immaterial value: 'le plus ou moins grand nombre: le plus ou moins poids social (ce qui veut dire ici considération, compétence reconnue) des personnes qui s'accordent à l'admettre, et le plus ou moins d'intensité de leur croyance en elle' (Tarde, 1902: 62).

The emergence of this general equivalent is the combined outcome of new measurement systems and an ongoing remediation of affective relations. Just as, according to Marx, the re-mediation of productive cooperation, through assembly lines, factory systems and ultimately a world market effectively made individual skills and competences measurable in terms of abstract labour time, so the remediation of affect, through the industrialization of culture and the emergence of a mass public and more lately social media, confers a general nature on what were previously particular and private manifestations of affect and renders them objectively comparable, measurable and visible as a manifestation of General Sentiment.

To Marx, the value-form that eventually emerged out of this process, the productivity of labour time, was a direct reflection of the objective reality of an underlying value-creating process. Can we claim that the value form of General Sentiment – affective proximity – is a direct reflection of the objective value-creating process that unfolds in the social media based public sphere? Maybe we can put it in a weaker way: the predominance of finance as the main mechanism of valorization and the strong link that is emerging between financial value and objectified forms of reputation, like brands; the importance of brands as intangible assets for companies and, increasingly, for individuals; the crucial role that connections and social capital plays in a networked economy; and the growing importance of social media are all factors that are likely to make a measure of value in terms of General Sentiment, as defined above, reflect perceptions on the part of important actors or groups of actors as to the nature of the processes subject to measure and calculation.

## Conclusion: politics after Parsons?

It would seem that the devices that are presently emerging as measurements of value in terms of General Sentiment are effectively paying heed to Tarde's call for a more multidimensional economic analysis. Ultimately this might lead to a recognition that value decisions are ever more based on multiple and diverse processes of public deliberation, rather than on universally valid rules; and that such decisions are essentially political, or perhaps better, ethical. In such a situation a political agenda could reasonably aim for the opening up and democratization of such deliberative processes, allowing them to reflect a multitude of different perspectives and value horizons. Conceivably this can be achieved through the construction of a multitude of different devices that allow for such extended forms of deliberation, by means of a *Dingpolitik*, to use Bruno Latour's (2005) term. For this to happen it is crucial that access to the underlying data remains open and free, so that actors that do not have the economic means to pay for such data, such as activist groups, consumer cooperatives or other non-profit organizations, will be able to construct and operate devices. To date, this has been the case in relation to Twitter (but not Facebook), but rumour has it that Twitter is now planning to charge for data access. In the light of this, an important political agenda, in for example, traditional parliamentary politics, must be to work for the regulation of social media 'utilities' (Boyd, 2010) in such a way that data access remains as open as possible.

## Notes

1 'Wealth Management Group' is a pseudonym. I have obtained permission to quote the document on condition that the identity of the actual companies involved is not revealed.
2 Concepts like 'Fordism' and 'post-Fordism' are to be understood as Weberian ideal types that help us to navigate a complex empirical reality, rather than as accurate representations of that reality. While 'Fordism' is generally used to indicate a model of economic and social organization that prevailed as a paradigmatic ideal in the postwar years, the argument also recognizes the actual diversity of prevailing modes of economic organization and the varying degrees to which the ideal of Fordism actually came to structure economic processes in different temporal and geographical contexts. For discussions of the theoretical status and empirical relevance of the concepts of 'Fordism' and post-Fordism see Amin (1994) and Harvey (1991).
3 In 1950 intangibles accounted for roughly 20 per cent of the market value of the S & P 500, today the figure is 70 per cent. Brands account for, on average, 30 per cent of market value, although this varies considerably between sectors and companies (Lev, 2001; Mandel *et al.*, 2006; Nakamura, 2001; Gerzema, 2008).
4 In other words, the argument in this article is organized around a weak version of the 'performativity paradigm' that is now near to hegemonic in economic sociology. I recognize that the performativity of economic theories and their embodiment in practical devices matter, but believe that, however important such performativity may be, it remains inscribed in a larger socio-historical context that limits and structures its scope and potential. For an excellent discussion of the performativity paradigm in economic sociology, see McKenzie *et al.* (2008).
5 See also Interbrand Corporation, Company History, available at http://www.funduniverse.com/company-histories/Interbrand-Corporation-Company-History.html (accessed 7 December 2010).
6 On BrandZ, see 'Cristiana Pearson explains the methodology behind the 2010 BrandZ Top 100', available at http://www.millwardbrown.com/Sites/mbOptimor/Ideas/BrandZTop100/VideoPlayer.aspx?Param=1124997e-0e18-4bc9-bc5a-29b2f964bb66 (accessed 7 December 2010), on the Brand Asset Valuator see http://www.brandassetconsulting.com/
7 https://www.generalsentiment.com/what-we-do.html (accessed 26 November 2010).
8 'La société est un tissue d'actions inter-spirituelles, d'états mentaux agissant les uns sur les autres. . . . Chaque action inter-spirituelle consiste dans le rapprot entre deux êtres animés, dont l'une impression l'autre . . . La société donc, en son essence intime, doit être définie une communion mentale' (Tarde, 1902: 1–2).
9 In the 1970s, Dallas Smythe would build on this model in developing his theory of the 'audience commodity' (2002 [1978]).

10 http://www.radian6.com/, http://www.sysomos.com/
11 http://www.streambase.com/, http://www.covalence.ch/
12 Of course, Marx saw gold as a fetish for labour. He argued that the value of gold is itself dependent on the socially average labour time needed in its production (Marx, 1976 [1867]: 188).

# References

Adler, P. and Heckscher, C., (2006), 'Towards collaborative community', in C. Heckscher and P. Adler (eds), *The Firm as Collaborative Community*, Oxford: Oxford University.
Amin, A. (ed.), (1994), *Postfordism: A Reader*, Oxford: Blackwell.
Arvidsson, A., (2003a), *Marketing Modernity: Italian Advertising from Fascism to the Postmodern*, London: Routledge.
Arvidsson, A., (2003b), 'The prehistory of the panoptic sort: mobility in market research', *Surveillance and Society*, 1(4), available at: http://www.surveillance-andsociety.org (accessed 14 December 2010).
Arvidsson, A., (2006), *Brands: Meaning and Value in Media Culture*, London: Routledge.
Baker, S., (2009), 'Putting a price on social connections', *Bloomberg BusinessWeek*, 8 April, available at: http://www.businessweek.com/technology/content/apr2009/tc2009047_031301.htm?link_position=link1 (accessed 16 December 2010).
Barabasi, L., (2003), *Linked: How Everything Is Connected to Everything Else and What it Means*, London: Plume Press.
Beale, M., (1991), 'Advertising and the Politics of Public Persuasion in France, 1900–33', unpublished PhD dissertation, Department of History, University of California at Berkeley.
Beccattini, G., (1989), *Distretti Industriali e Sviluppo Locale*, Torino: Rosenberg and Seller.
Bertin, G., (1985), *Multinationales et Proprieté Industrielle: Le Controlle de la Tecnologie Mondiale*, Paris: Presses Universitaires du France.
Boer, G. and Jeter, D., (1993), 'What's new about modern manufacturing? Empirical evidence of manufacturing changes', *Journal of Management Accounting Research*, 5(Fall): 61–83.
Boyd, D., (2010), 'Facebook is a utility: utilities get regulated', Zephoria.org, 15 May, available at: http://www.zephoria.org/thoughts/archives/2010/05/15/facebook-is-a-utility-utilitieget-regulated.html (accessed 15 December 2010).
Bradley, M. and Lang, P.J., (1999), *Affective Norms for English Words (ANEW): Stimuli, Instruction Manual, and Affective Ratings*, Technical Report, Center for Research in Psychophysiology, University of Florida, Gainesville, FL.
Callon, M., (1998), 'Introduction: the embeddedness of economic markets in economics', in M. Callon (ed.), *The Laws of the Markets*, Oxford: Blackwell.
Chandler, A., (1977), *The Visible Hand: The Managerial Revolution in American Business*, Harvard: Belknapp.
Chessel, M., (1995), 'L'Émergence de la Publicité: Publicitaires, Annonceurs et Affichistes dans la France de l'entre-deux-guerres', unpublished PhD dissertation, Department of History and Civilisation, European University Institute, Fiesole, Italy.
Converse, J.M., (1987), *Survey Research in the United States, its Roots and Emergence, 1890–1960*, Berkeley: University of California Press.
Cordazzo, M., (2007), 'IC statement vs. environmental and social reports: an empirical analysis of their convergences in the Italian context', in S. Zambon and G. Marzo (eds), *Visualizing Intangibles: Measuring and Reporting in the Knowledge Economy*, Aldershot: Ashgate.
Dave, K., Lawrence, S. and Pennock, M., (2003), 'Mining the peanut gallery: opinion extraction and semantic classification of product reviews', *WWW'03: Proceedings of the 12th International Conference on the World Wide Web*, 519–528, New York: ACM.
De Angelis, M., (2007), *The Beginning of History: Value Struggles and Global Capital*, London: Pluto Press.

Deleuze, G., (1978), 'Lecture on Spinoza's concept of affect', *Course Vincennes 24/1/1978* (transcript) eds. E. Deleuze and J. Deleuze, available at: http://www.webdeleuze.com/php/sommaire.html (accessed 10 December 2010).
du Gay, P., (2000), *In Praise of Bureaucracy: Weber, Organization, Ethics*, London: Sage.
Edvinsson, L. and Malone, M.S., (1997), *Intellectual Capital: Realizing Your Company's True Value by Finding its Hidden Brainpower*, New York: Harper Business.
Fox, J., (2009), *The Myth of the Rational Market: A History of Risk, Reward and Delusion on Wall Street*, New York: Harper Collins.
Frank, T., (1997), *The Conquest of Cool*, Chicago: University of Chicago Press.
Fuchs, C., (2010), 'Labor in informational capitalism and on the Internet', *The Information Society*, 26(3): 179–196.
Fumagalli, A., (2007), *Bioeconomia e Capitalismo Cognitivo: Verso un Nuovo Paradigma di Accumulazione*, Rome: Carocci.
Gardner, B. and Levy, S., (1955), 'The product and the brand', *Harvard Business Review*, March–April: 33–39.
Garriga, E. and Melé, D., (2004), 'Corporate social responsibility theories: mapping the territory', *Journal of Business Ethics*, 53: 51–71.
Gerlitz, C. and Helmond, A., (2010), 'Hit, link and share: organizing the social fabric of the web in a like economy', paper presented at the DMI mini-conference, Amsterdam, 24–25 January 2010.
Gerzema, J., (2008), *The Brand Bubble: The Looming Crisis in Brand Value and How to Avoid It*, New York: Jossey-Bass.
Glover, L. and Fitzgerald-Moore, D., (1999), 'Total quality management: shop floor perspectives', in C. Mabey, D. Skinner and T. Clark (eds), *Experiencing Human Resource Management*, London: Sage.
Gramsci, A., (1971), 'Americanism and Fordism', in Q. Hoare and G. Nowell-Smith (eds), *Selections from the Prison Notebooks*, New York: International Publishers.
Habermas, J., (1989), *The Structural Transformation of the Public Sphere: An Inquiry into a Category of Bourgeois Society*, Cambridge, MA: MIT Press.
Harvey, D., (1991), *The Condition of Postmodernity*, Oxford: Blackwell.
Harvey, D., (2010), *The Enigma of Capital and the Crises of Capitalism*, London: Enigma Books.
Hearn, A., (2008), 'Meat, mask, burden: probing the contours of the branded "self"', *Journal of Consumer Culture*, 8(2): 163–183.
Holdsworth, P., (2001), 'John Murphy walks out the retreads', *Brand Management*, May, available at: http://www.highbeam.com/doc/1G1-74336433.html (accessed 7 February 2010).
Kittler, F., (1990), *Discourse Networks 1800/1900*, Stanford, CA: Stanford University Press.
Landes, D., (2003), *The Unbound Prometheus: Technical Change and Industrial Development in Western Europe from 1750 to the Present*, Cambridge: Cambridge University Press.
Latour, B., (2004), 'Never too late to read Tarde', *Domus*, October available at: http://www.bruno-latour.fr/presse/presse_art/GB-DOMUS%2010-04.html (accessed 16 December 2010).
Latour, B., (2005), 'From Realpolitik to Dingpolitik', in B. Latour and P. Weibel (eds), *Making Things Public: Atmospheres of Democracy*, Cambridge, MA: MIT Press.
Lev, B., (2001), *Intangibles: Management, Measurement and Reporting*, Washington DC: Brookings Institution Press.
Levitt, T., (1983), 'The globalization of markets', *Harvard Business Review*, May–June: 92–103.
Linebaugh, P. and Rediker, M., (2000), *The Many-Headed Hydra: The Hidden History of the Revolutionary Atlantic*, London: Verso.
Liu, A., (2004), *The Laws of Cool: Knowledge Work and the Culture of Information*, Chicago: University of Chicago Press.
Lockley, L., (1950), 'Notes on the history of marketing research', *The Journal of Marketing*, 14: 733–736.
Lury, C. and Moor, L., (2010), 'Brand valuation and topological culture', in M. Aronczyk and D. Powers (eds), *Blowing up the Brand: Critical Perspectives on Promotional Culture*, New York: Lang.

MacMillan, D., (2010), 'Twitter targets one billion users, challenging Facebook for ads', *Bloomberg BusinessWeek*, 12 October, available at: http://www.businessweek.com/technology/content/oct2010/tc20101012_048119.htm (accessed 7 December 2010).
Maffesoli, M., (1995), *The Time of the Tribes: The Decline of Individualism in Mass Society*, London: Sage.
Mandel, M., Hamm, S. and Farrell, C., (2006), 'Why the economy is a lot stronger than you think', *BusinessWeek*, 13 February, available at: http://www.businessweek.com/magazine/content/06_07/b3971001.htm (accessed 25 November 2007).
Marwick, A. and Boyd, D., (2010), 'I tweet honestly, I tweet passionately: Twitter users, context collapse and the imagined audience', *New Media and Society*, 13(1): 114–133.
Marwick, A., Murgia-Diaz, D. and Palfrey, J., (2010), 'Youth, privacy and reputation', Harvard Law School Public Law and Legal Theory Working Paper Series Paper No. 10–29.
Marx, K., (1973 [1939]), *Grundrisse*, trans. Martin Nicolaus, London: Penguin.
Marx, K., (1976 [1867]), *Capital*, Vol I, trans. Ben Fowkes, London: Penguin.
McKenzie, D., (2006), *An Engine, Not a Camera: How Financial Models Shape Markets*, Boston, MA: MIT Press.
McKenzie, D., Muniesa, F. and Siu, L. (eds), (2008), *Do Economists Make Markets? On the Performativity of Economics*, Princeton: Princeton University Press.
Miller, V., (2008), 'New media, networking and phatic culture', *Convergence*, 14(4): 387–400.
Mitchell, A., (1984), *Nine American Lifestyles*, New York: Warner Books.
Morris-Suzuki, T., (1984), 'Robots and capitalism', *New Left Review*, 147: 109–121.
Nakamura, L., (2001), 'Investing in intangibles: is a trillion dollars missing from GDP?' *Business Review*, 04/2001: 27–37.
O'Hare, N., Davy, M., Bermingham, A., Ferguson, P., Sheridan, P., Gurrin, C. and Smeaton, A., (2009), 'Topic-dependent sentiment analysis of financial blogs', paper presented at *TSA'09, First International CIKM Workshop on Topic Sentiment Analysis for Mass Opinion Measurement*, Hong Kong, 6 November 2009.
Pang, B. and Lee, L., (2008), *Opinion Mining and Sentiment Analysis*, Boston: Now Publishers.
Pang, B., Lee, L. and Vaithyanathan, S., (2002), 'Thumbs up? Sentiment classification using machine learning techniques', *Proceedings of the 2002 Conference on Empirical Methods in Natural Language Processing, EMNLP*: 79–86.
Piore, M. and Sabel, C., (1984), *The Second Industrial Divide: Possibilities for Prosperity*, New York: Basic Books.
Rayport, J., (2009), 'How social networks are changing everything', *BusinessWeek*, 7 May, available at: http://www.businessweek.com/magazine/content/09_20/b4131067611088.htm (accessed 12 June 2009).
Roethlisberger, F. and Dickson, W., (1939), *Management and the Worker*, Cambridge, MA: Harvard University Press.
Rose, M., (1975), *Industrial Behaviour*, Harmondsworth: Allen Lane.
Salinas, G. and Ambler, T., (2009), 'A taxonomy of brand valuation practice: methodologies and purposes', *Journal of Brand Management*, 17: 39–61.
Smart, B. (ed.), (1999), *Resisting McDonaldization*, London: Sage.
Smythe, D., (2002) [1978], 'On the audience commodity and its work', in M.G. Duham and D. Kellner (eds), *Media and Cultural Studies: Key Works*, Oxford: Blackwell.
Stark, D., (2009), *A Sense of Dissonance: Accounts of Worth in Economic Life*, Princeton, NJ: Princeton University Press.
Stehr, N., Henning, C. and Weiler, B. (eds), (2006), *The Moralization of Markets*, London: Transaction Books.
Tarde, G., (1902), *Psychologie Economique*, Paris: Félix Alcan.
Taylor, F.W., (1896), *The Adjustment of Wages to Efficiency: Three Papers*, London: Schonnenshein and Co.
Veloso, F. and Kumar, R., (2002), 'The automotive supply chain: global trends and Asian perspectives', Asian Development Bank Working Paper, January.

Virno, P., (2004), *A Grammar of the Multitude*, London: Verso.
Vogel, D., (2005), *The Market for Virtue: The Potential and Limits of Corporate Social Responsibility*, Washington: Brookings Institution Press.
Watts, D., (2004), *Six Degrees: The Science of a Connected Age*, New York: Norton.
Wells, D.W., (1974), 'Foreword' in D.W. Wells (ed.), *Life Style and Psychographics*, Chicago: American Marketing Association.
Wells, W. and Tigert, D., (1971), 'Activities, interests and opinions', *Journal of Advertising Research*, 11: 27–35.
Zwick, D., Bonsu, S. and Darmondy, A., (2009), 'Putting consumers to work: "co-creation" and new marketing govern-mentality', *Journal of Consumer Culture*, 8(2): 163–196.

# The changing lives of measures and values: from centre stage in the fading 'disciplinary' society to pervasive background instrument in the emergent 'control' society

## Helen Verran

**Abstract:** This paper examines the work that measures and values do in policy in the context of an epochal change in the relations between knowledge and policy in Australia. I tell a story of successive attempts to rehabilitate a dying Australian river. The first attempt employs policy as the application of theoretically justified natural knowledge about rivers and their environs. The second attempt occurs after the evidence-based policy era has dawned in Australia. The contrast shows that measures, values and facts about the dying river justified by epistemic practices have been displaced. In an era of evidence-based policy and governance through market mechanisms, measures and values speak to policy through designs that can be bought and sold. In order to be able to better describe this shift I develop an analytic vocabulary to give an account of the intensive properties of what I call enumerated entities, and link the shift to the move from a disciplinary to a control society.

**Keywords:** control society, modern fact, number, design, enumerated entities, Peirce

## Introduction

In this paper I attempt to discern the liveliness of measures and values, or more precisely, 'enumerated entities', as they contribute to contemporary governmentality (Foucault, 2000).[1] My contention is that the status and contribution of measures and values in relation to governmentality has changed in recent times. Formerly a core element in the relation between knowledge and policy, the enumerated entities that comprise measures and values expressed and epistemically justified natural and social orders, as those orders in turn called up and reaffirmed particular forms of measures and values. The foregrounding of measures and values is, however, now receding as science increasingly functions as a service industry. Measures and values have gone from centre stage in a fading

© 2012 The Author. Editorial organisation © 2012 The Editorial Board of the Sociological Review. Published by Wiley-Blackwell Publishing Ltd, 9600 Garsington Road, Oxford OX4 2DQ, UK and 350 Main Street, Malden, MA 02148, USA

'disciplinary' society to pervasive background instrument in an emergent 'control' society.

## Rehabilitating a river and changing policy eras

The story of policy work that lies at the core of this paper concerns the rehabilitation of the Snowy River. The river flows, or used to flow, from the slopes of Australia's highest mountain, Mount Kosziusko, through the southern end of Australia's High Country, falling suddenly to a short, narrow flood plain before flowing into the Southern Ocean. In Australian folklore this river epitomizes the Romantic Bush, but oddly, also National Progress. The water from the top third of the river is diverted through the tunnels of the Snowy Mountains Hydroelectric Scheme to end up on the other side of the mountains to flow west into irrigation country.

The problem with the Snowy River is that, like most of Australia's rivers, it is dying. The Snowy's health has been seriously failing for thirty years. In contrast, during most of the previous century and a half, the Snowy River was 'virile' with snowmelt. Back then 'the problem of the Snowy River' was that its waters ran east and south 'to waste in the Southern Ocean'. Its perceived virility meant it entered Australia's popular imagination. As one concerned scientist put it, 'The Snowy, bless it, is an iconic river, so it has got considerable attention and it is one where if something goes wrong, you can raise the ante . . . [but] who cares [or has even heard] about the Campaspe?'[2]

The Snowy River's morbidity is caused by too little rain, exacerbated by well-documented human-induced conditions: silting associated with advanced soil erosion from excessive cattle grazing in the montane plateau got underway in the 1890s. Still, for 60–70 years the spring snowmelt surges pushed the sand to the banks and eventually washed most of it out to sea. From the 1970s, however, severely diminished flows resulting from the diversion of 99 per cent of its upstream water to generate hydroelectric power and provide water for irrigation farmers on the western side of the mountains pushed the Snowy River to the edge. It became a swampy trickle for most of its length. A 14 km long sand-plug built up near the flood plain town of Orbost. According to the Snowy Alliance, which advocates for the rehabilitation of the river, the promise made under a government agreement in 2006 that 28 per cent of the harvested water would be returned to the river has not yet been implemented.[3]

The dying Snowy River is not the only crisis the folk of Orbost are facing. They are also dealing with the consequences of the demise of a once-thriving farming economy and the end of Orbost's life as a timber town. The limited acreage of the lower Snowy River flood plain means that farming the rich soil is no longer economic in an era of large-scale agro-industry. Severe government limitations on logging in the nearby forest uplands mean that sawmills have closed. That industry too has become a mere remnant, reduced to the cutting and hauling of a few logs for woodchip export. Many Orbost families are losing their livelihoods. Divisions between sections of the community are rife: greenies against forest workers; farmers against anglers; the employed (mostly by government) against the unemployed. The activities of the Wilderness Society supporting ecotourism fuel rumours that greenies are taking advantage of the dire situation to make more land grabs to tie up large areas in National Parks.

The problems of Orbost and its river reach might well have remained just another instance of Australia's 'dying rural hinterland' problem – interlinked environmental and social decay – if the local advocacy group, the Snowy Alliance, had not managed to get their candidate elected to the Parliament of the State of Victoria in 1999. As it happened, the Snowy Alliance found itself holding the balance of power and precipitated a change in government by aligning itself with the social democratic Labour Party, forcing the conservative Liberal Party into opposition.

It seemed the Snowy's moment had come, and almost immediately a plan for a $1.7 million rehabilitation trial of the Snowy at Orbost was announced. This trial was to be undertaken under the guidance of scientists either employed or contracted to the newly expanded Department of the Environment. However, in a departure from past practice, the trial was to be administered by the East Gippsland Catchment Management Authority (EGCMA). This organization is one of nine semi-autonomous local environmental government commissions operating as non-profit organizations. It was established by the previous Liberal government as part of the civil service reform programme in Victoria instituting the 'new public administration' (Verran, 2009).[4]

Proper process was followed: a Memorandum of Understanding was reached with EGCMA. Feasibility studies, literature reviews and concept plans were commissioned. A Scientific Reference Panel for the trial was appointed in 2001. There was a small hiccup at this point when the Panel 'saw a need to resolve some knowledge gaps to allow more confident decisions to be made regarding the direction of the Trial'.[5] More consulting scientists and engineers were commissioned to produce a Scoping Study. Despite all the proper procedures being followed, still things did not go as planned. Administratively, an experimental trial of river rehabilitation techniques in the Snowy River at Orbost was initiated in September 2000. The trial expressed a long established policy of 're-naturalizing' rivers, a policy supported by well-established environmental theory. But long after the election that the trial was designed to speak to, the project was yet to get underway. The experiment in river rehabilitation never happened! What went wrong?

It seems that the EGCMA asserted its autonomy and diverted the money provided by the government for the trial to other projects. Powerful local interests opposed the experimental rehabilitation work on the grounds that the logs that were to be submerged in the river to encourage scour pools and variations in flow would break loose in a flood and destroy sheds, bridges and fences. The administrative innovation had provided a means for locals to resist the government policy of naturalizing rivers. A thwarted experiment, a never-achieved field laboratory, logs not anchored in the river: the sets of flows-values that would have epistemically justified the placement of the logs and simultaneously attested the rightness of the policy of (re)naturalization of the river were never registered. There were no values for river flows; knowledge was not produced; epistemic justification was never called into being.

What I want to draw attention to in relating this seemingly insignificant episode is not (only) the local politics in which vested agricultural interests trump established environmental policies, although that continues to be a major issue in Australian environmentalism. Instead, I want to use this expression of local power thwarting government policy to identify something that in the normal course of events could easily be missed: the taken for granted, 'normal', relation between knowledge and government policy, for, in the first decades of the twentieth century, that norm is about to be overturned.

My claim will be that from centre stage in warranting certainty about the characteristics of territory and populations in a 'disciplinary' society, measures and values are now the pervasive instrument choreographing performance of interventions over wealth creation in an emergent 'control' society. In formulating this claim I am adopting terms from Deleuze (1995). Following Foucault, Deleuze names 18th to early 20th century modernity as the 'disciplinary society', and using William Burroughs' term labels what has come after that, beginning in the 1970s, as the 'control society'. Deleuze exhorts us to begin the work of 'establish[ing] the basic socio-technological principles of "control mechanisms" as their age dawns' (1995: 182).

Here I take Deleuze as referring to Foucault's work on governmentality that formed the content of lectures he gave at the Collège de France in 1978–79. Foucault was interested in the emergence of political economy that he associated with the liberal principle that 'One always governs too much . . . [Liberalism asks] why after all is it necessary to govern?' (Foucault, 2008: 319). And he notes, in liberalism there is only successful and failed governance (not legitimate and illegitimate), where success is the generation of wealth. In beginning this series of lectures Foucault lists five points that are indispensible for understanding governmentality. The fourth insight he lists is that political economy:

> Discovers a certain naturalness specific to the practice of [liberal] government itself. The objects of governmental action have a specific nature. . . . Nature is not an original and reserved region on which the exercise of power should not impinge. Nature is something that runs under, through, and in the exercise of governmentality . . . It is not background but a permanent correlative. (Foucault, 2008: 15)

Using Foucault's terms to articulate the change in policy eras, I am asking whether there has been a significant change in the nature that runs under, through and in the exercise of governmentality in Australia. Has the nature that exists with its particular types of objects (measures and values, or as I will call them enumerated entities), as the permanent correlative of environmental government in Australia, changed over the past 15 years? And if so, how? Is it valid to see this in Deleuze's terms as a shift from a disciplinary to a control society? More specifically, is it valid to see this in terms of a shift from mechanisms which create a closed system or moulds, to those which modulate, continuously changing from one moment to the next, forming a system of variable geometry? (Deleuze, 1995).

## Enumerated entities

To answer this question I will foreground the assumptions about relations between knowledge practices and policy practices that are implicit in this story of a thwarted experiment in river rehabilitation. I do this by juxtaposing the first failed episode of river rehabilitation that I have just outlined, with a second episode. In particular I note (in relation to the first episode) the expectation of a direct connection between the facts that might have been produced about the river, and the actions of a government. The assumption was that policy should be directed by theory established by past experimental facts, and should in turn be able to produce new facts: the new facts would attest both theory and the policy.

The second episode, styled as government services for the environment, begins with a call for tenders as part of newly instituted forms of government procurement of an evidence base for river rehabilitation policy design. This form of governmentality proved more difficult to resist, and through a designed intervention the river was duly acted upon alongside the re-making of citizen identities as a 'community' (Verran, 2009). In calling for tenders the government specified the product it sought as the design and testing of in-stream structures to generate measures and values, but crucially also specified the need for extensive public consultation and involvement.

The group that won the tender centred their bid on a laboratory set-up they referred to as 'a physical model' – a model of the river-reach in a huge sand box in the grounds of a nearby university. This was the central methodological element that would gather values for river flows. This 'mobile bed' (25 metres in length and 5 metres wide) in which a scale version of the river-reach would be constructed, provided a strong scientific basis for in-stream structure design. One of the important benefits of this type of model, as described in the bid, was the capacity for members of the 'community' to visit the laboratory and study the model. They could watch the flow of water under various simulated conditions and see a scale model of the effects that the placing of logs in the river at various places would have. Best of all, these visitors could become experimenters themselves and put in simulated logs at their favourite fishing spot to see what would happen with river flow. Visits from various 'community' groups – the local land-care group, groups of school children, local anglers and so on – were to be arranged. And the results of informal experiments made by these groups were to be collated to promote and evidence community involvement in the trial.

The bid further described how the results that emerged from this modelling exercise would be work-shopped with scientists from various biological sciences

– those concerned with fish habitats, those who dealt with riparian vegetation, those whose special knowledge was about local indigenous plants, their propagation and establishment needs. Lists of requirements for meeting the biological needs of a river would be assembled. Groups of children and local volunteers to plant and tend this expanding natural habitat would be recruited and trained. The plans would be presented in several local meetings in a form of niche marketing, and feedback from those meetings was to be incorporated. Also important was an estimate of the total costs of the projected river works and a breakdown of what money should be spent where and when. This would go along with an elaborate schedule and time sequence of events and sub-events.

Following the success of this bid in competition, and the carrying out of the programme of activities it described, a full set of policy recommendations were handed over: designs for manufacture and placement of engineered logjams; lists of values and measures generated in the modelling of these designs in the huge sand-box; analysis of these findings identifying and specifying the hydraulic works needed; accounts of further river works needed to achieve full biological recovery of the river reach; plans for 'community' working bees to contribute to this; lists of plants and plans of their distribution; plans for a school syllabus in environmental studies that could be worked up with a consortium of several local schools.

What are the differences in the two episodes described here? To identify some of the most significant I want to introduce the notion of an enumerated entity, a term that speaks to the material-semiotic liveliness of the numbers that are brought into existence in ordering and valuing. To explain the significance of this term for my argument let me proceed by reference to the work of Mary Poovey on the history of modern facts (1998). In beginning her analysis, Poovey notes how early modern knowledge constituted facts that seemed to consist of non-interpretive numerical description (that is, uncontroversial values) embedded in systematic claims about orders that were somehow derived from, and derivative of, those categories so unproblematically and uncontroversially valued. Numbers, Poovey writes, 'have come to epitomize the modern fact . . . somehow non-interpretive [in valuing] at the same time as they have become the bedrock [order] of systematic knowledge' (Poovey, 1998: xii).

Poovey points to what identify as a peculiar three-step epistemic dance that numbers perform as modern facts and in so doing highlights the importance of my term enumerated entities as a way of acknowledging the ways in which numbering participates in ordering and valuing. In the first step (1) categories are derived as parts of a vague whole (this is the process of ordering); in the second step, (2) categories are (measured and) valued as parts become specified units or elements and are collected; and in the third step (3) the categories derived in step one, and valued in the second, are universalized as how things are. This third step naturalizes the modern fact: it reverses the ordering of step (1) through the dazzling formalism of step (2), and the collected units/parts are elided as an instantiation of a specified whole. An order of specific interests is thereby rendered as a natural order.[6] The achievement of valuing – very often through practices of numbering – attests the self-evident given-ness of the category valued. This dissembling step solidifies a partial order (in both senses of the term) as the given nature of 'nature' or 'society'. My use of the term enumerated entity (rather than merely number) is a way of insisting on the importance of locating number in relation to this work, of acknowledging numbers as *lively* semiotic-material actants in this three-step dance.

How they do this – how numbers as indices of a partial order become lively measurements of value that can then be put to work to produce a naturalized order – becomes important if we are to develop insights about the modern fact in a governmentality that has cut loose from epistemic practices by instituting market mechanisms at the core of governance. And to make this possible I need to make brief reference to the work of C.S. Peirce on signs[7] since it offers a typology that classifies semiotic affordances of signs as symbols, indexes or icons. These three types of sign are distinguished by Peirce in terms of how they are organized in the central unit of his investigation: the triad of sign-object-interpretant. It is this triad that Peirce understands as central to the empirical undertaking required to develop a normative scientific method.

A 'sign' might be the graphic numeral in a table of results, a spoken number name, or a set of coordinates in a line graph. The 'interpretant' is the material practices of constituting the 'reader of the sign' and the rationalities in which reading is possible and hence the meanings that might be made. The 'object', or more precisely the sets of material routines (such as the flowing of the river, or the floating away of logs) in which the object 'does itself', may be human or non-human, living or non-living. All three modes are deeply implicated in the others and something that acts as 'sign' in one situation might act as 'object' in another, or what is 'object' here can become 'interpretant' there. For those of us who wish to use Peirce's semiotics instrumentally, this triad effects a continuum and provides a basis from which to consider the participation of enumerated entities in assemblage. As noted above, it is the way this triad, or the way in which three-way relations are variously brought together, that allows Peirce to distinguish between icons, indices and symbols, with different strengths of linkage in relation to 'sign', 'object' and 'interpretant'. Crucially, it is indices where the relations between 'sign', 'object' and 'interpretant' within which the entity is constituted are open and available for reworking. It is thus in the indexical zone that the three-step epistemic dance of 'modern facts' is most easily undone.

**From symbol to icon**

So, now having put this conceptual apparatus of enumerated entities in place, let me start again with the first episode. Here we saw things proceeding in the expectation that natural sciences studying the various aspects of rivers – the waters and their flows, the physical and biological properties of river beds and banks and so on – would enable and justify the policy of (re)naturalizing the river reach. The plan to spend $1.7 million rehabilitating the Snowy at Orbost began with science, or more particularly with a theory about rehabilitating rivers that exists as a scientific literature. Some of the texts making up that literature contain numbers that represent or value a 'universal river' in terms of established facts. As universal values these numbers, which epistemically attest theories, denote: that is, they are symbols in Peirce's terms.

Embedded within theory, symbolizing numbers played a role in generating a river naturalization policy, along with political intuition and environmental ideology. But science and the enumerated entities that will be generated in its name also have a specific role in implementing the policy. There, however, semiotically at least, they are different to the numbers working as symbols in theory. Implementing policy involves indexicalizing the symbolic values of theory, and what in theory is purely values, will, in indexes, become evident as a tension, that is, indexicality is the site of the tension or liveliness of measures and values. It is this tension – the source of the liveliness of enumerated entities – I suggest, that is lost in the second case.

In the first episode – bringing river-flow to life as a specific matter of concern – values are put to work indexically: policy, engineering works, river, and measures and values, and the experimenter, the muddy hydraulic engineer (no longer the removed judging observer of theory), are ineluctably linked. And for policy and river, government and index to continue into the future, work must continually be put in. This is the work that keeps indexes alive, the work of particularizing (the order established in step 1 of the 3-step dance) and generalizing (the valuing of step 2), which is never simply given but must be reproduced. Particularizing and generalizing guide implementation and justify the assiduously attended workings of the elaborate laboratory field site in which they come to life. In the zone of indexicality they are organically co-constituting; you cannot have one without the other and changes to one side are inevitably expressed, sometimes in unexpected ways, in the other.[8]

Indeed, what the example of the Snowy River suggests is that the (re)indexicalizing of the symbolizing numbers of theory during policy implementation provides an opportunity for the partiality of the ordering that has been made invisible in theory to be made evident. What we saw in the first episode is that in the collective action of the policy experiment, the partial order of the working indexes was resisted.[9] The epistemic dissembling of such modern facts (effecting the categories of the 'natural' and hiding that accomplishment) in the first episode failed to achieve river rehabilitation, as powerful interests disturbed their performance so as to prevent the re-naturalizing of rivers from being realized.

The 'empire of expertise' in which the epistemic dissembling of the modern facts could be kept intact, and the partiality of their ordering hidden, had broken down. The institutions created as part of the process of establishing government by commission did not warrant the indexes that formerly were so carefully maintained. As the passage between the symbols of theory and the indexes of doing policy work occurred, the partiality of the ordering involved became evident as an order that favoured environmental scientists and not farmers. Coincidentally, the work of maintaining indexes with incessant actual messy ordering work, which necessitated the government retaining the services of scientists on a permanent basis, became evident as a government 'cost centre'.

Consider, then, what happened in the second episode, with particular attention to the zone of indexicality.[10] Nine or ten consultants retained by a large international consulting firm were occupied in various ways. Some tested the flows of water in a river-reach modelled in a huge sandbox, others consulted with various community groups in Orbost – the pensioners, school children, anglers clubs, the local land-care group, and so on – arranging for visits to the lab where the sandbox was located and for discussions of the issues, and explanations of the processes involved in these information-gathering exercises. After months of such activity many meetings are held and a further series of sandbox trials and meetings with individuals and groups takes place. Many sets of values concerning the likely responses of the river under varying conditions, and likely responses of this group of Orbostians to those river responses are generated.

Compared to the index of river behaviour as measures of river flow that the river scientists were prevented from assembling just a few years earlier, a far more complicated and demanding set of indexes is assembled here, indexes to the multiplicity of the people-place of Orbost and its river-reach. But, crucially, these indexes themselves have zero temporal extension; they are not lively. In generating a product to hand over to the purchaser – the government – the many accumulated indexes become a whole (proprietary) design that cannot sustain the future life of the indexes of which it comprises. What began as indexes growing from a particular (interested) reading of Orbost and its river-reach (the diagnostic intervention), becomes a solidified value icon – a design for 'a river-rehabilitating and community building intervention' – that is handed over to government.

In this product the enumerated entities whose ephemeral life indexed the collective life of Orbost and its river-reach, become not symbols (whose continuing relation to their past and to future rivers is sustained in the capacity of numbers as symbols to be put to work in law-like, naturalized ways) but an icon. The dissembling 3-step is now different. No longer will it contribute to the sustenance of the (universal) categories of a found natural world as a set of values. Instead, enumerated entities in the second episode are rendered recognizable in terms of resemblance, that is, as promoting an interested socio-political order of a people-place: Orbost as a community of stakeholders whose interests may or may not be served by the partial order the consultants' design promotes. And yet, despite its qualities of 'resemblance', supported by techniques of 'transparency' and 'risk management', this recognizable partiality is rendered irretrievable when the consultants' product is handed over to the government. There, those indexes that had ephemeral life as the consultants hurried about doing this and that, inventing categories and assembling values, come to be visible as icons, but in this glare of visibility, the enumerated entities are rendered lifeless.

Juxtaposing these two episodes, only one of which came to fruition, thus foregrounds the changing relations between knowledge and policy in 21st-century Australia. Had the first version of the river rehabilitation trial proceeded as expected, and measures and values been collected, the measures and values would have reported on the river. Embedded in existing knowledge practices produced elsewhere, these measures and values would have simultaneously contributed to a justification of a (re)naturalizing rivers policy, and the environmental theory on which it was based. In the second episode, however, measures and values were created *in situ* to generate a design to hand over to government, a proposed set of collective acts. In the privatized work of natural and social sciences, the ordering categories were rendered internal to proprietary design. In developing the design, we can imagine a group of consultants getting their feet wet in the river and having their patience tested by uncooperative community members. But when handed over to government officers at the end of the contract, the mess of the world, mud and non-compliant citizens, retreats. A design of a projected intervention that would resemble a newly ordered 'community' with various 'stakeholders', and in which the effectiveness and financial probity of the intervention were to be monitored, was what was bought and sold.

Indeed, the Orbost and its river-reach indexed in the product received by the government might no longer exist by the time the work has been completed and all the measures and values are neatly in their tables and graphs and the words assembled in reports. The product has already largely been paid for in an agreed schedule of payments, and was given no warranty by the company that produced it. When governments buy measures and values in generating evidence-based policy it is the customer – the government (not 'nature') – that provides warranty and guarantee. In the work of generating values on which design of a policy intervention might be based, enumerated entities do work indexically, but these indexes are not kept alive with respect to a theoretically informed policy. What the government buys is a customized intervention designed to be carried out by a firm of consultants.

It is evident to anyone who cares enough to examine the documents that policy expresses interested knowledge. At the beginning of the second episode 'Orbost and its river-reach' are a 'failing-people-place', a cost centre for the 'firm' that is the state, yet the design of the rehabilitation policy as a project, an intervention (a one-off, time-limited generation of indexical values that are tested for their capacity to resemble a place that is not yet but is designed to come into existence), will seek to ensure that 'Orbost and its river-reach' will stop being a 'cost centre' and may even become a 'centre of production'. In other words, where we may have thought there was only class politics and the (mis)use of government resources we now see how an ontological politics was also generated, resulting in a privileging of the practices effecting a 'productive' river over those that do a 'natural(ized)' river.

But my analysis has suggested that this is not all, or not only, what is at stake. Certainly, just as in the previous era of governmentality epistemic practices effected a singular order, so too do they in this newly instituted era. But in the new era this effecting of unimpeachability in design practices is located in the private sector rather than in a government constituted sanctuary for experts, whose knowledge is organized with the aim of keeping indices alive, by supporting their conversion into symbols. On becoming (government) property the enumerated entities not only lose their status as indexical and become instead icons, but cannot be reconstituted – brought to life again – as indexes. What I am suggesting, then, is that the iconicity effected in the practices of designing interventions achieves the solidification of an order, which is neither and both natural and social.

The policy-making that is at the heart of both episodes is environmental policy making. At first glance this seems to involve the natural sciences only. And in the first era that is a correct assessment: measures and values there would indeed report on the natural properties of the river and its environs. In the second era the constitution of the policy product offered for sale to the government certainly involved collecting values by interrogating a natural entity albeit indirectly via a model. But the crucial aspect of the product was the creative integration of the social and the natural. The bid that made the most of that element won the contract. Rather than natural or social sciences, the salient divisions in the second era are between the work of the natural and social sciences and the work that incorporates the information they both produce into a seemly and viable prototype policy design. The collective action that attends to the public problem of the Snowy River at Orbost dissolves the division between social and natural sciences in a form of government that shapes a particular community, or perhaps several, in a particular place.

In this second episode – evoking the newly hatched era of evidence-based market-mechanisms policy – the measures devised had two rather distinct elements: river flow rate data and data on how various resident groups and individuals feel about, and respond to, projected futures for their town and its river-reach. Both elements participate not only in entrepreneurial social and natural science in constituting a product to be sold to government, that is, a prototype policy design, but also, as part of that product they participate in project design of an intervention that will incorporate systematic measures of performance and financial probity. As such, in the second episode, we witness not only (to paraphrase Foucault once more) a change in the nature that 'runs under, through, and in the exercise of governmentality', but also how this change – and the move from the natural(ized) to the productive that it entails – sees measures and values working, not to create certainty about entities, but to produce entities whose intensive characteristics are the subject of design. As such they are inherently variable, and this variability of design is what makes them such able participants in the generation of new forms of wealth, at the same time that their liveliness is curtailed. In short, from first to second episodes we witness a shift in the involvement of enumerated entities in mechanisms of discipline to those of control.

## Conclusion

In this paper I set out with the intention of taking seriously Deleuze's exhortation to develop familiarity with the socio-technical workings of the means by which compliance is elicited in the newly hatched era of control governmentality. I examined changes in the intensive properties of enumerated entities as policy eras moved from instituting policy based on knowledge of the natural world to instituting policy through design of interventions. In a discussion of two instances of policy intervention I showed that there was a move from a policy in which the use of indexes that is obscured in a rubric of 'natural', to one in which the partiality of the ordering implied by indices is revealed. But I also showed that in the new era enumerated entities do not come to symbolize, but instead are icons; as such, they do not sustain the indexes from which they are produced. There is no longer the elaborate fiction that the knowledge embedded in policy is neutral – an impartial representation of reality.

The question posed by this analysis of the Snowy River is whether we should be calling for a return to a governmentality that secures collective social life through a use of indices, that, while adjudicated by experts, nonetheless requires epistemic dissembling around the making and valuing of an order of 'nature'. Or should we try to make the best of a new governmentality in which design practices constitute facts as icons that dissemble around the making and valuing of an order of politics? Perhaps – in the emerging control society – we have no choice but to engage in the zone of indexicality, wittingly negotiating with and through other participants in that zone.

## Notes

1 'Governmentality' is an awkward neologism deriving from Foucault's thinking about security, territory, and population in the late 1970s (Foucault, 2000). It imagines government as an ever-changing set of *practices*. I am following Miller and Rose (2008) in using a loose notion of the term governmentality, implying intersecting practices of 'doing knowledge' or 'rationalities', and the bewildering varieties of instruments devised in acting upon knowledge generated so as to transform it (Miller and Rose, 2008: 15).
2 Professor Sam Lake, quoted in *The Age*, 26 April 2003, p. 5.
3 http://www.snowyriveralliance.com.au
4 New Public Administration (NPA) swept through Australian governments in the 1990s. See http://www.apsc.gov.au/about/exppsreform2.htm
5 'Lower Snowy River Rehabilitation Trial, Consultancy Brief for Design and Evaluation of In-stream Structures', Department of Sustainability and Environment, Tender No. 103111, 15 March 2003, p. 3.
6 Hacking describes this peculiar three-step epistemic dance of modern facts in allegorical style: 'First there was this human thing, the making of representations. Then there was the judging of representations as real or unreal, true or false, faithful or unfaithful. Finally comes the world, not first, but second, third, or fourth' (Hacking, 1983: 196). Translating Hacking's terms to describe the generation of enumerated entities I identify these three steps: (1) 'the making of representations': the creation of a particular set of categories in an ordering step; (2) 'the judging of representations as real/true/faithful': the de facto defining of a unit of the property the cate-

gory creates; (3) 'Finally comes the world': being valued through the unitified category we get a single (valued) world. See Verran (2001: 166–169) for an empirical description of this three-step generation of enumerated entities in English language use and in Yoruba language use.

Law suggests that the problem is what I identify as the third step, which he labels 'reductionist reversal'. 'The predominant Euro-American mode . . . ends by authorizing a singular mode of out-thereness . . . [W]e should undo the reductionist reversal . . . nature should no longer be seen as the unique author of a single account but something that is produced along with social and cultural arrangements' (Law, 2004: 122). But giving up the third step is easier said than done.

7  See Hoopes (1991: 239) for a summary.
8  Crucial although they are in this form of governmentality, indexes are very risky things to have embedded at the core of doing policy, especially when there are no longer institutional mechanisms to tend them. Things to do with the here and now, or to do with the index are always floating off in one way or another, leaving policy, implementation, and evaluation in a shambles. Look at the recent bushfires in Victoria. The index at the centre of bush-fire policy, which had been carefully constituted not too long ago, was fatally exceeded by fire on 9 February 2009 leaving in its wake Australia's worst peacetime disaster.
9  And powerful landowners are able to make use of this indexical tension to prevent a river being re-ordered if they perceive it as not in their interest.
10 This section is imagined on some slender information I was given by the government communications officer. My hope in attending the tender bids hearing was that this would be the first stage in doing an ethnographic study of the rehabilitation policy experiment that the government was purchasing. For a number of reasons that turned out to be impossible. Large international consultancy firms are not much interested in having academics following their consultants around.

# References

Deleuze, G., (1995), *Negotiations 1972–1990*, trans. M. Joughin, New York: Columbia University Press.
Foucault, M., (2000), 'Governmentality', in J.D. Faubion (ed.), *Power: Essential Works of Foucault 1954–1984*, Volume 3, London: Penguin Books.
Foucault, M., (2008), *The Birth of Biopolitics: Lectures at the Collège de France 1978–1979*, ed. Michel Senellart, New York: Palgrave Macmillan.
Hacking, I., (1983), *Representing and Intervening: Introductory Topics in the Philosophy of Natural Science*, Cambridge: Cambridge University Press.
Hoopes, J. (ed.), (1991), *Peirce on Signs: Writings on Semiotic by Charles Sanders Peirce*, Chapel Hill, NC: University of North Carolina Press.
Law, J., (2004), *After Method: Mess in Social Science Research*, London: Routledge.
Miller, P. and Rose, N., (2008), *Governing the Present: Administering Economic, Social, and Personal Life*, Cambridge: Polity Press.
Poovey, M., (1998), *A History of the Modern Fact: Problems in Knowledge in the Sciences of Wealth and Society*, Chicago: Chicago University Press.
Verran, H., (2001), *Science and an African Logic*, Chicago: Chicago University Press.
Verran, H., (2009), 'Natural Resource Management's Nature and its Politics', *Communication, Politics and Culture*, 42(1): 3–18.

# Transactional politics

## Evelyn Ruppert and Mike Savage

**Abstract:** In spring 2009, revelations over the expense claims of British MPs led to one of the most damaging scandals affecting the legitimacy of parliamentary democracy in recent history. This article explores how this incident reveals the capacity of Web 2.0 devices and transactional data to transform politics. It reflects, graphically, the political power of identifying and knowing people on the basis of their transactions, on what they do rather than what they say. It also shows in practice how Web 2.0 devices such as Crowdsourcing, Google Docs, mash-ups and visualization software can be used to mobilize data for collective and popular projects. Basic analytic tools freely available on the Web enable people to access, digitize and analyse data and do their own analyses and representations of phenomena. We examine media and popular mobilizations of transactional data using the specific example of the MPs' expenses scandal and relate this to larger currents in online government data and devices for public scrutiny which give rise to a new politics of measurement. We argue that this politics of measurement involves the introduction of new visual devices based on the manipulation of huge databases into simplified visual arrays; the reorientation of accounts of the social from elicited attitudes and views to transactions and practices; and, the inspection of individuals arrayed in relation to other individuals within whole (sub) populations. It is also a politics that mobilizes new informational gatekeepers and organizers in the making and analysis of transactional data and challenges dominant or expert forms of analysis and representation.

**Keywords:** digital data, MP expenses, transactional politics, visualization, Web 2.0

## Introduction

Much has been written about how digital traces of our everyday transactions are recorded in commercial and government databases. In the UK, for instance, identifiers such as bank and loyalty cards, National Health Service (NHS) or National Insurance Numbers (NIN) mediate our transactions and make it possible to know much about who we are on the basis of what we do. Government databases track activities such as the registration of life events, income earned and taxes paid, licences obtained, cars purchased, borders crossed, benefits received, education attained, visits made to hospitals, and so on. Rather than identifying ourselves we are identified on the basis of data that is generated routinely as a by-product of our everyday activities. Commercial transactional databases also provide counts of the activities of whole populations through sales, subscriptions, loyalty cards, and online searches. There is now a lively debate about how such data might be making many of the orthodox tools of social science, notably the interview and the survey, somewhat redundant. What is the value of actually generating new data when so much data arises as the by-product of myriad transactional processes (see Savage and Burrows, 2007; Crompton 2008; Webber 2008; Savage 2009)?

Although there is currently an engaging academic debate about the power of transactional data, our paper breaks new ground by demonstrating how these data might be mobilized politically. Focusing on the 2009 British MPs' expenses scandal, we show how revelations about MPs' spending are indicative of the more pervasive mobilization of transactional data to know and evaluate the performance of populations. MPs' own shock and distress that their spending was exposed publicly is itself indicative of the unpredictable and transformative capacity of these new data sources. Bureaucratic procedure was also cast into question: expenses were 'unacceptable' or could 'not stand up to reasonable public scrutiny' even if they had been approved by the Fees Office or were within the Department of Finance and Administration's Green Book. Even though in only four cases was a case for criminal investigation warranted,[1] the power of the scandal needs no demonstration by us. It led to numerous resignations or decisions to stand down in the next election – from the Speaker of the House of Commons to several cabinet ministers – far more than any other single event or controversy. The *Guardian* reported that in the wake of the scandal almost 150 MPs quit (Glover, 2010). It is for these reasons that we are interested in analysing it here as an indication of an emerging form of transactional politics.

For, while the scandal could be construed as a classic instance of a media political exposé and investigative reporting (as presented in Winnett and Rayner, 2009), we argue that it is part of emergent politics in which Web 2.0 devices can be used by the media to engage the public in the digitization and analysis of data.[2] We are interested in how the very focus on transactional activity – in the form of expense claims – is not just a discrete, atypical political scandal, but evidence for a different kind of political activity. Our argument is developed in three phases. First, we begin by discussing the MPs' expenses scandal in March 2009, as first broken by journalists at the *Daily Telegraph* in order to show the limits of this as a traditional form of journalistic exposé of scandalous behaviour. Rather, we identify this as an emerging politics of measurement that is concerned with whole populations and the performance of MPs, not in relation to what they said, but in relation to their actual and individual spending practices, as revealed by traces left in expense claims. Secondly, we explore the *Guardian's* engagement, to reflect on how the focus on individuals and specifics is linked to methodological devices, notably 'relational visualizations'. We examine how the data was analysed and undertake our own analysis to address the deployment of methods for summarizing huge quantities of data through visual simplifications and arrays. Thirdly, we generalize from this specific case to reflect more broadly on how Web 2.0 devices are being deployed and are more generally being used for democratic political mobilization and engage the media and amateurs in data collection, digitization and analyses through mash-ups and data linkages in publicly visible and effective ways.[3] We situate this politics of measurement as different from that elicited by long-standing techniques such as surveys, which focus on knowledge of aggregate groups in relation to general issues and which rely on expert forms of analysis and representation.

Our general aim is to argue against two opposing views: first, that 'information' is superficial and does not allow critique (Lash, 2002), and secondly that such devices and data somehow allow more accountability. Rather, we show that it permits the formation of new constituencies of informational gatekeepers, organizers and interpreters who are at best only loosely attached to formal organizations and companies, perhaps resembling more of a mob rather than an organized form of political action. Rather than separating out these political actors and devices, we examine how they are mutually constituted by the socio-technical arrangements of which they are a part.

## Part 1: The MPs' expenses scandal

When Parliament passed the Freedom of Information Act in 2000, its members had not envisaged the possibility of using its provisions to make their own expense claims public information. However, following the lobbying of journalist Heather Brooke beginning in 2004, demands to reveal this 'private' data gathered pace, though with considerable resistance from parliament. Even following the UK Information Tribunal ruling in favour of disclosure on 26 February 2008, the House of Commons attempted to find strategies to avoid detailed information entering the public realm, preferring instead to release summary statements, which they thought would satisfy public interest. However, as part of this process, two dozen civil servants were seconded to a 'redaction unit' to process expense receipts into digital form, and to remove extraneous elements of the claims in this process. As they went about their work they became increasingly scandalized about the kinds of abuses they observed, and some of the detailed information and stories began to leak out.[4] In spring 2009, a series of scandals broke about particular well-known politicians, such as Home Secretary Jackie Smith (8 February) who had claimed £116,000 for a 'second home', which turned out to be her family residence.

These initial leaks, based on a sample of the redacted data, conformed to the traditional journalistic model of identifying specific scandalous individuals, rather than reporting expenses more systematically. Yet those working on the redacted data thought that the abuses they were processing were systemic and not to be easily identified as 'fingering' particular corrupt individuals. Those organizing the leak demanded that the newspaper that was to be given the disk would not cherry-pick the data but would promise to reveal abuses across the board. Most newspapers baulked at the idea of reporting this level of detail, since they realized they did not have the capacity – or expertise – to report it systematically, but eventually the *Daily Telegraph* with its unusually large corps of political journalists thought it could devote the resources to allow a comprehensive treatment. Some 25 journalists and their assistants were given just ten days by the source of the leak to detail the spending accounts. They began by publicizing the expenses of the entire cabinet and shadow cabinet and then moved on to opposition parliamentarians, along the way highlighting select expenses of MPs with particular egregious spending patterns.[5]

In the view of *Telegraph* insiders, Winnett and Rayner (2009), this was a heroic scoop of the traditional muckraking journalistic model. Thus, Gordon Brown, with his suspect bill for house cleaning, was one of the first to be exposed. Attention then was directed to apparently extreme cases such as Elliot Morgan, who claimed £16,000 for a loan which had been paid off. This kind of method can best be seen as a variant of conventional forms of journalistic investigation, of 'digging the dirt' through select and detailed inquiries into scurrilous individuals. And, as is the case for the traditional media exposé, the *Daily Telegraph's* deputy political editor and chief reporter eventually wrote up the controversy in a book (Winnett and Rayner, 2009).

One of the striking features of the exposé was the way that it juxtaposed accounts and actions. MPs, a group whose public role is nearly entirely concerned with providing narratives, were now treated as a population whose actual and individual spending practices were of public concern. In a similar way, there was an opposition between grandiose, general rhetoric, and specific, often minute forms of spending. Thus, Jackie Smith's claim for 88 pence to buy a plug, as well as her husband's interest in viewing pornography at taxpayers' expense, became a new kind of political allegory, which depended on using mundane details to activate broad concerns.

Indeed, Winnett and Rayner's account also relates to some intriguing issues, which suggest an emerging politics that could not so easily be appropriated to the scandal model. First, precisely because the source of the leaked disk made it clear that the *Telegraph* would only be given the disk if they were prepared to expose all MPs, we can see an interest in a politics of measurement of a 'whole population' that contravened journalistic norms. Secondly, Winnett and Rayner's (2009) account insists on how far the journalists work on the leaked expenses ran against their normal practices, not only in terms of their time commitments, but also in terms of the team working involved. It was only the suspension of journalistic norms, which permitted the exposé to take place. Thirdly, although Winnett and Rayner make much of the heroic role of the journalists, the key work in translating the paper-based expenses into digital data was done by redaction workers who had been mobilized into this work away from their main duties. The exposé hence depended on the additional mobilization of non-experts. It is possible, therefore, to read *The Daily Telegraph's* exposure as a residue of an older form of media politics which could only just cope with the challenge of an emerging kind of transactional politics, which focused on the whole population of MPs.

In the remainder of this paper we therefore want to explore how the *Guardian* took up this case, through mobilizing amateurs to transcribe and amalgamate data. Although lacking the spectacular effect of the *Telegraph's* exposé, it extended the potential ways that the transactional data could be deployed. For while the *Daily Telegraph* staff maintained ownership and control of the production, analyses and visualizations of the digitized data, the *Guardian* mobilized an army of anonymous and unorganized volunteers to do the work and made the database publicly available. Using a Crowdsourcing application, a Web 2.0 device that enables interactive information sharing and collaboration on the World Wide Web, the *Guardian* engaged over 20,000 participants in the review and digitization of MPs' expenses.[6] As of September 2009, more than 23,000 participants reviewed over 200,000 out of 500,000 pages of MPs expenses, producing a publicly accessible database on Google Docs that was constantly being updated. Access to the data was provided via the *Guardian's* OpenPlatform datastore on Google Spreadsheets. While the level of activity was very high during the initial months (June and July), by the end of the summer, digitization began to stall as interest in the issue started to wane. At the time of writing, only half of the pages had been digitized.

This digitization of MPs' expenses drew on prior expertise involving the categorization of the conduct of parliamentarians. For several years, the website TheyWorkForYou (run by volunteers and part of the charity mySociety) has been tracking voting patterns, policy positions, committee attendance, public appearances and generating a numerology of debates and written questions including the level of readability of speeches. More recently, the site has also added links to the Parliamentary website's tabulations of each MP's aggregate expenses with links to the original scanned claims.[7] The expenses scandal is therefore only the culmination of a much longer process of digital scrutiny in which the practices of MPs – such as their voting records – command attention.

However, the form of data in this case is unique in that it consists of transactions and enabled analyses of the whole population of MPs. We now turn to investigate how this kind of data constitutes a different politics of measurement, which might burst from the bounds of more conventional modes and involves the mobilization of both data and publics.

## Part 2: Mobilizing data: visualizing aggregates and individuals

Let us consider the potential of political exposure using transactional data. Here we argue against the view that vast amounts of information entail the loss of critique (Lash, 2002). Rather, we are interested in the way that transactional data can be deployed not to mobilize data on social, political or cultural aggregates, but specificities of the kind that destabilize the political arena which is not used to dealing with these. We are particularly interested in the way that 'relational visualizations' which highlight outliers against more usual patterns and hence focus on aberrant cases are an important device.

Table 1 is extracted from the *Guardian* and represents how the data can be deployed using the format of a standard cross-tabulated table, where aggregate categories (Labour, Conservative and Liberal Democrat) are highlighted. This is, in effect, treating data on expenses analogously to that from a conventional social survey or census. Table 1 shows that Conservatives spend much more on carpets and on housing costs (mortgages or rent) than do Labour MPs. So far, so stereotypical. It turns out that Labour MPs have more of a relish for running up a food bill, Liberal Democrats are especially keen on expensive TVs, whereas Conservatives prefer cheaper tellies and Labour MPs are somewhat in the middle. Liberal Democrats are much keener gardeners than those from the other two parties. But in fact, there is no telling general message from this table. Aggregate differences largely balance out between the parties: one cannot say in general terms that Tories are more 'on the make' than are Labour or Liberal Democrat MPs. In fact, there is not much of a story here if the data is used in a standard social scientific form as a means of examining aggregate properties of the political parties.

This all looks rather different, however, when more advanced visuals are deployed, so that specific individual MPs can be highlighted. This of course, is where the *Daily Telegraph* exposé has been most effective, not in placing generalized blame but in fingering particular MPs. This is a politics of 'whole populations', one in which individuals can be singled out vis-à-vis their peers and their idiosyncrasies revealed in all their mundane splendour. However, whereas the *Daily Telegraph* exposé depends either on the exposure of well-known politicians, or the use of exceptional cases, the methods of the *Guardian* allow more mundane exposure.

A further example is to see how the database has been analysed using IBM's online Many Eyes Wikified visualization software to produce bar charts, block histograms, scatterplots and maps.[8] Visualization software enables the detection of patterns that might not otherwise be apparent in a Google Docs spreadsheet. Such visualizations reduce all of the detail and 'noise' of data to simplified relational patterns.[9] One visualization illustrates the location of each MP and their total travel expenses thus illustrating MPs who appear to be claiming disproportionately more than other MPs with constituencies in a similar area (Figure 1).

This first visual gives remarkable detail on the spending of every MP, on a range of different headings. By scrolling the cursor across the figure, every MP can be highlighted. Again, the overarching impression is that there is not very much of a story here. There is in fact rather little variance in terms of MPs' expenses excluding travel. The most miserly MP is Holbourne who claimed £40.4k, and the most spendthrift are Borrow and Wallace, with £158k – but the graph shows very little variance around the mean figure of £90k or so. However,

**Table 1:** *Aggregate MP expenses*

| Party | Lab total | Lab avg | Con total | Con avg | LibDem total | LibDem avg |
|---|---|---|---|---|---|---|
| Carpet | 97,960.57 | **907.04** | 74,799.68 | **1,739.53** | 9,351.93 | 668.00 |
| Food | 1,625,039.51 | **507.98** | 444,424.25 | 402.92 | 248,068.32 | 393.76 |
| Garden | 88,708.96 | 469.36 | 231,439.70 | 460.12 | 19,856.97 | **902.59** |
| Kitchen | 276,661.85 | 722.35 | 63,231.13 | 405.33 | 52,621.83 | 657.77 |
| Mortgage or rent | 4,879,773.24 | **1,415.66** | 3,334,659.29 | **2,014.9** | 978,588.88 | 1871.11 |
| Petty cash | 285,151.58 | 256.89 | 199,984.96 | 280.09 | 17,655.45 | 223.49 |
| Soft furnishings | 268,297.8 | 508.14 | 82,616.48 | 425.86 | 52,409.89 | 647.04 |
| TV | 164,917.25 | 455.57 | 31,598.61 | **292.58** | 48,401.16 | **780.66** |
| Tech | 993,234.04 | 323.74 | 518,409.18 | 306.57 | 159,297.24 | 367.04 |

*Notes:* Figures in $, running total as of 5 September 2009.
*Source:* http://spreadsheets.google.com/pub?key=rqW4cYeDb2zt5q_nu0DcBQA&single=true&gid=0&output=html

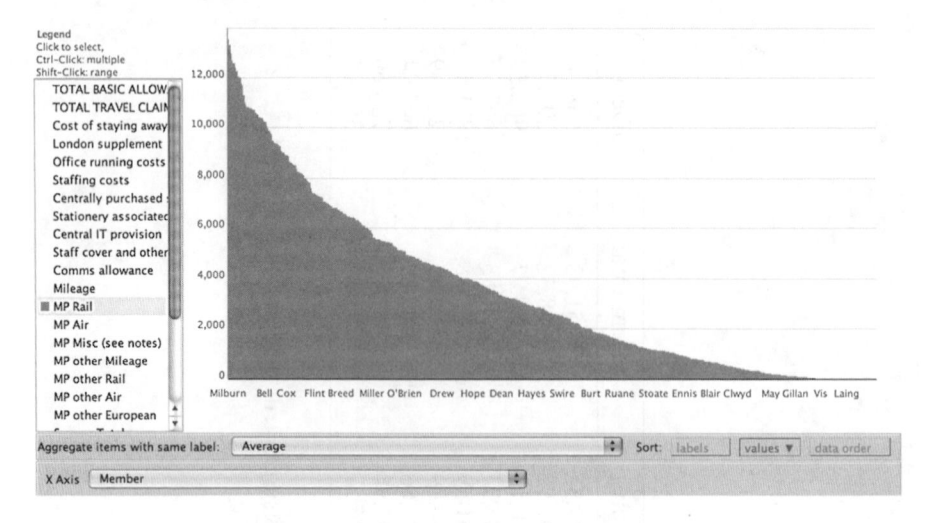

Figure 1: *Visualization of MP expenses – rail.*

by distinguishing more specialized categories, apparent differences can be detected. Thus airfare is highly variable with McNeil charging £28k but most MPs claiming nothing. Rail fares give a more linear distribution, with Milburn topping the list with £13,650.

These data sources, allied to appropriate visualizations, allow the analysis of specifics and permit apparently telling contrasts in spending to be revealed. In fact, as we have suggested above, these differences are often only germane to specific headings and aggregate differences tend to balance each other out. There are very few genuine outliers, particularly scandalous MPs or especially abstemious ones. However, what we see here is the mobilization of data on whole populations that supplants aggregate categories and highlights all individuals in relation to each other as well as the outliers. Figure 2 shows how all MPs can be individually located on a grid with two axes. Here, if we compare office running costs with staff costs we do encounter a few outliers with Dennis Skinner and Tony Blair (who presumably had all his costs paid for through his Prime Ministerial role and hence had no need to claim as private MP) standing out as the most abstemious.

If we compare the two most broadly defined headings, travel expenses and total basic allowances including travel we can see the huge clustering towards the right with a few outliers who spend little: Holbourne, Skinner, Blair and Martin (Figure 3).

And finally, the data can also be plotted spatially (Figure 4). One example is through the production of 'heat maps' of Britain showing those areas with the highest (hottest) expenses down to the lowest (coolest).[10] One blogger linked the expenses database with a georeferenced database to create a map that represents each MP as a colour-coded pinpoint.[11] This again shows the power of

*Transactional politics*

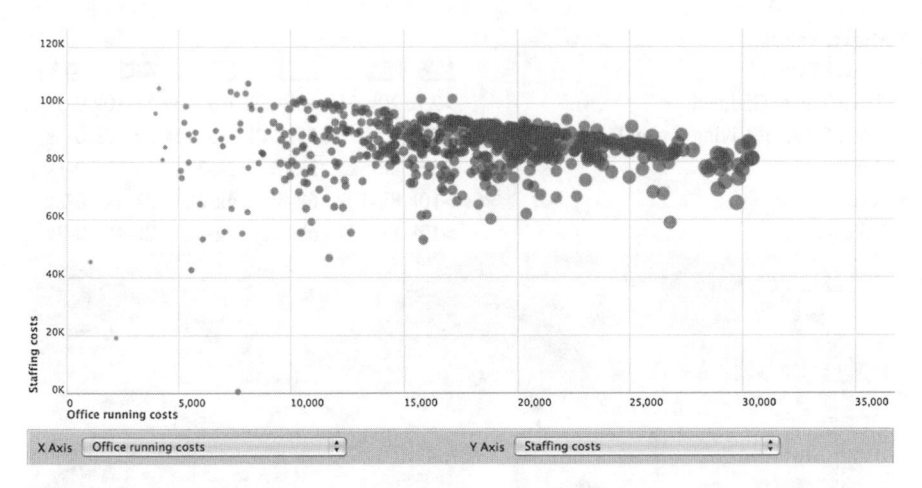

**Figure 2:** *Visualization of MP expenses – staffing costs and office running costs.*

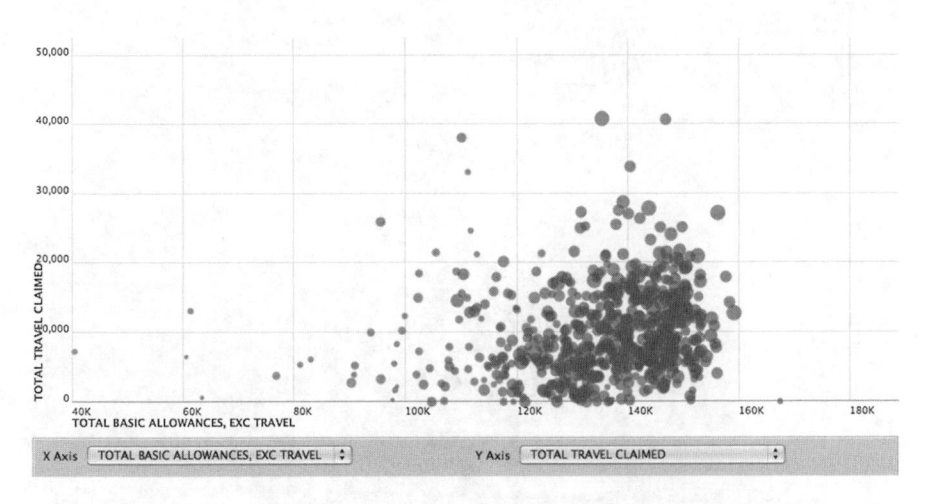

**Figure 3:** *Visualization of MP expenses – total travel and total basic allowances.*

these data sources to spatialize processes, in a manner germane to the arguments of Savage and Burrows (2007).

As the blogger noted, 'what's nice about this view is that it's quite easy to see which MPs appear to be claiming disproportionately more than other MPs with constituencies in a similar area'. In this visualization, individual transactions were spatially located and outliers defined and identified by arraying the individual in relation to the general. But additionally the device reveals how the aggregate is patterned (assisted by colour coding) and consists of shades of difference. In this example geographic location was also linked to total travel

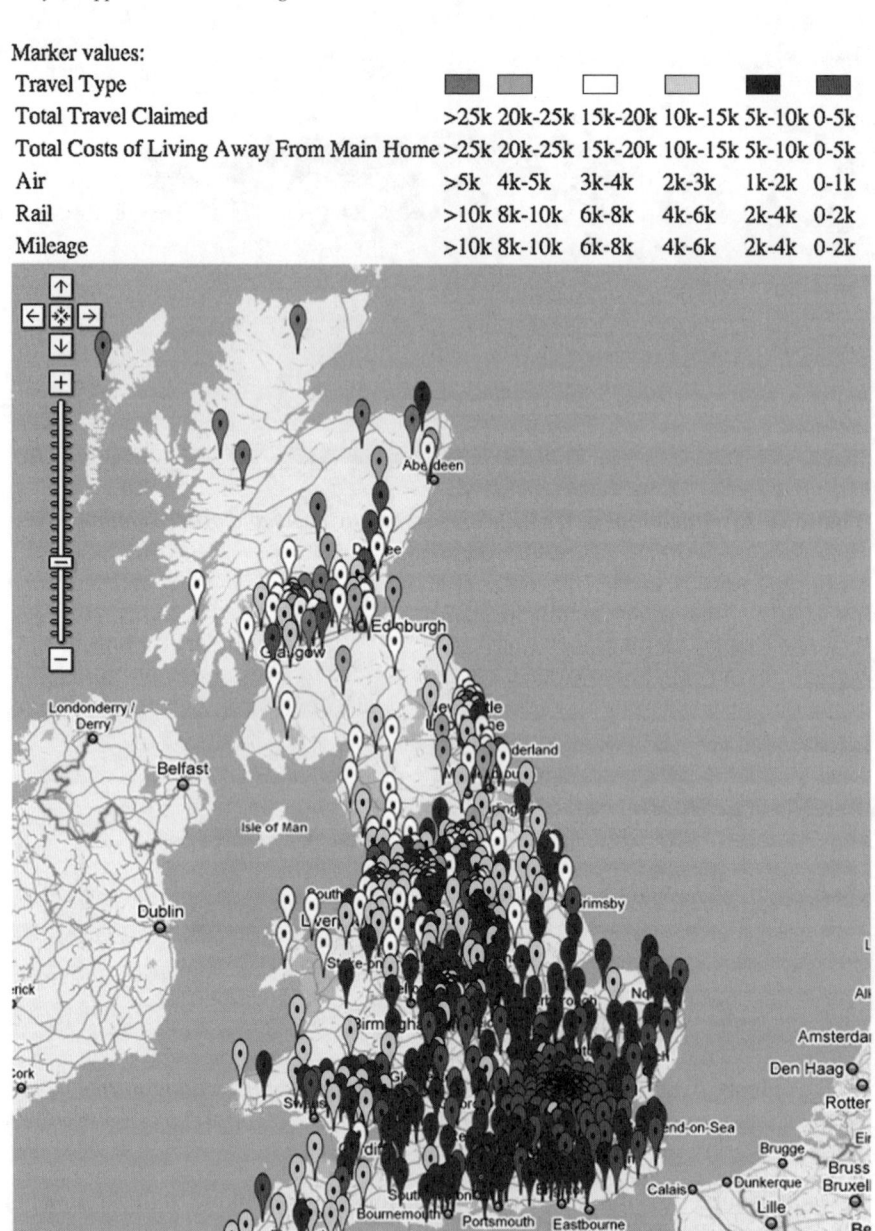

Marker values:
Travel Type
Total Travel Claimed                                  >25k   20k-25k  15k-20k  10k-15k  5k-10k  0-5k
Total Costs of Living Away From Main Home  >25k  20k-25k  15k-20k  10k-15k  5k-10k  0-5k
Air                                                   >5k    4k-5k    3k-4k    2k-3k    1k-2k   0-1k
Rail                                                  >10k   8k-10k   6k-8k    4k-6k    2k-4k   0-2k
Mileage                                               >10k   8k-10k   6k-8k    4k-6k    2k-4k   0-2k

**Figure 4:** *Visualization of MP expenses – mapping of travel expenses.*

expenses, then mileage claims and finally total expenses claimed for living away from the primary home. In each case when individuals are arrayed against the aggregate different patterns emerge and new outliers pop up for inspection.

Whereas these methods allow spatial analyses, they however prove opaque with respect to issues of time. This is true in two senses: first, it is difficult to represent items of spending temporally. It would certainly be possible to deploy time categories (eg breaking down expenditure in 2005, 2006 and so on), but this relies on a form of aggregation which we have shown has been eclipsed by these methods. Since time cannot be easily graphed or mapped two dimensionally, it turns out to be difficult to render it, other than as a kind of flat, homogeneous time. Secondly, time is critical to the analyses since the data sources change on a daily basis as more work is done on them. It is thus never entirely clear when the work is completed or how the analysis changes as additional analysis is conducted.

In sum, we highlight two matters of interest in this emerging politics of measurement. Through these techniques, forms of knowledge based on textual and numerical manipulation are fused through the visual as a fundamental point of mediation. Visualizations of transactions reveal the particular and the outlier as fundamental features of transactional data. In this regard, digitized transactional data allow the deployment of specifics rather than aggregates, through allowing the mobilization of highly individualized and discrete measurements. Such a politics of measurement allows particularistic attention to be used in pervasive and powerful ways. The traceability of transactions and the availability of tools to identify patterns, enable the interpreter to move from individuals to aggregates and back again. But as the various visualizations above attest, 'the "whole" is now nothing more than a provisional visualization which can be modified and reversed at will, by moving back to the individual components, and then looking for yet other tools to regroup the same elements into alternative assemblages' (Latour, 2010: 158). This is different from standard social scientific forms of measurement that consist of samples and deal with categories and statistical means and averages.

This concern with MP transactions is compellingly similar to the increasing pervasiveness and deployment of transactional data to know individuals and whole populations on the basis of what people do rather than what they say. In both the commercial and government sectors traceability through digital data is being used to know and evaluate the performance of individuals in relation to aggregates. For example, law enforcement and intelligence agencies 'connect the dots' in databases using techniques such as profiling, data mining, social network analysis, risk analysis and other predictive technologies. The US Department of Homeland Security's US VISIT programme integrates existing databases, from police authorities, to health, financial and travel records to identify aberrant and suspect individuals (Amoore, 2006). With UK social programmes such as Every Child Matters, patterns in transactional data across government agencies (education, housing, training, counselling) mediate the identification and needs of individual children potentially 'at-risk' (Ruppert,

2011). At issue in all of these examples is the individual and not a group or category, or the one person in relation to an average. Rather, as promoted in the popular book *Outliers* (Gladwell, 2008), it is how individuals constitute their own category.

Second, transactional data are a fundamentally different register which focus on practices rather than elicited attitudes and views. Whereas the postwar social sciences sought to elaborate popular accounts through the questionnaire or interview, new digital data focuses instead on peoples' transactions and practices. What matters is not what is said, but what is done – or more precisely what is done through commercial and governmental transactions which have become liable to leave traces and are increasingly digitized. And through this reorientation, the boundary between what is deemed private and public is reconfigured. Whereas devices for eliciting accounts inherently distinguish public (ie recorded) from 'private' (ie not recorded, possibly not even articulated) accounts, there is no such thing as a private transaction. The boundary between public and private is not erased, however, but reconfigured. Whereas traces can be recorded of any transaction, some of these remain private property while others enter the public realm, a distinction that is fundamentally concerned with the commodification and mobilization of data itself, and a matter for political contestation. For example, with the digitizing of online activities records of all individuals (whole populations) engaged in an activity are recorded and in some cases public and can be analysed as data (Twitter, blogs, chatrooms, websites). Even if sequestered in private databanks (eg, Amazon, Google) private transactions of whole populations become data that inform individuals about their similarities to others (through devices such as pop-up messages identifying the preferences of shoppers who make similar purchases) and can also be marketed and sold. In the next part of this article we broaden our discussion to explore in greater detail the Web 2.0 devices which were taken up to digitize and analyse the expenses data and how these are intervening in politics by mobilizing and producing new data analysts and interpreters.

## Part 3: Mobilizing publics: crowdsourcing the mob

While the journalists at the *Daily Telegraph* attracted the plaudits for their disclosure of MPs' expenses, we have argued that the *Guardian's* use of Web 2.0 devices in association with the labour of thousands of volunteers may be more of a pointer to emerging political trends. There are many examples of how Web 2.0 devices have been mobilized for collective political action, such as social networking sites (Facebook for US elections) and micro blogs (Twitter for Iranian protests). In this instance, Crowdsourcing, Google Docs, mash-ups and visualization software were organized to engage the public in a politics of measurement that did not involve eliciting 'popular' views but instead mobilized publics, where people were invited to participate and 'see for themselves' what secrets were hidden in the data.

This form of engaging publics is different from conventional practices conceived by democratic political regimes, which have commonly been understood as being dependent on devices for eliciting 'popular' views. Political theorists emphasize the role of public deliberative processes as central to the functioning of democracy. The most visible of such devices – the 'vote' – is only one, rather marginal device, though it remains the most fundamental to democratic legitimacy: take it away, and claims to democratic politics look thin. It is widely recognized that irregular elections have little role in the management and administration of the kinds of complex public institutions, which characterize the governmental complex of neo-liberal capitalism (Rose, 1991). Collective meetings, campaigns in public locations, and social movements, have always been important to political mobilization (Vernon, 1993; Lawrence, 2009) and continue to be seen as an important public right. Much has been written by political scientists about the need for pressure groups and voluntary associations to provide the right kind of 'social capital' that allows the population to learn the skills of democratic deliberation and also find vehicles to express their views (Putnam, 2000). Public inquiries allow further mechanisms for concerned members of the public to make their feelings manifest.

Since the 1930s, it has also become clear that the delineation of 'public opinion' has become critically dependent on the mobilization of data from polls and surveys, which can be construed as machines and mediators for arraying popular feelings in a 'flat' format, reduced to cell counts in a contingency table (Osborne and Rose, 1999). From the 1960s, surveys have been widely used to render scientific and objective accounts of popular practices and values, as a means of managing public attitudes on issues ranging from the reform of local government through local planning issues (Savage, 2010). Sample surveys are now used routinely as a means of eliciting consumer satisfaction in the public sector, such as in higher education (through the National Student Survey) and user questionnaires are mundane practices in hotels and restaurants.

By the early 21st century, however, the example of the MPs' expense scandal shows the power of devices for popular democratic mobilization and directly engaging people rather than simply eliciting views.[12] The use of Web 2.0 devices to digitize, analyse and visualize transactional data on MPs' expenses reveals their potential for construing democratic accountability in new and powerful ways. Whereas analyses of data have usually been the jurisdiction of experts, who typically conduct the relevant fieldwork and analyse the data, these devices constitute a kind of popular mobilization that does not rely on experts or interest groups, but make life public by mobilizing unorganized and anonymous individuals in what Rheingold (2002) has called mob-like cooperative action. However, in this instance the mob was primarily engaged in the digitizing of the data while a smaller cadre of analysts intervened to interpret and visualize it. The *Guardian* produced many of the visualizations as well as promoted a competition for the best visualizations, which they displayed on their Datablog site.

We therefore suggest that the MPs' expenses scandal is indicative of a broader emerging politics in which the collection and storage of digitized datasets as well as the availability of relatively simple analytic software has made the sharing, linking, analysis and visualization of transactional data a feature of modern technological life. This not only includes data collected by organizations (Google, Amazon and so on) and institutions as in the case of MPs' expenses but also that collected by individuals in relation to their own performance and activities. There are numerous tools and applications that people can use to 'self-track' and visualize their individual transactions and in some cases share and exchange these with others.[13] In addition to particularistic and individual transaction data, there are also other forms of publicly available data on the Web that are being organized in ways that invite individuals to do their own analyses and interpretations.

In relation to government and politics a significant development involves recent initiatives to liberate data from the confines of government administrative offices and make them publicly available on the Internet along with applications and tools for citizens to do their own analyses of 'raw data'. From the US Data.gov and San Francisco DataSF.org to the UK Data.gov.uk and Data.london.gov.uk, governments are embracing Web 2.0 technologies to change the traditional ways that they communicate and disseminate official statistics.[14] Transparency, democracy, accountability, engagement, collaboration, participation – these are just a few norms that politicians and administrators attach to the project of providing open access to government data along with tools and methods for analysing, visualizing and interpreting that data. For example, the London Datastore (data.london.gov.uk) describes this practice as a way to ensure that 'data belongs to the people'.

The US lead the way with the Obama administration's Data.gov, which is now the main repository for all US public databases. In an interview, the administration's Chief Information Officer Vivek Kundra commented that everyone – and at the forefront, the news media – can take advantage of this initiative for the public's benefit: 'The key is recognising that we don't have a monopoly on good ideas and that the federal government doesn't have infinite resources. . . . Democratizing data enables comparative analysis of the services the government provides and the investments it makes, leading to a better government' (quoted in Thompson, 2009). It is promoted as an instrument of participatory democracy whereby the public can participate in government by downloading Federal datasets and conducting their own research and analysis. Just as the digitizing of MPs' expenses engaged the public in data analysis so too does Data.gov. The 'raw data' catalogue includes everything from consumer expenditure surveys to benefits data. A 'tool catalogue' provides hyperlinks to tools that allow you to mine datasets and produce graphs, charts and histograms and a 'geodata catalogue' that enables you to undertake spatial analyses.[15] In all instances data is also understood as a commodity, a good that not only contributes to an engaged and active political community but also one that has commodity value, an aspect of what Thrift (2005) characterizes as 'knowing capitalism'.

## Conclusion

With the digitization of MPs' expenses we can now categorize MPs according to their transaction patterns. We can identify the most expensive MP, whether this be the one who spends the highest on office expenses or travel or earned the largest windfall from a property transaction. We could develop amusing categorizations such as the 'profligate spender', 'frequent diner', 'excessive nepotist', 'world traveller' or 'wannabe property developer'. Just as data about ourselves can be used to detect fraud and criminal activity so can we examine MPs' transactions. The gaze has been turned from the governed back onto the governors where the subjects of dataveillance now engage in 'sousveillance' – a 'watchful vigilance from underneath' (Dennis, 2008).[16] Clearly, and for understandable reasons, many MPs don't like it. We have shown how this new politics of measurement enacts novel and original kinds of political stakes which move beyond the aggregate and which locate individuals in a wider relational field. It is a politics that raises questions about what devices make both possible and impossible in the name of democracy and what it means for how we know and make up the social world.

Let us conclude by highlighting three issues. First, just as the technology of public opinion research in the early twentieth century was active in creating 'opinioned or opinionated people', (Osborne and Rose, 1999) these techniques and devices are active in creating new informational gatekeepers and data interpreters, actors with the capacities and competencies to interpret, analyse, represent and enact the social world. Web 2.0 applications enable people to engage in social science types of analysis without realizing it and challenge and contest dominant or expert forms of analysis and representation. Promoters of open government data sites argue that these devices can make it easier for the public to make better choices about the services that they want and to produce analyses such as their own local crime maps to hold the police and local councils to account (Howes, 2009). But these technological devices do not merely mobilize already existing actors but are active in making them up.[17] That is, actors are constituted through their actions in relation to the sociotechnical arrangements of which they are a part and the ways that devices get taken up and intervene are not predetermined (interestingly, Data.gov describes this as 'Evolving data.gov with You', whilst data.gov.uk sees it as 'unlocking innovation'). Technology and the social are ontologically relational rather than independent categories that come into play with each other: that is, they are mutually constitutive (Halford and Savage, 2010).

Amongst the new data analysts are the media. Government data sites are heralded by some (such as Simon Rogers, editor of the *Guardian*'s Datablog) as an opportunity to revitalize journalism by providing unprecedented access to publicly available data, which can be processed and used to construct in-depth analyses of immigration, crime, finance and so on (Filloux, 2009). Rather than reporting on the analyses produced by government authorities or researchers, journalists can undertake their own research as in the example of MPs' expenses. Data and their devices are thus making up a new breed of journalist. These do not need to be 'a statistician to understand what a dataset is about' but would be well advised to undertake some technical training (Filloux, 2009).

A second point is that these devices are not only involved in the making up of new data analysts and political actors but also mediate the making up of the social world. Through the interactions between actors and devices 'new' social relations and correlations can be discovered and made into objects of political scrutiny and debate. From Crowdsourcing and other Web 2.0 tools to the methods by which data is collected, categorized and organized, there are numerous devices and mediators in the long chain of relations engaged in not just representing but also enacting the social world (Law and Urry, 2004; Mol, 2002). While devices preconfigure the kinds of analyses that are possible they do not foreclose or determine them.[18] For one, devices involve many actors in making choices about what is deemed important, what should be included and excluded, how people and things should be categorized, all of which form the basis of comparisons and rankings. And such practices often get things wrong. For example, some MPs have come to their own defence arguing that classifications and interpretations of their transactions have been erroneous. Tom Brake MP contacted the *Guardian* to provide an explanation for an apparent anomaly in his claims concerning a payment his office made to a stationery company. His explanation illustrated how transactions are not as straightforward as they might appear. Just as border screening systems may misidentify 'risky' travellers, so too can transaction patterns misidentify dodgy expenses.

Yet, in Berners-Lee's conception (as well as that of others) data is represented as 'raw' and awaiting neutral analysis.[19] Re-stating an old argument about the difference between qualitative and quantitative data Filloux (2009) advances that the revolution for journalism is that 'Data treatment raises the objectivity of a story; instead of – or in addition to – a piece about the economic context of an event, based on interviews with their human limitations, a clever presentation of raw data can be a great tool to offer facts in a unbiased way.' Analyses are represented as 'flat' descriptions and visualizations, and simply objective accounts of the 'real' world, a kind of 'descriptive assemblage', which is also highly artefactual, and which is becoming dominant in key social arenas such as security, marketing, finance, medicine and government (Savage, 2009). These devices are also not anchored in establishing causal relationships but in producing 'useful' information as 'telling' indicators. The interest is in 'surfaces rather than depths' and of performance indicators, measurements and profiles. For example, the website TheyWorkForYou states that the quantity and type of activities of MPs reveals little about the quality of their work (and acknowledges that they do many other things not counted). Users are advised to read actual speeches and attend meetings and thereby use the site only as a 'gateway' to more detailed inquiry. However, the data alters the nature of political stakes and the politics of measurement by focusing on expenses and voting records rather than policies and platforms.

Third and finally, the new reality of large volumes of digitized data in both the commercial and government sector presents a significant challenge to the methods and future of empirical sociology (Savage and Burrows, 2007). New information gatekeepers, organizers and interpreters challenge the jurisdiction and power of 'traditional' experts. From journalists to amateurs and political activists, new data generators and interpreters are reconfiguring the field of social knowledge. Zygmunt Bauman (1987) suggested that the metaphor of legislator best captures modern intellectual practice whereas the interpreter best describes the postmodern. The former was based on the certainty of intellectual knowledge, the forsaking of critique and alignment with the state as part of an aspiration to power and commitment to change the social world. In contrast the latter represents a crisis of confidence brought on by a belief in the uncertainty and contingency of knowledge. That crisis has now taken on a new dimension and as suggested elsewhere calls for rethinking the role and repertoire of empirical sociology (Savage and Burrows, 2007). Rather than retooling either the meta-theoretical or methodological repertoires of the discipline we would endorse a critical engagement in the ontological politics of these new forms of data and analysis, not an internal politics but one that engages with the various communities of analysts and interpreters to provide reflexive accounts of the work that devices do in enacting versions of the social world. For example, this may involve engagement in a new politics of measurement that brings into question the assumption that 'popular', anonymous and collective analyses are infallible or transparent. It could also involve analysis of the underlying normativities of presumably unbiased or neutral analyses.

## Notes

1 Consider how many weeks the MPs' expenses were the object of media analysis compared to the transactions that led to the current financial crisis. Or consider how the Department of Works and Pensions routinely matches housing benefit records with social security, national insurance and tax systems, along with customer data from gas, electricity and telephone companies to identify 'benefit thieves'.
2 Web 2.0 devices are applications that enable interactive information sharing and collaboration on the World Wide Web and include wikis, blogs, mash-ups, etc.
3 A mash-up is a web page or application that combines data from two or more external sources to create a new representation.
4 Remarkably, the redaction process was not subject to the Official Secrets Act.
5 See http://www.guardian.co.uk/politics/2009/jun/18/mps-expenses-crowdsourcing-app.
6 Crowdsourcing is a method that enables large, undefined and unsupervised groups of people to collectively perform tasks, the most popularly known example being Wikipedia. In relation to data there are several examples such as 'Automated Genealogy', a Wiki that enables volunteers to participate in the digitization of the names of every person enumerated as well as their personal data for the 1901–1911 censuses of Canada. Using simple web forms volunteers transcribe

census data from pdf images into a database, with the entered data being immediately available on the site. Each transcribed page has a 'split view' option that allows further volunteers to proofread and make corrections. And finally links for individuals are provided to other records such as censuses from other years, birth, marriage and death. While the purpose is to support genealogical research, the project engages people in the practice of interpretation, data entry and coding.

7 The scanned claim forms in pdf were the documents ('edited to remove information which could cause serious security issues and breach the privacy of the MP, their staff and other third parties') collected by the *Daily Telegraph* and the *Guardian* from the Parliamentary website (published on 18 June 2009). The original forms provide greater detail and allow for more scrutiny of specific claims. It should be noted that data on Excel spreadsheets can also be downloaded from the Parliamentary website but only for stationery and postage expenses; incidental expenses (additional cost allowances for staying overnight and away from main home, travel, office, staff and other costs) are not provided as digitized data and only as pdf images of the claim forms. However, as of 2011, all MP expenses are provided in digital format via the website of the Independent Parliamentary Standards Authority.

8 The visualizations are from the blog of Tony Hirst, a part-time Associate Lecturer at the Open University, who operates OUseful.info, 'a blog in part about . . . things that I think may be useful in an higher education context, one day'. See: http://ouseful.wordpress.com/about/.

9 'The greatest value of a picture is when it forces us to notice what we never expected to see.' John W. Tukey (Exploratory Data Analysis, 1977) cited on the website Flowing Data, which 'explores how designers, statisticians, and computer scientists are using data to understand ourselves better – mainly through data visualization'. See http://flowingdata.com/about/.

10 A heat map is a two-dimensional representation of data where the values of a variable are represented in colours. This example was produced by Shoothill, a software developer 'with a passion for unlocking more power from complex data through new visualisation technologies' (see http://www.shoothill.com/).

11 Tony Hirst used an API provided by TheyWorkForYou. APIs are Application Programming Interfaces. For example, Google Maps API enables users to embed Google Maps on their own web pages as well as a number of utilities for manipulating maps and adding content to maps. See http://ouseful.wordpress.com/2009/04/02/visualising-mps-expenses-using-scatterplots-charts-and-maps/. The heat map is best viewed in colour by following this link.

12 See, for example, discussions in Lanier (2006) and Rheingold (2002).

13 For example, the Graffito Data Project (http://www.graffito.org/#) grabs the places you have been by looking at information you can download from your credit card site, then filling in details like address and phone number and plots those places on a time-map to visualize your activities. More generally on self-tracking, see http://www.kk.org/quantifiedself/.

14 In the UK, the establishment of data.gov.co.uk followed a 2007 report, *The Power of Information*, written by Tom Steinberg, director of MySociety (the organization that operates TheyWorkForYou), and Ed Mayo, chief executive of the National Consumer Council for the Home Office (Steinberg and Mayo, 2007).

15 In DC, someone combined several of the data sets released by local government – maps, liquor license info, crime statistics – into an app called Stumble Safely, which shows users the safest way to walk home when drunk' (Thompson, 2009).

16 Dennis (2008) outlines how 'Sousveillance' was coined by Mann (1998) who describes it as form of 'reflectionism' or as a 'watchful vigilance from underneath', which is a form of inverse surveillance. Yet it more than inverses the notion; it embellishes it with a self-reflective responsibility (Dennis, 2008: 349).

17 In this regard we use mobilization in distinction to the dictionary definition, which refers to how an individual or group is enabled or incited to be active or capable of action (eg, see *Oxford English Dictionary*, 'mobilization, n.' 3rd edn, September 2002; online version December 2011 available at: http://www.oed.com.libezproxy.open.ac.uk/view/Entry/120497; accessed 6 February 2012. An entry for this word was first included in *New English Dictionary*, 1907).

18 For example, inscription devices such as SPSS configure what forms of analysis and knowledge of populations are possible (Uprichard *et al.*, 2008).
19 Berners-Lee is credited as the founder of the World Wide Web.

# References

Amoore, L., (2006), 'Biometric borders: governing mobilities in the war on terror', *Political Geography*, 25: 336–351.
Bauman, Z., (1987), *Legislators and Interpreters: On Modernity, Post–Modernity and Intellectuals*, Ithaca: Cornell University Press.
Crompton, R., (2008), 'Forty years of sociology: some comments', *Sociology*, 42(6): 1218–1227.
Dennis, K., (2008), 'Keeping a close watch – the rise of self-surveillance and the threat of digital exposure', *Sociological Review*, 56(3): 347–357.
Filloux, F., (2009), 'Can data revitalise journalism?' *Monday Note: Media, Tech & Business Models*, available at: http://www.mondaynote.com/2009/06/28/can-data-revitalize-journalism/.
Gladwell, M., (2008), *Outliers: The Story of Success*, New York: Little, Brown and Company.
Glover, J., (2010), 'Tories 2.0: Cameron's new breed', *The Guardian*, 20 March, available at: http://www.guardian.co.uk/politics/2010/mar/20/new-tories-cameron-conservatives-election.
Halford, S. and Savage, M., (2010), 'Reconceptualizing digital social inequality', *Information, Communication and Society*, 13(3): 937–955.
Howes, A., (2009), 'An information revolution', available at: http://www.adamsmith.org/think-piece/government/an-information-revolution-/.
Lanier, J., (2006), 'Digital Maoism: the hazards of the new online collectivism', in *Edge: The Third Culture*, available at: http://www.edge.org/3rd_culture/lanier06/lanier06_index.html.
Lash, S., (2002), *Critique of Information*, London: Sage.
Latour, B., (2010), 'Tarde's idea of quantification', in M. Candea (ed.), *The Social after Gabriel Tarde: Debates and Assessments*, London: Routledge.
Law, J. and Urry, J., (2004), 'Enacting the social', *Economy and Society*, 33(3): 390–410.
Lawrence, J., (2009), *Electing our Masters: The Hustings in British Politics from Hogarth to Blair*, Oxford: Clarendon.
Mann, S., (1998), '"Reflectionism" and "diffusionism": new tactics for deconstructing the video surveillance superhighway', *Leonardo*, 31(2): 93–102.
Mol, A., (2002), *The Body Multiple: Ontology in Medical Practice*, Durham, NC: Duke University Press.
Osborne, T. and Rose, N., (1999), 'Do the social sciences create phenomena? The example of public opinion research', *British Journal of Sociology*, 50(3): 367–396.
Putnam, R.D., (2000), *Bowling Alone: Collapse and Revival of American Community*, New York: Simon & Schuster.
Rheingold, H., (2002), *Smart Mobs: The Next Social Revolution*, Cambridge, MA: Perseus.
Rose, N., (1991), 'Governing by numbers: figuring out democracy', *Accounting, Organizations and Society*, 16(7): 673–692.
Ruppert, E., (2011), 'Population objects: interpassive subjects', *Sociology*, 45(2): 218–233.
Savage, M., (2009), 'Contemporary sociology and the challenge of descriptive assemblage', *European Journal of Social Theory*, 12(1): 155–174.
Savage, M., (2010), *Identities and Social Change in Britain since 1940: the Politics of Method*, Oxford: Clarendon.
Savage, M. and Burrows, R., (2007), 'The coming crisis of empirical sociology', *Sociology*, 41(5): 885–899.
Steinberg, T. and Mayo, E., (2007), *The Power of Information*, London: Home Office.
Thompson, N., (2009), 'And data for all: why Obama's geeky new CIO wants to put *all* gov't info online', *Wired*, 18 June.
Thrift, N., (2005), *Knowing Capitalism*, London: Sage.

Uprichard, E., Burrows, R. and Byrne, D., (2008), 'SPSS as an "inscription device": from causality to description?' *Sociological Review*, 56(4): 606–622.
Vernon, J., (1993), *Politics and the People: A Study in English Political Culture, 1815–1867*, Oxford: Clarendon.
Webber, R., (2008), 'Response to "The Coming Crisis of Empirical Sociology": an outline of the research potential of administrative and transactional data', *Sociology*, 43(1): 169–178.
Winnett, R. and Rayner, G., (2009), *No Expenses Spared: The Inside Story of the Scoop which Changed the Face of British Politics – By the Team that Broke It*, London: Bantam Press.

# Dirty data: longitudinal classification systems

## Emma Uprichard

**Abstract:** Typically in longitudinal quantitative research, classifications are tracked over time. However, most classifications change in absolute terms in that some die whilst others are created, and in their meaning. There is a need, therefore, to re-think how longitudinal quantitative research might explore both the qualitative changes to classification systems as well as the quantitative changes within each classification. By drawing on the changing classifications of local food retail outlets in the city of York (UK) since the 1950s as an illustrative example, an alternative way of graphing longitudinal quantitative data is presented which ultimately provides a description of both types of change over time. In so doing, this article argues for the increased use of 'dirty data' in longitudinal quantitative analysis, a step which allows for the exploration of both qualitative and quantitative changes to, and within, classification systems. This ultimately challenges existing assumptions relating to the quality and type of data used in quantitative research and how change in the social world is measured in general.

**Keywords:** classification, classification systems, longitudinal quantitative analysis, York, food

## Introduction

Longitudinal data analysis has been taking place for over three centuries (Menard, 2002). Over the past decade, however, within the social sciences in particular, quantitative longitudinal research has gained a growing currency and witnessed a flourishing level of interest. This is because of the increased public access to large-scale longitudinal surveys and the fact that longitudinal techniques have become more available in standard quantitative software packages (Hosmer *et al.*, 2008). At the heart of much of this work lies the problem of how to capture *trajectories*. Typically, such endeavours involve the combined attempt to understand: (a) *what* has changed, (b) *how* that thing has changed, and at least implicitly if not explicitly, (c) *why* that thing has changed the way it has. The onus, then, is often on developing retrospective historical descriptions in an attempt to consider issues of causality, which in turn feed into developing prediction(s) about possible future trajectories.

Whereas a lot of attention has been paid to the difficulties in determining causal models in longitudinal research, this article focuses instead on the problems involved in developing *descriptions* of classifications over time. This is not to say that issues of causality and prediction are unimportant or that they can be easily disentangled from issues of description – as C. Wright Mills (1959: 170) argues, prediction and description 'are not to be sharply separated'. Rather, the view here is that to even begin exploring issues of causality within the complex social world, it is necessary to first trace a rich description of the changes to the classifications *as they exist*, that is, without any 'cleaning up', however problematic that may be.

In effect, the argument is a simple one: when it comes to exploring, describing, measuring quantitative change longitudinally, it is necessary to use 'dirty data' – a term used deliberately to argue against 'cleaning up' classifications. This contrasts with current practices in quantitative (and increasingly qualitative) longitudinal research, which tend to entail the more or less rigorous merging, recoding of 'suitable' categories that would seemingly facilitate measuring change longitudinally. Instead, by leaving the data alone, and using the categories in their raw form as much as possible, descriptions of both qualitative *and* quantitative changes to social classifications systems are rendered possible.

Analysing classifications over time is, after all, where the money is. Predicting changes and continuities to classifications – *not* to variables, but to polythetic *cases* – is what the global commercial enterprises, such as the large supermarket chains, insurance and credit card agencies, etc. are now doing with quantitative data collected via our transactions. Even quantitative software packages such as SPSS – re-branded by IBM as PASW in version 18, reflecting precisely this shift in 'Predictive Analytical Statistics' where classification and visualization are sold as its forte – are in on the game (see Uprichard *et al.*, 2008). Commercial enterprises are doing it; social scientists, however, are rather embarrassingly lagging behind and merely thinking or talking about it – see Savage and Burrows (2007) on the 'empirical crisis' within sociology specifically. As Byrne (2002: 35) suggests, 'the movement of systems of classes and indeed even more importantly, changes in classification systems over time, is exactly what should interest us most'. Abbott (2000: 299) goes as far as stating that a 'central challenge for the future of all social research is to figure out how to handle this category change without simply sweeping it under the rug'. In this article, category changes are *not* swept under the rug; they are moved to centre stage.

To be sure, there are plenty of quantitative techniques used to describe changing social objects of study over time. Crudely speaking, existing approaches vary according to the extent to which they focus on the variable(s) rather than the case(s) (see Byrne and Ragin, 2009). Many time-based statistical techniques, for instance, tend to zoom in on the change of one or more variables or the timing of events (Singer and Willett, 2003). Other procedures, such as agent-based, cellular-automata or mathematical modelling (eg Schelling, 1971; Batty, 2005; Allen, 1997; Gilbert and Troitzsch, 1999) have been developed, which arguably also tend to simulate change in one or more variables, albeit in different ways. Then there are narrative approaches used to combine qualitative and quantitative methods (Elliott, 2005), and temporal qualitative comparative analysis (Caren and Panofsky, 2005; Chaplain *et al.*, 1999; Ragin and Strand, 2008). The list continues, but the point is that, whilst different in detail, the existing approaches tend to share a focus on describing quantitative change in one or more variables, without paying attention to the qualitative changes to those variables. As Abbott (2000: 205) notes, 'Work involving data over time often boils down to "trends and counts," with little sensitivity to historical context or contingency, and less to qualitative temporal fluctuations in the social categories or attributes analyzed.'

There is nothing wrong with describing 'trends and counts'. This may well be all we can meaningfully do and, as will be seen, is also the basis for what is proposed here. However, what needs to happen alongside such a description is an explicit exploration of category changes that may underpin that description vis-à-vis *what* is counted, *how* those things are counted, and in turn *why* the trends which are based on those counts are as they are. After all, irrespective of the approach employed, and whether or not the desired data(set) exists (which often it does not), data are themselves part and parcel of that changing object of study. Quantitative data are *always and necessarily* manifestations of the processes involved in describing a changing object of study; data do not exist in a vacuum independent of our knowledge any more than the objects they represent (see Desrosières, 1998). Therefore, whatever is described in whatever way it is described, a quantitative description says as much if not more about the method used as it does about the social world it reveals. Ideally, then, any chosen methodology must consider the nature of the abstractions whilst also attempting to maximize the probability that the object is adequately and accurately described and explored (see Reed and Harvey, 1996; Sayer, 2000). In turn, in order to develop any meaningful longitudinal description of change, it is necessary to consider the co-construction of the actual description obtained and the historical contingency involved in the construction of that empirical description (see Dupré, 2006; Desrosières, 1998, 2000, 2001; Hacking, 1999, 2002).

These issues are discussed here specifically in relation to the changing classification of food outlets in the city of York (UK) between 1951 and 2001. Although the example of food outlets is quite specific, the methodological issues discussed are ones that are likely to be present when exploring change in other substantive topics. Perhaps a more politically loaded example might have been occupational, class, race and ethnicity classifications in the census. Whatever example is used though, classification, which gets used as variables (see Tryon's (1939) early work on clustering cases versus variables), need to be tracked over time; the qualitative changes *to* the classification or variables are just as important as the quantitative changes *within* them. Hence, many of the challenges involved in studying social change empirically are arguably methodological ones rather than substantive ones to do with the nature of the object of study. This is not to say that the nature of the object of study is unimportant, but that there are methodological issues that relate to *longitudinal* social research, irrespective of what case is being examined, precisely because studying something that changes inevitably raises its own methodological issues. The argument, therefore, relates to any attempt to explore the social world over time and the many classification systems through which change happens (see Bowker and Star, 2002, on this issue).

Three points are worth noting before moving on to discuss the study. First, the discussion is much informed by Bhaskar's (1975, 1979) critical realist philosophy. There is plenty of scope to argue that other approaches might have been preferable. Indeed, there may be a good case to argue that what is presented is compatible with alternative philosophical perspectives or authors. Ultimately, the positions of authors arguing against Kant's transcendental argument about the extent to which we can deduce the world based on our (limited) knowledge of it will probably not be incompatible with many of the views presented here. Nevertheless, since this paper relates to the practice of studying social change empirically, the discussion places more value on how to measure change than it does on the value of understanding how change occurs. In turn, therefore, Bhaskar has been used because he deals explicitly with the empirical problems of knowing the social world, specifically by adapting a hard empiricist perspective to the study of society, and offers therefore some useful hinge-pins to the discussion here, since hard empiricism arguably still underpins the legacy of much variable driven quantitative analysis.

Secondly, in contrast to authors such as Hacking, Bowker and Star, and Dupré – who also inform this argument in important ways – here it is suggested that exploring changes in measurement and classification needs to be an *empirical* enterprise. It is not enough to merely reflect on classifications, which is arguably what these authors have done. Instead, the value of obtaining a rigorous empirical description of a changing classification system is underscored here. Third, what is presented here is a little different to the two major schools of thought that, Bowker (2002: 8) suggests, are typical of researchers exploring historical classifications. Whereas one approach involves using 'classifications available to actors at the time' (see, for example, Hacking (1995) on child abuse), the other approach is to 'use the real classifications that progress in the arts and sciences has uncovered' – the example he gives is 'Tort's (1989) work on "genetic" classification systems, which were not so called at the time, but which are of vital interest to the Foucauldian problematic'.

Here, the approach is more similar to Hacking's work on the history of child abuse, inasmuch as the food retail categories are collated *as they appear* in the directories, irrespective of whether or not they are meaningful now. However, the approach is also sensitive to the locality to which they refer. In other words, it has a foot in both of the major schools of thought insofar as the aim is to note both the changing nomenclature of the classifications, for example 'bakers' versus 'bakers and cakeries', whilst at the same time considering what these classifications mean within the local context of York itself. The effort to consider the inter-dynamics between the changing classifications and the changing city is key, Bowker (2002: 10) argues, to understanding 'classification systems according to the work that they are doing – the network within which they are embedded'.

## Category and frequency change in food retail outlets

In the discussion that follows, the obstacles, and importantly, the resolutions, involved in what first appeared to be a simple exercise of counting the change of food outlets over time are explicated. Thus, the argument is derived from the genuine difficulties that emerged as part of a wider study relating to understanding changes in food and eating practices since 1945 in the city of York and the UK. From the outset, certain changes relating to contemporary urban regions were assumed to have occurred, such as the shift from industrial small sector retail outlets to a more service-based economy that relates to reorganization of the global financial, cultural and political economy (see Mérenne-Schoumaker, 1996; Sassen, 1994; Zukin, 1995). For example, it was expected that the number of local inner-city bakeries had declined, whereas the number of local restaurants increased, and that the changes reflected a general qualitative change to the city and surrounding urban regions. However, *empirically* exploring how these general changes manifest themselves specifically with respect to the food retail outlets at the *local* level of York itself was deemed to be a fundamental part of understanding how change may manifest itself locally and through time.

In order to sketch the changing numbers of local food outlets, two key sources were used: *Kelly's Directories* and the better-known *Yellow Pages*; the latter replacing the former in 1975. Both sources require a fee for traders to be listed, and although there are issues that one needs to consider when using them to do with their content and reliability for reasons which are discussed below, they nevertheless provide an accessible and continuous source of local trade data (see Shaw, 1978; Timmins, 1978) and have therefore frequently been used as a way of studying local change (eg Jopson and Reeder, 2008; Shaw, 1984; Shaw and Alexander, 1994).

Although each directory appears annually, the UK national population census dates were taken as the same time-points used to explore the food retail industry, thus allowing the census to provide an additional source with which to understand other socio-economic changes at national, regional and local level levels. Thus, snap shots at 1951, 1961, 1971, 1981, 1991 and 2001 were taken. This entailed using the local *Kelly's Directories* for 1951, 1961, 1971 and the *Yellow Pages* for 1981, 1991 and 2001. (The *Yellow Pages* moved to a 'split year' publication in 1991, so instead of a 1991 publication, there was a 1991/1992 version, which was used as the 1991 snap-shot; likewise 2001/2002 is used to reflect 2001.)

*Emma Uprichard*

Once the basic logistics of the research design were chosen, the next stage was to examine what the categories were and to, quite simply, count the number of entries under each category. This proved to be a classifier's nightmare, or a classifier's dream, depending on which perspective is taken. Taking 'bakers' as a first example, the category changes, as well as the quantitative changes within each category, made what was first thought to be a simple exercise into one that signalled many difficulties to come in other categories also (see Table 1). In 1951, 'bakers' are classified under 'bakers & pastry cooks', of which there are a total of 98. In 1961, as expected, the number of entries listed under this same category decreases, to just 66. In 1971, however, the category, 'bakers & pastry cooks', is no longer available, but 'bakers' now is; this time there are 64 listed entries, just two entries fewer than the decade before, suggesting that these same organizations were possibly the same entries in the previous two decades also despite the different wording of the categories. In 1981, the category 'bakers' disappears and is replaced with 'bakers & confectioners', a category which lasts until 2001, going from 31 units in 1981, up to 35 in 1991 and then back down to 32 in 2001.

Similar issues are present with regards to 'green grocers' over the same time period. However, instead of a total of four different categories appearing between 1951 and 2001, there are a total of ten categories over the same time (see Table 2), making the category change more complicated, as well as the difficulty of measuring change, greater. The changes to 'cafés and restaurants' (see Table 3) are similar, albeit greater still. In 1951, there is just one category, namely 'cafés, restaurants and caterers', which has morphed into seven categories by 2001, with another eight other categories appearing in between; fifteen categories are altogether created over the total time period, each supposedly accounting for a different kind of business at the local level.

Note that the categories have been ordered in each table quite specifically. Just as in the visualization of boxplots it is necessary to first rank the cases

**Table 1:** *Category and frequency changes to 'bakers' in York, 1951–2001*

| 'BAKERS' | 1951* | 1961* | 1971* | 1981** | 1991/92** | 2000/01** |
|---|---|---|---|---|---|---|
| Bakers & Pastry Cooks | 98 | 66 | | | | |
| Bakers | | | 64 | | | |
| Bakers & Confectioners Retail | | | | 31 | 35 | 32 |
| Bakers & Confectioners Sundriesmen | | | | 1 | | |

*York Directories; **Yellow Pages

**Table 2:** Category and frequency change in '(Green)grocers' in York, 1951–2001

| '(GREEN)GROCERS' | 1951* | 1961* | 1971* | 1981** | 1991/92** | 2000/01** |
|---|---|---|---|---|---|---|
| Grocers, tea and coffee provision merchants | 280 | | | | | |
| Fruiterers (retail) | 90 | | | | | |
| Greengrocers (retail) | 59 | | | | | |
| Grocers | | 236 | | | | |
| Fruiterers & Greengrocers | | 66 | 53 | 44 | | |
| Grocers – Retail (e.g. Jacksons) | | | | 65 | | |
| Grocers – Licensed | | | | 18 | | |
| Greengrocers & Fruit Sellers | | | | | 41 | 16 |
| Grocer & General Stores | | | | | 41 | |
| Grocers & Convenience Stores | | | | | | 42 |

**Table 3:** Category and frequency change in 'Cafés & Restaurants' in York, 1951–2001

| 'CAFES/RESTAURANTS' | 1951* | 1961* | 1971* | 1981** | 1991/92** | 2000/01** |
|---|---|---|---|---|---|---|
| Cafes, Restaurants and Caterers | 54 | | | | | |
| Restaurants, Cafes & c. | | 31 | | | | |
| Snack Bars | | 2 | | 2 | | |
| Fried Fish Shops | | | 47 | | | |
| Restaurants | | | 28 | 64 | 97 | 126 |
| Fish & Chip Shops & Restaurants | | | | 45 | 42 | 36 |
| Cafes & Cafeterias | | | | 11 | 32 | |
| Take Away Food Shops | | | | 11 | 39 | |
| Coffee Bars | | | | 9 | | |
| Take Away Food | | | | | | 75 |
| Cafes | | | | | | 41 |
| Sandwich Shops & Delivery | | | | | | 14 |
| Pizza Delivery & Take Away | | | | | | 8 |
| Internet Bars & Cafes | | | | | | 1 |

according to absolute values of the particular variable to be plotted, so too have the categories been assigned a particular row based on the year they appear and the frequency of entries within them. The first row in each table, for example, is a 1951 category, namely whichever has the highest frequency of entries listed within it. Thus, in Table 2, 'Grocers, tea and coffee provision merchants' has 280 entries in 1951, the highest frequency of all the included categories in that year, so it is also the first row in that table. For each year, then, as far as was possible, the order of the categories in each table also reflects something about the frequency within particular categories. (Note that the ordering of cells needs to be a bit flexible, since the degrees of freedom decrease within the table with every previous entry, ie the positioning of rows for each column is determined by both the frequency and sequence in which a category appears, but each category is itself determined by all the antecedent cells.)

The careful reader will already detect three patterns within each of these tabular stories of change. First, categories present in 1951 do not tend to exist any more by 2001. Second, some categories are created in one year but then disappear immediately afterwards and become replaced by others that then in their turn also 'die' and become replaced by other newer ones as time goes on. Third, visually, a kind of 'step' pattern is observed between the categories over time, which is shaded in the tables to make it more visible – more about this shortly. At this point, as a purely exploratory exercise, and also because it became apparent that the 'death' and 'birth' of categories was relative to all the categories within each year as well as across the years, it was decided to place all the categories between 1951 and 2001 in one table – see Table 4 below. From this table, a total of 46 categories are seen dying, adapting, emerging all together in relation to one another.

What is interesting, although perhaps not surprising, is that these three patterns are even more visible when exploring *all* the categories. Now, we not only observe that out of the nine categories that appear in 1951, only one – namely 'Butchers' – survives through to 2001. No other category shows such longevity. 'Fishmongers' is next in terms of category durability, appearing in 1961 and lasting through to 2001. The next longest surviving categories include 'restaurants', which lasts for four successive decades, appearing for the first time in 1971, whereas 'Fish & chip shops and restaurants' lasts for three successive decades. All the rest die out quickly after just one or two decades.

Note that 'Confectioners (retail)' also lasts four decades, but this also signals a possible issue with the 1971 data as a whole, inasmuch as it seems that this particular category has been missed out for just this year. It would certainly make sense within the context of the city of York and its industrial history in chocolate making with *Rowntree's* (now *Nestlé–Rowntree*, from *Nestlé*'s takeover in 1988) and *Terry's* (which finally closed in 2005) playing a key part in the lives of families across several generations, that 'Confectioners', as a category, is relatively robust.

The same 'hole' in the 1971 data is present for at least another two categories. There are only two 'Snack Bars' in 1961 and again in 1981, suggesting that there

Emma Uprichard

**Table 4:** *Category and frequency changes to food retail outlets in York, 1951–2001*

| | 1951 | 1961 | 1971 | 1981 | 1991/1992 | 2000/2001 |
|---|---|---|---|---|---|---|
| Grocers, tea and coffee provision merchants (retail) | 280 | | | | | |
| Confectioners (retail) | 156 | 80 | | 21 | 16 | |
| Butchers | 122 | 99 | 76 | 62 | 56 | 33 |
| Bakers & Pastry Cooks | 98 | 66 | | | | |
| Fruiterers (retail) | 90 | | | | | |
| Fried Fish Dealers | 70 | 56 | | | | |
| Green Grocers (retail) | 59 | | | | | |
| Cafes, Restaurants and Caterers | 54 | | | | | |
| Fishmongers, Poulterers etc | 28 | | | | | |
| Grocers | | 236 | | | | |
| Fruiterers & Greengrocers | | 66 | 53 | 44 | | |
| Restaurants, Cafes & c. | | 31 | | | | |
| Fishmongers | | 16 | 11 | 4 | 5 | 3 |
| Snack Bars | | 2 | | 2 | | |
| Poulterers | | 1 | | 1 | | |
| Health Food Stores | | 1 | | | | |
| Bakers | | | 64 | | | |
| Fried Fish Shops | | | 47 | | | |
| Restaurants | | | 28 | 64 | 97 | 126 |
| Pork Butchers | | | 27 | | | |
| Grocers – Retail (ie Jacksons) | | | | 65 | | |
| Fish & Chip Shops & Restaurants | | | | 45 | 42 | 36 |
| Bakers & Confectioners Retail | | | | 31 | 35 | 32 |
| Grocers – Licensed | | | | 18 | | |
| Dairies | | | | 17 | 11 | 4 |
| Take Away Food Shops | | | | 11 | 39 | |
| Supermarkets (1 Tea Cos) | | | | 11 | 36 | 26 |
| Cafes & Cafeterias | | | | 11 | 32 | |
| Coffee Bars | | | | 9 | | |
| Frozen Food & Freezer Centres | | | | 6 | | |
| Delicatessens & Cooked Meats | | | | 5 | | |
| Health Food Shops | | | | 4 | 9 | 6 |
| Bacon & Ham Curers and Suppliers | | | | 1 | | |
| Bakers & Confectioners Sundriesmen | | | | 1 | | |
| Greengrocers & Fruit Sellers | | | | | 41 | 16 |
| Grocer & General Stores | | | | | 41 | |
| Dellcatessens | | | | | 7 | 10 |
| Freezer Centres | | | | | 5 | 4 |
| Pick your Own Fruit & Vegetables | | | | | 2 | 0 |
| Take Away Food | | | | | | 75 |
| Grocers & Convenience Stores | | | | | | 42 |
| Cafes | | | | | | 41 |
| Sandwich Shops & Delivery | | | | | | 14 |
| Pizza Delivery & Take Away | | | | | | 8 |
| Internet Bars & Cafes | | | | | | 1 |
| Organic Foods | | | | | | 1 |

were probably still at least two snack bars in 1971, but they were just not counted. Similarly, there is one entry under 'Poulterers' in 1961 and 1981, but the entry does not appear in 1971. Another issue is raised with respect to 'Health food store' recorded in 1961 and then 'Health food *shop*' in 1981, 1991 and 2000/1, as if it was missed out in 1971, but then picked up again in 1981 under a slightly (perhaps careless) adjustment to the wording, suggesting possibly a preference for British terminology of a 'shop' as opposed to the more American sounding 'store'. Merging these categories was considered, but for the purposes of continuing the initial exploratory examination of the classifications themselves, it was decided to leave them all exactly as they appear in the directories and *Yellow Pages*.

Now, it is possible that these are data errors. Some categories were perhaps just forgotten about, double counted, or carelessly renamed (see Shaw, 1978 for further examples of this in relation to the trade directories). Data entry mistakes do happen and this is perhaps all that is observed here also. These 'issues' may or may not be highly significant. There is really no way of knowing. But this is precisely why it is safer to leave them in *as they are* rather than trying to clean, merge, code, recode, or measure some new 'made up' category which is *not* there. 'Dirty data' are arguably more valid than 'cleaned up' data, if only because they are what we *do* know *was* recorded and counted, irrespective of the extent to which they are interpreted as meaningful. Even where data entries are presumed or known to be 'dirty' errors, there is value there too. Like patterns in missing data, patterns in data entry errors over time may be interesting. They may for instance, appear more frequently in some years than others. 1971 here, for example, marks itself out from the other years precisely because of its possible data entry errors, signalling perhaps the start of the rift of change that was to become more visible later on. Dirty data provide clues to the context in which the data were constructed and it is in accessing this context that the numbers themselves can be better understood.

In any case, it is worth noticing the 'shape' of the shading. Like the histogram, it is the *overall* distribution of the data that is perhaps more important than the precise details of each row. 'New' categories appear each decade. In fact, at each decade, at least as many categories emerge as disappear. 1981 has the most categories. Again, whether or not this is significant is difficult to tell, but what is interesting is that this is also the year in the census data that shows important socio-economic 'ripples' of change (Uprichard, 2005), suggesting that around this time, change was taking place locally across multiple dimensions. By 2000/1, there are nineteen categories compared to just nine in 1951.

It is possible that there is something about the category itself that makes some survive longer than others. One of the anonymous reviewers of this article, for instance, pointed out that 'it seems to be broader, more general, categories that survive' and that we might expect this 'since they are going to find it easier to collect members than more narrowly defined categories, *ceteris paribus*'. How one defines whether a category is 'broader' or 'more narrow' is debatable, but the point remains an interesting one for of course if there is a pattern in the level of abstraction to do with whether categories survive or do not survive over time, that would surely have implications on how one might try to predetermine possible future change and continuity as well. Be this as it may, there is certainly a need to do more comparative work within other cities in the UK and elsewhere to know what all this may mean.

That said, if we think of the 'food retail industry in York' as the case and the categories of food retail outlets as the variables, then this quantitative 'growth' in the number of categories from nine in 1951 to nineteen in 2001 – but a total of 46 categories between 1951–2001 – may point not only to the need for polythetic descriptions of the case, but that more attributes are actually necessary the more complex the case becomes. Conversely, the qualitative continuity in certain categories is of interest also. Why, for example, is it that 'Butchers' is the only surviving category throughout 1951–2001? Would this be the same in other cities? Is there something particular about the business that makes it meaningful to the city itself?

Pig farming and pork butchers are indeed renown in the Yorkshire region, and after speaking with a couple of local butchers to ask them whether they had any comments about the local meat industry, it quickly became clear that there was a sense that the meat industry in general had changed considerably, now making it increasingly difficult for them to 'specialize' in particular meat products (such as 'pork' or 'poultry' which are other meat-related categories in 1971, and in 1961 and 1981 respectively). There was also a point made about butchers in York being very much a family enterprise, which had therefore maintained a sense of continuity in ownership as the family business was passed down the generations. Of course, two conversations are by no means sufficient to make confident interpretations, but examining category changes raises other questions, which are precisely about understanding the *local context* in which the categories are situated. Using 'dirty data' allows for the historical contingency of the qualitative changes *to* the categories to be investigated, which ultimately underpin the quantitative changes also – precisely the kind of approach that authors such as Abbott (2000), Bowker and Star (2002) and Hacking (1995, 1999, 2002) advocate.

A word of caution, however. Let us be very clear about the quality of the data used here: neither the *Kelly's Directories* nor the *Yellow Pages* are perfect records. On the one hand, they share similar, but not identical geographies, although the geographical changes are relatively small. Technically speaking, though, the available data on York does not allow for detailed like-for-like longitudinal comparisons between the time-points. Yet even if the geographies were comparable, they probably would not be as useful as might appear anyway, since the administrative geography does not reflect the growing city anyway. Indeed, when it comes to studying change of a dynamic entity, it is oxymoronic to strive for like-for-like comparisons anyway. The very fact that something is understood as *dynamic* implies that over time it is also understood to have changed, so seeking for like-for-like comparisons of a changing thing arguably needs to be abandoned in longitudinal research anyway. On the other hand, there is no way of knowing that the listed entries represent *all* the outlets under any category. It must be assumed that there are sampling errors within each directory, but then we also need to assume that these errors are of a similar kind in each directory, making the 'dirty data' nevertheless meaningful. However imperfect they are, both sources provide the most accessible source and to this extent they offer similar advantages and disadvantages.

Whilst it is important to be aware of the various issues within 'dirty data', from an ontological and epistemological perspective, *the data as they are available* remain informative. The key is to move away from the notion of the variable as a measure of a thing in itself and instead towards the idea of the variable as a *trace* – a left-over mark, if you like – of that dynamic thing which it measures (Byrne, 2002). Byrne explains:

> The dynamic systems which are our cases leave traces for us, which we can pick up. We can, as it were, track them, and we can infer from the traces what it was that left them. From the traces we can reconstruct a version of the real entities *and* of the relationships among those entities *and* of the emergent forms which are the product of and the producers of the relationships among those entities. We can glimpse the entities and the systemic relationships among the entities. (Byrne, 2002: 36)

Note though that there are time and space issues intrinsic to 'variate traces'. Byrne does not say anything explicit on this, even though they are implicit in his work elsewhere. Three are important to us here. First, there is always a 'disjuncture' between the temporality of the data and its production. In other words, the category is likely to only ever be recorded *after* it has come into being. So even though a new category might 'appear' in the Directories, we can be sure that people were using this category at ground level in York beforehand, even if we cannot determine when it first appeared. Of course, it may be that some categories were used more widely than others, but the point here is what is counted becomes a category. Second, it is worth paying attention to the temporality of traces, for example duration – this might show 'grooves' in which particular trajectories are 'stuck'. Alternatively it could mark a possible future phase shift. When the last butcher closes in York, this will mark a quantitative shift in butchers, but it will also mark a symbolic qualitative shift in how food retail outlets in York have changed. Third, the changing spatiality intrinsic to the traces is important. That is, the geography of each of the categories is not insignificant; even the geography of the resource is significant. The York Directories, for instance, which were in use between 1947 and 1975, and focus primarily on York ward, were replaced by the Yellow Pages, which include many other surrounding areas too, reflecting the changing nature of what was deemed to be 'local' or 'accessible' to the York resident. In other words, as the city of 'York' grew so did the 'pages' from which local residents accessed services and facilities; bigger and thicker sources also mean the bigger and more diverse geography of 'York'.

What we have here, then, as we do with any measures over time, is a complex interaction going on between the thing that is counted, how that thing is perceived, how it changes in absolute terms and how it is perceived to have changed – at the same time the context in which that thing is changing (or not) may or may not be changing as well. Conceptualizing measurable tangible change as Byrne's 'variate traces' is helpful in grasping some of this complexity, especially with regards to understanding what it is that is measured when measuring quantitative change. In some ways, it has been phrased in different ways since Plato's allegory of the cave, for at its heart lies the tension between the epistemological versus the ontological complexity of the world and our efforts to relate one to the other – or more accurately perhaps, it has to do with the extent to which one believes it is possible to abstract one from the other. Byrne's point is reminiscent of other authors (eg Cilliers, 2001; Bhaskar, 1998), who each argue, albeit in different ways, that to think of the epistemological realm (which in this case has to do with quantitative descriptions) and the ontological as independent of one another, is a mistake. This is because, as Cilliers (2001) spells out, there is 'a constant to and fro between them in which our models and, especially in the case of the human sciences, the world itself is transformed'. Cilliers continues:

> Boundaries are simultaneously a function of the activity of the system itself, and a product of the strategy of description involved. In other words, we frame the system by describing it in a certain way (for a certain reason), but we are constrained in where the frame can be drawn. The boundary of the system is therefore neither purely a function of our description, nor is it a purely natural thing. (Cilliers, 2001: 141)

In other words, the measures are representations *both of the system and a representation of our description of it*. This is a crucial point and is central to this argument. Simply put, it is important to think about the data as re-presentations of the re-organization of social life. That said, Bhaskar's epistemological logic about measurement is also worth citing here, precisely because it affirms the sequential ordering of what variables are or are not representing:

> To be is *not* to be the value of a variable; though it is plausible (if, I would argue, incorrect) to suppose that things can only be *known* as such. For if to be were just to be the value of the variable we could never make sense of the complex processes of identification and measurement by means of which we can sometimes represent some things as such. *Knowledge follows existence*, in logic and in time; and any philosophical position which explicitly or implicitly denies this has got things upside down. (Bhaskar, 1998: 29, italics added)

That is, in order to obtain a description of a thing, that thing first needs to exist, and then we need to become sufficiently aware of it in order to know about it in order to measure its frequency as a variable. Conversely, a variable needs to exist first as a variable in order to know more about it and to understand what it represents. This is not to say that knowledge and existence are not recursively constituted or that variables do not have impact on the things that they measure. Rather, it is to underscore the ontological dimension of both variables and the things that they describe and that in order for a variable to come into being, the thing it describes necessarily is already perceived to exist. Of course, once a variable comes into being then it too takes on both an ontological and epistemological dimension which impact on both the ontology and the epistemology of the thing that it describes, and so on. But either way, knowledge follows existence.

The reason Bhaskar's point about existence preceding knowledge is important to bear in mind with respect to methods of understanding change in the social world is because it assumes that despite a constant recursivity between a thing and how it is measured, particularly over time, that relationship is asymmetrical. For example, the reason 'bakers' were counted was that they were there to count in the first place (and not because they were counted that they existed). This is the case, even though once 'bakers' were formally counted, it was also possible to know more about them. In other words, there is always an assumed temporal direction between existence and knowledge, between a thing and the variables that describe it. Hence the time-lag between variate traces and the thing it represents. Like the tracks in the sand signalling the passage of a particular kind of animal, variables are necessarily better at telling us what has happened (in the past) compared to it happening (in the present) or what will happen (in the future). Using variables for predictive purposes becomes a tall order once the temporal nature of the variable is acknowledged.

Guérois and Paulus (2001) raise this issue in an interesting paper about the history and chronology of the main urban geographies in French census and administrative statistics (eg *l'unité urbaine* or *l'aire urbaine*, etc.). They argue that the timing of when new terms and concepts become officially recognized coincides – *and is a direct consequence of* – what is happening directly at ground level, often as a widespread phenomenon across cities and urban regions throughout France. Similarly, the records of change in the food retail outlets reflect something about what was currently happening at the ground level around that time.

As Desrosières (2000: 176) puts it in relation to the construction and selection of variables, the categories were 'chosen and constructed because they were 'judged socially to be of social importance'. In other words, at a given moment in history society judges that 'something' is an issue for intervention by that same 'society' through action taken by its public authorities and its institutions.' There is much value, therefore, in employing 'dirty data' to explore longitudinal change precisely because they also contain within them information about political judgements of the actors that were involved in its construction. The importance of actors remains an implicit component in this kind of quantitative data analysis.

## Re-thinking longitudinal quantitative research

The dialectical relationship between the empirical description of the object of study (the realm of epistemology) and the actual object of study (the realm of ontology) is arguably an intrinsic component of any social investigation. It is worth, therefore, discussing these issues a little further before bringing this article to an end. Certainly, with regards to developing quantitative longitudinal descriptions, these debates tend to be played out in the epistemological-ontological interface relating to 'measurement', 'classification', and of course the subsequent operationalization of the 'variable' and the 'case'. The point being that quantitative data are socially constructed, and just as for any social construction, attention needs to be paid to the processes involved in the construction of quantitative data.

This is not a new argument; it has been well presented elsewhere (eg Bateson, 1984; Cicourel, 1964; Hindess, 1973; Irvine *et al*., 1979). However, even though it is a well-known perspective, it is strangely overlooked in *longitudinal* quantitative research. Yet when all the issues involved in quantitatively describing change over time are put together, it becomes a wonder that any internal validity within measurement systems are left at all. For instance, the number system and the property to be measured need to 'match up'. That is, there needs be an isomorphism between a number system and a property to be measured whereby 'a one to one relationship must be obtained between certain characteristics of the number system involved and the relations between various quantities (instances) of the property to be measured' (Togerson, 1958, cited in Cicourel, 1964: 10–11). For example, to say that there are $x$-many 'bakers' assumes a one-to-one relationship between the number system used to count the number of 'bakers' (usually this is the base ten number system, but it could be another) and that this number system can work adequately in relation to what it may mean to count 'bakers'. It is meaningful to employ integers to reflect 'bakers' since it is not possible to have a fraction of a 'baker'. Simple counts, therefore, become one of the most powerful tools to any longitudinal quantitative researcher.

Yet social scientists tend to have a very bad habit of ignoring the fact that number systems also need to be appropriate to the things they measure and focus predominantly on the social construction of that thing. This may be an acceptable omission, except of course that most classifications do not change in the same way as the number systems that measure them. Most of the time, when a classification changes, it rarely does so in this 'crisp' way suitable to the integer number system used to measure them. Instead, most classifications go through a transitional phase where they are 'fuzzy'. Thus, it is difficult to place 'all bakers' in a 'baker' category; some bakers may be a 'kind of bakers, but also sell takeaway food, such as fresh sandwiches'. Likewise, census classifications have evolved over time making it rather difficult to measure key changes with many of the core demographic categories. As Marsh *et al.* (1988: 854) note, the core issue in calculating change between censuses is being 'able to distinguish real trends from artefactual change brought about by altering census definitions'.

Consequently, in practice, Cicourel argues, measuring the social world involves measurement by fiat, instead of literal measurement. He explains the two ways of measuring the social as follows:

> *Literal* measurement refers to an exact correspondence between the substantive elements and relations under study and the ordered elements and relations of the measurement system. Measurement by *fiat* is an arbitrary or forced correspondence between elements, relations, and operations. (Cicourel, 1964: 225–226)

Although literal measurement is by far the most preferable kind of measurement, it is measurement by fiat that takes place in (and in relation to) the social world. This is not because social scientists are inherently 'bad measurers', but rather the nature of the social world itself renders it difficult to do otherwise. Taking the example of simple frequency counts, before even being able to assign a number to 'bakers', the classification 'baker' itself needs to be identified. Of course, identifying 'bakers' is more than simple nomenclature; it requires a set of (often legal) standards. As Hacking argues, classifications and standards are 'two sides of the same coin': 'classifications are containers for the descriptions of events – they are an aspect of organizational, social and personal memory – whereas standards are procedures for how to do things – they are an aspect of acting in the world' (quoted in Bowker, 2002: 7).

Making valid and reliable longitudinal comparisons over any meaningful length of time becomes, then, extremely problematic, even at the level of acquiring simple changes in counts. Classifications are in and of themselves insufficient in determining either the nature of the isomorphism required to measure them or the descriptions and mechanisms that helped to produce them. The classification 'baker', for example, is not sufficiently precise to indicate how to measure 'change in the number of bakers'. After all, 'change in the number of bakers' depends on the classification ('bakers') and standards that litigate what 'bakers' are both real in their consequences and in themselves. Hence, to measure 'change in the number of bakers' requires the definition of 'baker' to remain static over time, which in turn assumes that all things being equal, to be a 'baker', whatever that might involve, is both epistemologically *and* ontologically constant, which in the context of a dynamic social world is unlikely.

The changing classifications of any object of study themselves become meaningful, then, so long as it is recognized that: (a) the number system used to count a particular classification is itself a social construct, which (b) is only appropriate to that object of study if there is also an isomorphism between (c) the construct of that classification and the number system itself. In addition, following Bowker and Starr (2002), (d) the ways in which these classifications work and how they are interpreted is subject to historical change, which is (e) also regulated by standards which maintain or force changes to those classifications. All these points work together and have a number of implications for what is measured, how measurement is interpreted, and the re-ordering of the social world.

All that said, it is worth bearing in mind Bhaskar's (1998: 29) point that 'Knowledge follows existence, in logic and in time' and that however classifications are constructed, the ways in which they emerge and are subsequently made to hold has much to do with their ontological properties as well. Thus, following Bhaskar (1979), it is because 'bakers' exist at all and are real in their consequences that they *can* be classified and maintained according to a set of standards and that they can also be identified and counted over time (though that they can be handled in this sort of way may be a contingently necessary condition for our knowledge about 'bakers'). However, the meanings associated with the classification and the underlying object, 'bakers', or any other classification or object for that matter, is subject to historical change as well. In turn, therefore, in order to examine something as relatively simple as 'change in number of bakers', it is also necessary to consider other related classifications that may or may not have helped to create, maintain or destroy them too. As Abbott (2000: 226) puts it, 'looking at the social world not in terms of simple variables but in terms of complexes of variables may be not only more important than we think, but may be all we are able to do'.

## Conclusion

Using 'dirty data' to explore qualitative changes to classification systems and quantitative change within classifications over time is meaningful for two main reasons. First, it is at that level of abstraction that further patterns of change and continuity may be empirically captured. Second, any patterns within the trajectories of the categories themselves may point to shifts in the rate of change, the momentum involved in that change, and dimensions of change that may or may not be path dependent. 'Dirty data' – that is, using the categories as they exist *without* any recoding or merging etc. – is meaningful when exploring longitudinal change precisely because they allow for both quantitative and qualitative changes to be explored *together*. Leave the data and categories alone, even if this creates more mess in practice!

The upshot of all of this is that we need to rethink the kind of social research we are doing. As Abbott wrote over a decade ago:

> A quiet revolution is underway in social science. We are turning from units to context, from attributes to connections, from causes to events. The change has many antecedents: the exhaustion of our old paradigm, our inherent desire for change, the power of computers. It also has many consequences: new areas for empirical work, new methodologies, rediscovery of important old theories. (Abbott, 1995: 93)

We might add to this list that there is a shift to focus on the case rather than the variable and using variables differently to classify cases. As Byrne (2002: 127) suggests, 'It is as much a matter of reinterpreting what we are doing as of doing something differently'. The methodological revolution in the social sciences is here and it is already happening. Let us no longer be quiet about it, but rather discuss it openly and honestly. The social world has changed and so too must our ways of knowing change with it.

## Acknowledgements

This research was supported by a grant from the Economic and Social Research Council. Some initial parts of the paper were presented at the *Measure and Value* conference at Goldsmith's College, London, 18 September 2009. I am also grateful to Sarah Nettleton for commenting on earlier drafts of this paper. Thanks also are due to Sarah Shrive-Morrison for the (very time consuming) data collection without which this article could not have been written.

## References

Abbott, A., (1995), 'Sequence analysis: new methods for old ideas', *Annual Review of Sociology*, 21: 93–113.
Abbott, A., (2000), 'Reflections on the future of sociology', *Contemporary Sociology*, 29(2): 296–300.
Allen, P., (1997), *Cities and Regions as Self–Organising Systems: Models of Complexity*, Amsterdam: Gordon and Breach Science Publishers.
Bateson, N., (1984), *Data Construction in Social Surveys*, London: Allen and Unwin.
Batty, M., (2005), *Cities and Complexity: Understanding Cities with Cellular Automata, Agent–Based Models, and Fractals*, London: MIT Press.
Bhaskar, R., (1975), *A Realist Theory of Science*, London: Version.
Bhaskar, R., (1979), *The Possibility of Naturalism*, 3rd edn, London: Routledge.
Bhaskar, R., (1998), 'Philosophy and scientific realism', in M. Archer, R. Bhaskar, A. Collier, T. Lawson and A. Norrie (eds), *Critical Realism: Essential Readings*, London: Routledge.
Bowker, G., (2002), 'How things work', paper posted at the eScholarship Repository, University of California, available at: http://repositories.cdlib.org/ucsdcomm/bowker.
Bowker, G. and Star, S.L., (2002), *Sorting Things Out: Classification and its Consequences*, Cambridge, MA: MIT Press.
Byrne, D., (2002), *Interpreting Quantitative Data*, London: Sage.
Byrne, D. and Ragin, C. (eds), (2009), *Handbook of Case–Based Methods*, London: Sage.
Caren, N. and Panofsky, A., (2005), 'TQCA: a technique for adding temporality to qualitative comparative analysis', *Sociological Methods & Research*, 34: 147–172.
Chaplain, M., Singh, G. and McLachlan, J., (1999), *On Growth and Form: Spatio–Temporal Pattern Formation in Biology*, Chichester: Wiley & Sons.
Cicourel, A., (1964), *Method and Measurement in Sociology*, New York: Free Press.
Cilliers, P., (2001), 'Boundaries, hierarchies and networks in complex systems', *International Journal of Innovation Management*, 5: 135–147.
Desrosières, A., (1998), *The Politics of Large Numbers*, Cambridge, MA: Harvard University Press.
Desrosières, A., (2000), 'Measurement and its uses: harmonization and quality in social statistics', *International Statistical Review*, 68: 173–187.
Desrosières, A., (2001), 'How real are statistics? Four possible attitudes', *Social Research*, 68(2): 339–355.
Dupré, J., (2006), 'Scientific classification', *Theory, Culture and Society*, 23: 30–32.
Elliott, J., (2005), *Using Narrative in Social Research*, London: Sage.
Gilbert, N. and Troitzsch, K., (1999), *Simulation for the Social Scientist*, Buckingham: Open University Press.
Guérois, M. and Paulus, F., (2001), 'Commune centre, agglomération, aire urbaine: quelle pertinence pour l'etude des villes?', paper presented at *Géo–évènement* conference, Paris, April.

Hacking, I., (1995), 'The looping effects of human kinds', in D. Sperber, D. Premack and A. J. Premack (eds), *Causal Cognition: A Multidisciplinary Debate*, New York: Clarendon Press.

Hacking, I., (1999), *The Social Construction of What?* Cambridge, MA: Harvard University Press.

Hacking, I., (2002), 'How "natural" are "kinds" of sexual orientation?' *Law and Philosophy*, 21: 335–347.

Hindess, B., (1973), *The Use of Official Statistics in Sociology: A Critique of Positivism and Ethnomethodology*, London: Macmillan.

Hosmer, D., Lemesow, S. and May, S., (2008), *Applied Survival Analysis: Regression Modeling of Time–to–Event Data*, 2nd edn, New Jersey: John Wiley and Sons.

Irvine, J., Miles, I. and Evans, J. (eds), (1979), *Demystifying Social Statistics*, London: Pluto Press.

Jopson, J. and Reeder, A., (2008), 'An audit of Yellow Pages telephone directory listings of indoor tanning facilities and services in New Zealand, 1992–2006', *Australian and New Zealand Journal of Public Health*, 32(4): 372–377.

Marsh, C., Arber, S., Wrigley, N., Rhind, D. and Bulmer, M., (1988), *'Research policy and review 23': The view of academic social scientists on the 1991 UK Census of Population*, London: Economic and Social Research Council.

Menard, S., (2002), *Longitudinal Research*, London: Sage.

Mérenne-Schoumaker, B., (1996), *La Localisation des Services*, Paris: Nathan.

Mills, C.W., (1959), *The Sociological Imagination*, London: Oxford University Press.

Ragin, C. and Strand, S., (2008), 'Using qualitative comparative analysis to study causal order: comment on Caren and Panofsky', *Sociological Methods and Research*, 36: 431–441.

Reed, M. and Harvey, D.L., (1996), 'Social science as the study of complex systems', in L.D. Kiel and E. Elliott (eds), *Chaos Theory in the Social Sciences*, Ann Arbor: University of Michigan Press.

Sassen, S., (1994), *Cities in a World Economy*, Thousand Oaks, CA: Pine Forge Press.

Savage, M. and Burrows, R., (2007), 'The coming crisis of empirical sociology', *Sociology*, 41(5): 885–899.

Sayer, A., (2000), *Realism and Social Science*, London: Sage.

Schelling, T., (1971), 'Dynamic models of segregation', *Journal of Mathematical Sociology*, 1: 143–186.

Shaw, G., (1978), 'The content and reliability of nineteenth-century trade directories', *Local Historian*, 13(4): 205–209.

Shaw, G., (1984), 'Directories as sources in urban history: a review of British and Canadian material', *Urban History Yearbook 1984*: 36–44.

Shaw, G. and Alexander, A., (1994), 'Directories and the local historian III: directories as sources in local history', *Local History*, 46: 12–17.

Singer, J. and Willett, J.B., (2003), *Applied Longitudinal Data Analysis: Modeling Change and Event Occurrence*, New York: Oxford University Press.

Timmins, G., (1978), 'Measuring industrial growth from trade directories', *The Local Historian*, 13(4): 349–351.

Tryon, R., (1939), *Cluster Analysis: Correlation Profile and Orthometric Analysis for the Isolation of Unities of Mind Personality*, Ann Arbor: Edward Brothers.

Uprichard, E., (2005), 'Studying complex places: change and continuity in York and Dijon', unpublished PhD thesis, Department of Sociology, Durham University: Durham, UK.

Uprichard, E., Burrows, R. and Byrne, D., (2008), 'SPSS as an inscription device: from causality to description?' *Sociological Review*, 56(4): 606–622.

Zukin, S., (1995), *The Culture of Cities*, Oxford: Blackwell.

# The economy of social data: exploring research ethics as device

## Ana Gross

**Abstract:** The following article argues that research ethics and data regulatory frameworks can be understood as devices that articulate a particular kind of social data economy. Following Waldby and Mitchell's (2006) work on biological material economies it explores how social research ethics and data regulatory frameworks in the United Kingdom, organized around the notions of informed consent and anonymization, have favoured a model in which privacy is disentangled from the human agency to which it makes reference in order to be converted and objectified as data. Informed consent and anonymization are hence here analysed as devices which enable the circulation, exchange and valuation of data, or in other words, as devices which enable the conversion of privacy into property. In particular, the paper argues that informed consent enacts a legitimate transaction between data subject and data controller and can be therefore understood as a surrogate property contract. On the other hand, anonymization, which works by suppressing the author function, renders singular data units commensurable and aggregatable in the form of databases, a procedure which supports the emergence of a specific set of property rights. Finally, the conclusion critically addresses the work of ethics as a device as new datascapes organized by the principle of traceability produce 'the human' as disaggregated and distributed.

**Keywords:** data economy, ethics, anonymity, informed consent, value

## Introduction

Creating value out of the qualities or capacities inherent in life or living entities has become a pervasive practice as part of the production of biovalue (Waldby, 2000, 2002; Waldby and Mitchell, 2006; Rose, 2006). It is described by Waldby as 'the yield of vitality produced by the biotechnical reformulation of living processes' (Waldby, 2002: 310). Rose similarly identifies the emergence of economies of vitality, which he describes in terms of the molecularization of vitality: 'vitality is decomposed into a series of discrete and distinct objects – that can be isolated, delimited, stored, accumulated, mobilised, and exchanged, accorded a discrete value, traded across time, spaces, . . . in the services of many objectives' (Rose, 2006: 135). In extending Foucault's concept of biopolitics, the practice of governance that brought 'life and its mechanisms into the realm of explicit calculations' (Foucault, 1978: 143), Rose claims that such calculations no longer organize the state, but instead increasingly shape economic spaces that take as their object the creation of value out of life itself. In these processes, the somatic entities that are produced and stabilized are no longer either individuals or populations, but fragments: cells, molecules, genomes and genes (Helmreich, 2008).

Rendering calculable the value of life is, however, a controversial practice, and it is often argued that life resists inclusion in market exchange (Zelizer, 1978, 1985; Tober, 2001; Dickenson, 2007; Scheper-Hughes, 2001; Fourcade, 2009). In any case, this resistance has not meant that life and its fragments have remained outside market valuation mechanisms; on the contrary, specific devices have served to articulate its valuation and circulation (Rose, 2006; Karpik, 2010). This article explores the possibility that these and other forms of valuing life are not limited to or exclusively produced in the unfolding of the bio-sciences within biocapital, but are also implicated in the practices which social scientists have undertaken in their empirical research with human subjects.

The claim being made here then is that creating value out of life itself has also been and continues to be a characteristic of the practices of social scientists, as vital emissions such as utterances, actions, opinions or interactions are detached, fragmented, recombined and transformed into valuable aggregates with the aid of a series of devices. Specifically, it is suggested that sociologists, across a range of epistemological approaches, manipulate, qualify and aggregate individuals and their vital emissions in order to construct the large collective beings so as to produce 'what has conventionally been called society since the first half of the nineteenth century' (Boltanski and Thevenot, 1991: 2), or in other words, in order to create an aggregate that is required to be qualitatively distinct from its individual components (Latour, 2010). In what follows, the focus will be on sociologists, and more widely social researchers. Such a focus demonstrates how in current social science practices the relations between individuals and collectives are being consequentially extended.

Indeed it will be argued here that there is emerging a newly enhanced productivity of living entities in social research, linked to what Savage and Burrows (2007) have described as a new reality of large volumes of digitalized transactional data and data fragments, previously inexistent or considered informational waste, that are being alienated, circulated and reincorporated in increasingly complex economies. Here, value is being created out of what previously were considered human by-products as new technologies appear to be enabling the capturing and extraction of vital emissions, such as commercial transactions or movements in space and time, which humans produce as part of their living process and which can be now fixed into biographical, biometric and transactional classifications (Ruppert, 2009), usually in the form of databases. In these practices, vital emissions are extensively captured and attached, duplicated in their flux by either the intervention of new technologies or through their incorporation into other value regimes (Appadurai, 1988): they are, in short, being rendered economic (Callon et al., 2007; Callon, 1998; Caliskan and Callon, 2009).

The article focuses on describing how the conversion of the individual into the aggregate, that is, the conversion of vital emissions into data is not without effort, but is, rather, a highly mediated operation in which the devices of ethics have played a key role. The article thus explores the mediation of data through a focus on the use of the devices of *informed consent* and *anonymization* principles as a way of showing how ethical practices participate in the creation of value within social scientific and commercial research. It aims to demonstrate that what has created value within these economies is the mediated conversion of vital emissions into data, in such a way as to enable the emergence and disentanglement of data as an entity distinct from the human agency to which it makes reference, thus enabling the circulation of vital emissions in regimes where they can be made commensurable[1] to one another and rendered of economic value.

In analytically opening up ethics as an economic device I am not attempting to reveal what is hidden in ethical principles or questioning the moral stance they impose, but to 'rediscover the strangeness of what has become all too familiar' (Karpik, 2010: 10) as part of a questioning of the emergence of data as an unmediated expression and function of human agency (Lezaun, 2007). In the exploration of ethics as a device, I consider how informed consent and anonymization procedures may equip human agency with the properties of autonomy and privacy so as to enable the extraction and manipulation of data. The effect of so doing is to reveal that there is no natural, *a priori* human essence to be located in research subjects but instead that humanity lies in the entanglements which affect and move those it envelops (Callon and Rabeharisoa, 2004). In other words, following Callon (2007), what a 'subject' is in the term 'research subject' is the outcome of a specific performance in which ethics play a key role.

But ethics do not only enable the bringing into existence, or making visible of the entity 'research subject', but also support the emergence of something that is extractable out of the research subject, that is, the entity 'data' as a separate, objectified thing. Ethics allow for vital emissions (otherwise entrenched in networks of subjectivity and privacy) to circulate, 'to alternate between detachments and (re) attachments' (Callon, 2007: 343).

To this end, the article analyzes the economic function of informed consent and anonymization procedures as laid out in four key documents involved in the regulation of sociological practice and the extraction and manipulation of data in the United Kingdom: the Economic and Social Research Ethics Framework (2009); the British Sociological Association *Statement of Ethical Practice* (2002); the Social Research Association Ethical Guidelines (2003); and the Data Protection Act (1998). The focus on sociological research regulations is purposeful not only because of the increasingly important role that ethics is called upon to play in contemporary scientific and commercial data landscapes, but also because of the role of ethics in the articulation of a particular kind of data economy, which in turn produces and requires particular forms of property and value. This is especially important if sociology is to be able to embrace a redefinition of the relationship between the individual and the aggregate, between the ingredients and the structure as Latour (2010) suggests. Any solution to what has been described as an empirical crisis must not only address the 'politics of method' (Savage and Burrows, 2007; Law and Urry, 2004) but also critically look at the political economy of data and the ethics devices which contribute to articulate its present and future economic functioning.

## Informed consent, or the sidetrack to property over privacy

Within both biomedical and social research, informed consent has played a central role in ethics codes and is at the core of ethical research practices established by most professional codes of conduct. The first and most prominent principle established by the Nuremberg Code (1948) states that:

> The voluntary consent of the human subject is absolutely essential. This means that the person involved should have legal capacity to give consent; should be so situated as to be able to exercise free power of choice, without the intervention of any element of force, fraud, deceit, duress, over-reaching, or other ulterior form of constraint or coercion; and should have sufficient knowledge and comprehension of the elements of the subject matter involved as to enable him to make an understanding and enlightened decision. This latter element requires that before the acceptance of an affirmative decision by the experimental subject there should be made known to him the nature, duration, and purpose of the experiment; the method and means by which it is to be conducted; all inconveniences and hazards reasonable to be expected; and the effects upon his health or person which may possibly come from his participation in the experiment (Nuremberg Code, 1948: 181).

The fundamental claim that 'informed consent' or 'freely given' consent by research subjects is a legitimate basis for research put forward in the Code has been central to most subsequent regulations governing scientific research and data extraction and handling practices[2] (Manson and O'Neill, 2007). It primarily entails the right of the research subject to be fully informed about his or her participation in any research or data experiment, including possible dangers and risks, as well as granting him or her the right to refuse participation. It sometimes also includes the consented waiving of any proprietary claims over the data extracted. The information deemed necessary for consent to be given 'freely' usually refers to the purpose, methods and intended possible uses of the data gathered. The type of informed consent advocated by the Economic and Social Research Council (ESRC) *Ethics Framework*, the Social Research Association (SRA) *Ethical Guidelines*, and the British Sociological Association (BSA) *Statement of Ethical Practice*, for example, assign human agents with freedom of choice. In doing so, they assume human agents can and should be autonomous from any external sources which might influence their desires, beliefs and decision-making processes. In this regard, the implementation of the practice of informed consent enacts the existence of human agency as sovereign from the influences of other agents, either persons or things: for example, 'research participants must participate in a voluntary way, free from coercion' and 'consent has to be freely given in order to be valid' (ESRC, 2009: 25). The BSA *Statement of Ethical Practice* advises that 'as far as possible participation in sociological research should be based on the freely given informed consent of those studied' (2002: 5), while the SRA *Ethical Guidelines* propose that research with human subjects should be based on the freely given informed consent of subjects. So, for example, 'in voluntary inquiries, subjects should not be under the impression that they are required to participate. They should be aware of their entitlement to refuse at any stage for whatever reason and to withdraw data just supplied' (SRA, 2003: 27).

The Data Protection Act 1998 also takes informed consent as one of its pivotal requirements for enforcing the lawful acquisition, possession and use of what are defined as either personal or sensitive personal data. Indeed, informed consent is implicitly required for both personal and sensitive data types in order for the data controller to comply with the Data Protection Act's first principle,[3] that is, that such data should be processed fairly and lawfully. In the case of sensitive personal data, the Data Protection Act requires explicit informed consent from the research subject, usually established through a written or recorded medium. Informed consent can be obtained in writing through a detailed consent form which usually includes an informative statement, or visually or audio recorded or simply verbally, depending on the nature of the research, the type of data to be gathered and the format in which the data will be inscribed. For in-depth interviews for example, the use of written consent forms is usually recommended, whereas for surveys obtaining written consent may not be required (UK Data Archive, 2009).

While explicitly formulated as a way of *recognizing* the autonomy of individuals, when understood as a device as is done here,[4] informed consent can be seen as a means to make explicit the sort of connections or attachments, the sort of dependences, which *produce* human activity as autonomous; specifically, it demonstrates that for consent to be autonomous, it also needs to be produced as informed. In all research regulations analysed, including the Data Protection Act, it is advised that information regarding the research process and data-processing procedures should at all times be provided in order to allow data subjects to arrive at an informed decision regarding their involvement in social research activities. Moreover, the information provided should not be deceptive, should not withhold material or methodological facts about the research process while at the same time not 'overwhelm[ing] potential subjects with unwanted and incomprehensible details about the origin and content of a social inquiry' (SRA, 2003: 35). It is therefore assumed that the provision of the right type and amount of information regarding the research process equips research subjects as free and self-determined agents, that it endows research subjects with specific capacities which enable them to conduct themselves as particular types of persons.

It could therefore also be argued that the device of informed consent produces the conditions necessary for the market ideal of pure and perfect information display, where it is assumed that an appropriate distribution of information between agencies can lead to and legitimate exchange, otherwise considered fraud or unlawful. It provides research subjects with enough information to help them make autonomous and rational choices, but these choices are, nevertheless, not possible without the 'preliminary framing not only of the choices, but also of the freedom of the framed actors' (Cochoy, 2007: 115). It can be argued, then, that it is the act of giving informed consent, mediated by the display of information, that is what produces autonomy and the ability to make free, rational choices by framing subjects, and not autonomy which provides for the possibility that an informed and consented decision will be made. It is thus the device that enables giving consent to be rendered an explicitly human form of agency.

As with autonomy, research ethics also make privacy visible, insofar as it produces a private sphere that can and must exist before the practices of research and data collection. In all four documents, research ethics presuppose a secluded private sphere that it is explicitly specified must not suffer intrusion. The British Sociological Association *Statement of Ethical Practice*, for example, states that 'in many of its forms social research intrudes into the lives of those studied. While some participants in sociological research may find the experience a positive and welcome one, for others, the experience may be disturbing . . . This can be particularly so if they perceive apparent intrusions into their private and personal worlds . . .' (BSA, 2002: 4). The Social Research Association *Ethical Guidelines* state, for example, that in observation studies 'where behaviour patterns are observed without the subject's knowledge, social researchers must take care not to infringe what may be referred to as "the private space" of an individual or group' (SRA, 2003: 31).

Research should also preserve both the physical and subjective well-being of its subjects: 'people can feel wronged without being harmed by research: they may feel they have been treated as objects of measurement without respect for their individual values and sense of privacy' (SRA, 2003: 25). Harm is therefore defined both by reference to potential physical or psychological destabilization, discomfort or stress that research might inflict upon human subjects and as action which might put at risk 'a subject's personal social standing, privacy, personal values and beliefs, their links to family and the wider community, and their position within occupational settings' and where the researcher must also consider 'the adverse effects of revealing information that relates to illegal, sexual or deviant behaviour' (ESRC, 2009: 21).

While privacy is not explicitly defined within the Data Protection Act 1998, its meaning is linked to what is described as personal and sensitive personal data. Personal data is defined as data that relates to a living individual who could be identified from the data, or from the data and other information which might be in the possession of, or is likely to come into the possession of, the data controller. Sensitive personal data on the other hand is defined as data which might incriminate a participant or third party, such as an individual's ethnic origin, political opinion, religious beliefs, trade union membership, physical or mental health, sexual orientation and criminal proceedings or convictions.

In making the personal or privacy data visible as sensitive data, the device of research ethics creates and signals the existence of (potentially extractable) data as deeply entangled in networks of subjectivity, sociality and humanity; specifically, its movement or extraction from research subjects is defined in relation to restrictions of access to such substantial attachment. Informed consent thus can be thought of as a device that also enables what would otherwise be an illegitimate detachment and transfer of that which is considered personal (private) from a research or data subject to researcher or data controller. As in market exchange settings, research transactions are framed as consensual (the work of framing is what the device does), otherwise they are considered illegitimate, as theft or fraud, for example, acts in which property is dishonestly appropriated, without the freely given consent of one party, or where agents are either not given the necessary information or deceived regarding the type of transaction they are committing to. The difference, however, is that while in market transactions the parties involved are recognized as already holding property rights over what is being exchanged, research or data subjects do not, strictly speaking, hold property rights over their personal data,[5] although they are constituted as subjects possessing legal and moral rights to exclude others from accessing and processing what is considered private. In this respect, informed consent acts as a 'surrogate property contract' (Waldby and Mitchell, 2006), enabling what would otherwise be the illegitimate detachment and transfer of privacy into value regimes from which it is protected (Appadurai, 1988). This surrogate property contract is enacted, however, without compromising privacy's status as a secluded sphere, a sphere where the market encounters its limits (Karpik, 2010). Informed consent as a device therefore reconciles the epistemic and economic potentiality of privacy through its circulation and detachment in the form of data, at the same time as it preserves the ontological significance of privacy and its perpetuation as an economically valueless sphere if encountered in its raw or 'natural' form.

## Anonymization: disentangling personal traits and the suppression of the author function

One of the ways in which a division between persons and things is established within Euro-American societies is by means of the assertion of property rights (between persons and with respect to things) 'as the paradigmatic exemplification of ownership – so that when one talks of property ownership one implies that rights are being exercised over [in relation to] some "thing" or the other' (Strathern, 2004: 111). Indeed, Strathern further argues that the more entities approximate to things, then the more legitimate ownership appears. Within the following section I argue that anonymization can be understood as erasing previous attachments and facilitating new appropriations and reconfigurations of vital emissions, aiding in the process of making vital emissions more thing-like, and thus more amenable to ownership. This involves an exploration of how anonymization aids in the production of databases (and their ability to be copyrighted): specifically, in being anonymized vital emissions can effectively change from being singular and incommensurable, unique and identifiably human, to being data which can be rendered comparable, and may be measured, stored, transmitted and traded.

Confidentiality and anonymity have been deployed in both social and bio-medical research as two foundational principles in making research ethical, where anonymity is primarily understood as the vehicle by which confidentiality is operationalized. All the examples of research ethics frameworks discussed here[6] and the Data Protection Act stipulate that personal data acquired during the process of research should not be disclosed, unless a research or data subject has given specific consent for this possibility. So in order to enable disclosure and circulation, anonymization is typically deployed in order to remove links that could be used to identify research subjects. This is described as the protection of subjects' privacy. Two main types of anonymization procedures are deployed: reversible anonymization entails working over data extracted so it does not contain any identifying keys, although researchers retain information that can be used to link back the data to the research subject. Alternatively, data can be de-linked irreversibly, so that the research subject remains unidentifiable not only by other agents but also by the researcher and indefinitely in time.

Ethics frameworks stipulate that the confidentiality of information supplied by research subjects and their anonymity should be respected (ESRC, 2009; BSA, 2002; SRA, 2003), although it is proposed that in some cases it might become necessary to decide whether it is actually appropriate at all to record and fix certain kinds of sensitive information as data (BSA, 2002). A number of measures are put forward to ensure the link between data and identifiable individuals is broken. In relation to quantitative datasets, for example, it is recommended that they be anonymized by removing direct identifiers, such as for example name or address, by aggregating or revising the precision of a variable, for example by replacing date of birth by age groups, or in the case of geo-referenced data, by replacing point coordinates by larger, non-disclosing geographical areas which typify the geographical position. Anonymizing qualitative datasets containing transcriptions or textual data is mainly achieved by using pseudonyms or replacing identifying characteristics in those data fragments that are considered to reveal personal traits, and by identifying those replacements in a meaningful way, usually in the form of typographical brackets. Finally, voice alteration and image blurring can also make audio and image data anonymous (UKDA, 2009). However, as the Social Research Association guidelines also note, it is not only particular and individual identifiers which need to be removed, but researchers also need to look at those particular configurations and associations of attributes that can, 'like a fingerprint, frequently identify its owner beyond doubt' (SRA, 2003: 30). In those cases where it is a particular configuration of attributes that might enable identification, researchers might need to regroup data in such a way so as to disguise identities, or to employ a variety of available measures to impede the detection of identities without inflicting serious damage on the aggregate dataset (SRA, 2003: 30).

Anonymization, however, becomes irrelevant if the actual or potential identification of research participants is made acceptable via informed consent: 'researchers cannot . . . be held responsible for any subject that freely chooses to reveal their participation in a study' (SRA, 2003: 30). Anonymization therefore becomes unnecessary if informed consent is given to the disclosure of personal and private traits. This is seen as especially desirable in those circumstances in which research participants possess a combination of attributes that make them readily and easily identifiable and where it is difficult to disguise their identity without introducing an unacceptably large measure of distortion into the data (BSA, 2002: 5).

Anonymization on the other hand renders the applicability of the Data Protection Act principles irrelevant, as the latter is only enforceable and applicable to data which makes explicit reference to living individuals: in this case if data is anonymized it is no longer considered personal. It should be noted though that true and genuine anonymization of data extracted from human agents is difficult to achieve in practice. Weak forms of anonymization tend not to satisfy the requirements of the Act, whereas stronger forms usually do not satisfy the requirements of social research which often requires not fully eliminating traces of the person from the aggregate sets. Anonymization techniques thus operate the border of this economy of data: too little anonymization and vital emissions cannot be converted into data as they are still entangled in the research subject's activities; on the contrary, if anonymization is too effective, then data is stripped of value.

The disentanglement of vital emissions thus requires not only the mediation of informed consent but also the detachment of certain elements, attributes or signs, considered to denote personhood. Only if the products of human living processes can be disconnected from subjects can they become data, and start to be stabilized as thing-like. Like body parts and tissues, personal data, if understood as an extension of the self, needs to take a separate existence from that of the original person to which it is linked (Waldby and Mitchell, 2006), a separateness that is enabled by anonymization. Furthermore, as well as making vital emissions more thing-like, anonymization can also be thought of as a technique that suppresses the author function (Foucault, 1970; Lury, 2005), a function concerned with sustaining conceptions of the individual in terms of self-possession and subjectivity. It was through 'the author-function that cultural value became a thing, a product and a possession caught in a circuit of property values' (Lury, 1993: 23). However, within the economy of social data, it is not in the association, but instead in the suppression of signs which indexically stand as a trace of a certain person's existence, such as a name, that produces a similar effect. That is, such suppression enables the detachment and circulation of vital emissions in regimes where they can be rendered appropriable.

What effectively enables the conversion of that which once was inalienable into a thing and therefore potentially the object of property claims is not the name but its deletion. In this movement, value is redefined 'not in terms of the relations of personhood but in relations external to the person' (Adkins, 2005: 119), that is, vital emissions become valuable not because they were emitted by a creative and unique self or, rather, an author, but because they are *potentially* detachable, malleable and convertible into a thing – data, a thing that needs to be (re)animated in order to acquire a value that is not 'personal' although it is 'alive' or 'vital'.

Anonymization here performs another important function for the emerging economy of data: it enables the transformation of vital emissions, located in the private domain and qualified as singular (as possessing unique properties) and incommensurable (as not equivalent to any other) to data which in fact can be aggregated, compared and rendered commensurable with other data units, albeit paradoxically and originally produced by differently unique research subjects. It renders possible the manipulation of vital emissions, their reordering, classification and grouping under databases, protected under copyright law. And it is interesting to note here that 'single' facts do not have copyright protection, but that collections of facts may enjoy copyright protection as literary works, databases and compilations which, by virtue of the selection or arrangement of the contents, are considered to be the data controller's own intellectual creation, excluding then the individual as a recognized source of value.[7]

Anonymization thus aids in the emergence of the database, in the construction of 'categories or classes of equivalence through which individuals pass from their singularity to a generality' (Ruppert, 2009: 7). As Ruppert notes, generalizing the individual into the population partly involves 'classifying and identifying her difference and resemblance to numerous categories (male, female, married, single, etc.)' (2009: 7). However, the passage from singularity to generalization also entails and requires the omission of certain categories, such as personal name, which might make traceable the original individual components. That is, categories which render too individual the elements constituted in the aggregate need to be omitted as they might problematize the generalization of the individual into the aggregate as such.

The argument being made here, then, is that data is not granted value by the sole fact of having been detached. If data remains detached but inert, that is, if it is preserved as a singular data unit, intellectual property rights cannot generally be awarded, either to the data subject or the data controller. In the creation of value, the act of processing data becomes key, as it is in the practices of 'animating' the data extracted that potential economic value resides. So, for example, the Data Protection Act makes clear that processing in relation to information or data not only means obtaining, recording or holding data but also carrying out an operation or set of operations on the data. These include the organization, adaptation or alteration of the data; retrieval, consultation or use of the data; disclosure of the information or data by transmission, dissemination or otherwise making available; and alignment, combination, blocking, erasure or destruction of the information or data (DPA, 1998).

The passage from individual to aggregate enabled by anonymization thus creates value by provoking not only a disentanglement of vital emissions, but also by invoking a conceptual transformation of vital emissions, a transformation necessary for the production of the aggregate. The de-personification of vital emissions renders them comparable and commensurate to each other; in such processes, they are made aggregable and therefore valuable. Singular, non-aggregated vital emissions are economically valueless; they are, rather, produced as an abundant resource, highly reproducible and easily replicable. The requisite for vital emissions to become economically valuable under research and data extraction and processing settings is, paradoxically, that they need to be encountered and qualified as singular in their mode of production and then lose (some of) their human qualities in the process of becoming visible as value.

## Conclusion

This article has focused on exploring the capabilities of the ethical techniques of informed consent and anonymization in the articulation of a particular kind of data economy. It began by showing how informed consent enacts a transaction between data subject and data controller in terms of legitimacy and enabled that transaction to become the basis of a surrogate property contract (Waldby and Mitchell, 2006). It went on to describe how anonymization facilitates the conversion of vital emissions into data by suppressing the author function, enabling the rendering of singular data into units commensurable to one another, able to be aggregated in the form of databases, a procedure that also supports a specific set of intellectual property rights. To conclude, I would like to point in two directions. On one hand I want to suggest that the fragmentation of data and the intensification and extensification of what is extractable as data from human agents, in line with what might be called the molecularization of vitality (Rose, 2006), should entail a rethinking of ethics as a device that creates 'the human' as it is disaggregated and distributed within new datascapes. On the other hand, I also suggest that the principle of *traceability* (Latour, 2010) might usefully be developed in ways that have the potential to alter how value is produced within data economies by redefining the devices that sustain value production.

The economy of digital data traces has been lately portrayed as a fertile empirical terrain over which sociology should claim some jurisdiction (Savage and Burrows, 2007; Latour, 2010). For Savage and Burrows, for example, digital data presents both a challenge and an opportunity for a discipline that is looking at redefining itself through a concern with research methods, 'not as particular techniques but as themselves an intrinsic feature of contemporary capitalist organization' (2007: 890). Latour's concern, by contrast, is with the forms of traceability that digital data offers to the researcher. He aims to develop techniques of traceability that debunk the aggregate, the law or the structure as a totality, and to explore the possibilities for social research of technical developments that enable always provisional visualizations of the 'whole', 'which can be modified and reversed at will, by moving back to the individual components, and then looking back at other tools to regroup the same elements into alternative assemblages' (Latour, 2010: 116). In short, Latour argues that what sociologists have tended to do is to observe and identify the individual and the aggregate as two separate and incompatible entities, where the more focused one would be on aggregates, the less individual variations one could trace. New datascapes, he suggests, allow for a redefinition of the relationship between the 'ingredient and the structure' in which the aggregate loses 'the privilege it maintained for one century' (2010: 14). This new 'technical' phenomenon enables the development of principles of traceability, that is, enabling individual components to be followed in such a way as to produce highly unstable aggregates, which may be continually dis- and re-aggregated enabling the researcher to map multiple trajectories in relation to a variety of assemblages.

In both cases, it is proposed that the new reality of digital data traces expands that which can be made measurable for sciences whose object of study are the relations between individuals and aggregates. For Latour, thanks to new technical developments, the principle of traceability is already being put in motion for 'opinions, rumors, political disputes, individual acts of buying and bidding, social affiliations, movements in space, telephone calls, and so on' (Latour, 2010: 116) while Savage sees the potential for 'descriptive assemblage' to be 'dramatically enhanced by the infrastructure of information technology and more particularly the digitalization of social relations' (Savage, 2009: 155). This expansion of what is measurable in social scientific and commercial research produces, on the one hand, a reorganization of the elements and boundaries of what are to be considered sociological units of analysis; and on the other, due to the scale and diversity of increased traceability, a redefinition of how the trajectory from the individual to aggregate can and should be understood (Latour, 2010). Both changes, I suggest, should be thought of in parallel with a discussion of how current and future ethics might articulate what appears as an original and novel way of qualifying data (Callon and Muniesa, 2003).

One can start by thinking of units of analysis, that is, the entities taken as objects of study, as being redefined, in line with biomedical practices and the molecularization of vitality, as new technical advancements facilitate an unprecedented and rather uncomplicated multiplication of vital emissions. This expansion and intensification of what it is possible to extract from human agency and the relationships that can now be established between different data points destabilizes both the individual and the aggregate as the paradigmatic, but discrete, units of analysis of social investigation, as it becomes possible instead to trace the constitution and trajectories of 'monads'. By this term is meant an entity that is 'a representation, a reflection, or an interiorisation of a whole set of other elements borrowed from the world around it' (Latour, 2010: 10). In his reading of Tarde, Latour rejects traditional sociological understandings of the 'individual' as whole, composite sites of social investigation, and instead proposes taking as units of analysis monads in their relationality. As Latour says, 'If there is nothing especially structural in the "whole" it is because of a vast crowd of elements already present in every single entity' (Latour, 2010: 10): new datascapes make visible such relationality, and constitute such relations as sources of value.

However, what I want to suggest is that if such new data reality produces a redefinition of what could be considered sociological units of analysis (or what the object of sociological enquiry should be) it should present a challenge not only to traditional methodologies and analytical frameworks (Savage and Burrows, 2007; Law and Urry, 2004) but also to the current governing ethics frameworks, either professional or legal, which regulate and enact the practice of the sociological (and more broadly social scientific) empirical enterprise. The emergence of such new units of analysis destabilize fundamental ontological considerations which are naturalized in most ethics regulations: is data 'personal' when actions, utterances, traits or bodily descriptions are not physically joined or found in or through the individual? Is the individual the site or source of data when he or she is multiplied in a conglomerate of extraneous self-duplications? Is the individual or the society to be found in the action, the purchase, the gesture, the location, the time frame, the opinion, the conversation, the discourse?

While current regulations may be ethically relevant in relation to a conception of the human as an individual whole that is indivisible, singular and private, it is debatable whether they are still relevant in a context where the distinction between the public and the private is being blurred and where the signs that denote personhood are changing. In this context – that of what Marilyn Strathern (1988) describes as the *dividual*, ethics understood as the 'application of moral principles to concrete social facts' (Fraser, 2008: 14) appears to be emptying out, its function becoming solely economic. It becomes important then to rethink ethics for a sociology of the dividual or post-human, for research subjects which are the action, the purchase, the gesture, the location, the time frame; to rethink ethics for data who/which are no longer envisaged or enacted as static, but mobile, constituted in traces, fragments potentially valuable in their futurity, transformed and rearticulated in the processes of dis- and re-aggregation. Following Fraser, this is to propose rethinking the ethics of the virtual, that is ethics not solely for 'entities that are physically or conceptually present somewhere (just not here), but to virtual multiplicities or singularities that have no corporeal presence at all' (2008: 19).

At the same time, if ethics principles can indeed be thought of as economic devices as the article suggests, it also becomes necessary to rethink their capabilities in a context where there is a more generalized mode of value production emerging within social and commercial data research. If the aggregate or structure is 'what is imagined to fill the gaps when there is a deficit of information as to the ways any entity inherits from its predecessors and successors' (Latour, 2010: 11), traceability enables the focus to be put on circulation, making the tracing of the *trajectory* from the individual, to the aggregate and back. What might create value here are not any of the provisional steps, that is, the individual or the aggregate taken separately and independently from each other, as informed consent and anonymization principles currently contribute to produce, but the trajectories that constitute the individuals and aggregates as processes and not as things. In this sense, if traceability, as Latour suggests (2010), should become a new terrain for the jurisdiction of sociology, the discipline needs to consider whether current ethics devices are appropriate for the creation of new forms of (economic) value. It needs to ask whether the creation and design of the range of devices which intervene in the production of data economies and the type of value forms they enact are too crucial to be overlooked. This article has proposed that the coming crisis of empirical sociology (Savage and Burrows, 2007) is also a crisis over data ownership and the devices which facilitate and secure specific forms of value. If this is indeed the case, the jurisdiction that sociology should aim to secure in relation to new datascapes should not only be concerned with reflecting on the 'politics of method' (Savage and Burrows, 2007; Law and Urry, 2004) but also with the political economy of data and the devices which serve to articulate its particular forms of property and value.

## Acknowledgements

I would like to thank Lisa Adkins, Lucia Ariza, Celia Lury and anonymous reviewers for many insightful comments on earlier versions of the article.

## Notes

1 It is worth noting, however, that incommensurability, as a measure which excludes comparisons, is not necessarily incompatible with market practices. On the contrary, as Karpik (2010) notes, incommensurability is an important asset in what he characterizes as an economy of singularities, that is, markets dominated by goods and services which are 'multidimensional, uncertain and incommensurable' (2010: 10). In not accepting the idea of a discontinuity between culture and the market, Karpik argues that under certain conditions incommensurability and commensurability are indeed mutually convertible *within* the market; he says: 'the oscillation between a relatively common stable reality and the multiplicity of the constructions associated with individual and collective points of view is constitutive of markets of singularities. It authorizes equivalence without calling incommensurability into doubt' (2010: 10). He further argues that incommensurabilities cannot furnish the bases of a general theory whose requirement is to make singular products equivalent entities, that is, 'to require to give up precisely that which makes them desirable' (2010: 31), but that emphasis should be put precisely on analysing the mechanisms by which incommensurability becomes a quality of singular products that are exchanged within the confines of market settings.

## The economy of social data: exploring research ethics as device

2 Both informed consent and anonymization principles have been part of the regulation of scientific research practice since the establishment of the Nuremberg Code in 1948 when ten standards were set up for investigators undertaking research with human subjects. Based on these Nuremberg Code principles, The World Medical Association Declaration of Helsinki released in 1964 a universally applicable set of rules aimed at regulating medical practice in both clinical and non-clinical settings. These two landmark documents have subsequently been unfolded and expanded into multiple international, national and local ethics codes. In the UK, for example, they were drawn on in the establishment of (medical) Local Research Ethics Committees in 1968, while the social sciences made use of the principles established in biomedical ethics (Beauchamp and Childress, 2001). Research with human subjects has thus been organized around a number of self-regulatory standards, which are often adopted by researchers as part of professional codes of conduct. Both informed consent and anonymization principles have also been incorporated into the Data Protection Act which was adopted in the United Kingdom in 1998 as part of the European Union Data Protection Directive, an initiative mainly aimed at promoting personal data privacy rights and harmonizing the data protection laws of its member states. So while research ethics frameworks limited their scope to the governance and regulation, in principle, of scientific research practice, the Data Protection Act became a legally enforceable regulation for any 'data controller', that is, either persons or institutions that potentially determine the purposes and the manner in which what is defined as personal data is processed. This Act therefore extended the applicability of informed consent and anonymization procedures to commercial data activities.

3 Other DPA principles include: (2) Personal data shall be obtained only for one or more specified and lawful purposes; (3) Personal data shall be adequate, relevant and not excessive for the purpose of processing; (4) Personal data shall be accurate and up to date; (5) Personal data shall not be kept for longer than necessary; (6) Personal data shall be processed in accordance with the rights of the data subject; (7) Personal data shall be kept secure; (8) Personal data shall not be transferred to countries without adequate protection.

4 Research ethics are not here considered as textual or discursive representations or renditions of the institutions they were created by, but instead as devices which enact particular versions of what research subjects are and can do and also importantly, on how data is ultimately constituted and qualified. Understanding research ethics as a device entails looking at the workings of specific assemblages where 'it is very often the discrete, visible or invisible arrangements that work to influence the action' (Karpik, 2010: 44). Callon *et al.* (2007) have argued for an understanding of devices as *agencements* where persons or things emerge as such as part of the encountered and contingent compound which assigns specific properties to each other, as opposed to encountering themselves already and in an *a priori* 'agenced' state. A device therefore emphasizes the distribution of agency between persons and things, it brings materiality to the front by assigning objects with agency, and devices 'articulate actions, they act or make others act' (2007: 2) and they also position subjects as not external to the devices but as enacted in and through them, so that, for example, subjectivity emerges in encounters with multiple device assemblages. In this sense, I understand research ethics frameworks and their operationalization in research practice as documents which do things, which articulate and make certain actions possible, which facilitate and shape in particular ways the 'making of data social' (Michael, 2004), that is, as Callon (1998) outlines in relation to economics and the economy, I propose taking research ethics not as moral principles in themselves which regulate an already existing state of affairs, but instead as instruments which contribute to the construction of data as an economically valuable and viable product.

5 It is indeterminate whether research subjects can establish property rights over their own privacy, unless, under current conditions, their emissions happen to meet the requirements stipulated in the Copyright, Designs and Patents Act 1988; that is, first, as long as privacy can be legible in material embodiments and supports or subside outside research subjects; secondly, as long as private acts can be considered authored solely by the research subject; thirdly, as long as privacy can be considered original; and finally, as long as privacy can be considered work. If all conditions are met, then copyright gives human agents 'exclusive legal control over certain acts in

relation to their work – not acts of use as such, but only certain acts of replication and repetition' (Barron, 2008: 3), that is, copyright assigns a non-exclusive form of property geared towards the potential circulation and multiplication of vital emissions, but not the right to their physical possession and as such, as in this sense they are still not strictly own-able.

6 The Economic and Social Research Council third principle requires that 'researchers take steps to ensure that research data and its sources remain confidential unless participants have consented to their disclosure, and in this latter case ensure that plans have been made for their storage and access to them' (ESRC, 2009: 25). The British Sociological Association code states: 'sociologists should be careful, on the one hand, not to give unrealistic guarantees of confidentiality and, on the other, not to permit communication of research films or records to audiences other than those to which the research participants have agreed' (BSA, 2002: 3). The Social Research Association outlines: 'data should not routinely be released to clients (even responsible public authorities) in any form that could identify respondents, unless explicit consent was given by the respondents and guarantees of anonymity and/or confidentiality had not been made' (SRA, 2003: 38).

7 JISC/TLTP Copyright Guidelines state that 'under UK law, each item added to a database may be protected under copyright as a work in its own right. Thus, items of which the author died more than 70 years ago are free from copyright, but all recent non-factual items are in copyright. Single facts, including bibliographic citations and URLs do not have copyright protection, but collections of facts enjoy copyright as literary works, databases or compilations. This means that even if a large number of individual items in a database are non-copyright, one cannot necessarily copy a significant number of them without infringing either the literary copyright, database right or compilation copyright afforded to the collection as a whole' (1998: 20).

# References

Adkins, L., (2005), 'The new economy property and personhood', *Theory Culture and Society*, 22(1): 111–129.
Appadurai, A., (1988), *The Social Life of Things: Commodities in Cultural Perspective*, Cambridge: Cambridge University Press.
Barron, A., (2008), *Copyright Infringement, 'Free Riding' and the Lifeworld*, LSE Law, Society and Economy Working Papers, No. 17.
Beauchamp, T. and Childress, J., (2001), *Principles of Biomedical Ethics*, Oxford: Oxford University Press.
Boltanski, L. and Thevenot, L., (1991), *On Justification: Economies of Worth*, Princeton, NJ: Princeton University Press.
British Sociological Association, (2002), *Statement of Ethical Practice*, available at: www.britsoc.co.uk
Caliskan, K. and Callon, M., (2009), 'Economization. Part 1: Shifting attention from the economy towards processes of economization', *Economy and Society*, 38(3): 369–398.
Callon, M., (1998), *The Laws of the Market*, Oxford: Blackwell.
Callon, M., (2007), 'What does it mean to say that economics is performative?' in D. MacKenzie, F. Muniesa and L. Siu (eds), *Do Economists Make Markets? On The Performativity of Economics*, Princeton, NJ: Princeton University Press.
Callon, M., Millo, Y. and Muniesa, F. (eds), (2007), *Market Devices*, Oxford: Blackwell.
Callon, M. and Muniesa, F., (2003), 'Les marchés économiques comme dispositifs collectifs de calcul', *Réseaux*, 21(122): 189–233.
Callon, M. and Rabeharisoa, V., (2004), 'Gino's lesson on humanity: genetics, mutual entanglements and the sociologist role', *Economy and Society*, 33(1): 1–27.
Cochoy, F., (2007), 'A sociology of market things: on tending the garden of choices in mass retailing', in M. Callon, Y. Millo and F. Muniesa (eds), *Market Devices*, Oxford: Blackwell.
Dickenson, D., (2007), *Property in the Body: Feminist Perspectives*, Cambridge: Cambridge University Press.

Economic and Social Research Council, (2009), *Framework for Research Ethics*, available at: www.esrc.ac.uk
Foucault, M., (1970), 'What is an author?' in A. Davidson (ed.), *The Government of Self and Others (Michel Foucault: Lectures at the Collège de France)*, New York: Palgrave MacMillan.
Foucault, M., (1978), 'The confession of the flesh', in C. Gordon (ed.), *Power/Knowledge: Selected Interviews and Other Writings*, New York: Palgrave MacMillan.
Fourcade, M., (2009), 'The political valuation of life', *Regulation and Governance*, 3: 291–297.
Fraser, M., (2008), 'Facts, ethics and events', in C. Bruun Jensen and K. Rödje (eds), *Deleuzian Intersections in Science, Technology and Anthropology*, New York and Oxford: Berghahn Books.
Helmreich, S., (2008), 'Species of biocapital', *Science as Culture*, 17(4): 463–478.
JISC/TLTP (Joint Information Systems Committee and Teaching and Learning Technology Programme), (1998), *Copyright Guidelines*, Portsmouth: CPC Lithographic Printers.
Karpik, L., (2010), *Valuing the Unique: The Economics of Singularities*, Princeton, NJ: Princeton University Press.
Latour, B., (2010), 'Tarde's idea of quantification', in C. Mattei (ed.), *The Social after Gabriel Tarde*, London: Routledge.
Law, J. and Urry, J., (2004), 'Enacting the Social', *Economy and Society*, 33(3): 390–410.
Lezaun, J., (2007), 'A market of opinions: the political epistemology of focus groups', in M. Callon, Y. Millo and F. Muniesa (eds), *Market Devices*, Oxford: Blackwell.
Lury, C., (1993), *Cultural Rights: Technology, Legality and Personality*, London: Routledge.
Lury, C., (2005), 'Contemplating a self-portrait as a pharmacist: a trade mark style of doing art and science', *Theory, Culture and Society*, 22(1): 93–110.
Manson, N. and O'Neill, O., (2007), *Rethinking Informed Consent in Bioethics*, Cambridge: Cambridge University Press.
Michael, M., (2004), 'On making data social: heterogeneity in sociological practice', *Qualitative Research*, 4(1): 5–23.
Rose, N., (2006), *The Politics of Life Itself: Biomedicine, Power and Subjectivity in the Twenty First Century*, Princeton, NJ: Princeton University Press.
Ruppert, E., (2009), 'Number regimes: from censuses to metrics', CRESC Working Paper Series No. 68, Milton Keynes: Open University.
Savage, M., (2009), 'Contemporary sociology and the challenge of descriptive assemblage', *European Journal of Social Theory*, 12(1): 155–173.
Savage, M. and Burrows, R., (2007), 'The coming crisis of empirical sociology', *Sociology*, 41(5): 885–899.
Scheper-Hughes, N., (2001), 'Bodies for sale – whole or in parts', *Body and Society*, 7(2–3): 1–8.
Social Research Association, (2003), *Ethical Guidelines*, available at: www.the-sra.org.uk/documents/pdfs/ethics03.pdf
Strathern, M., (1988), *The Gender of the Gift*, Berkeley, CA: University of California Press.
Strathern, M., (2004), 'Losing (out on) intellectual resources', in A. Pottage and M. Mundy (eds), *Law, Anthropology and the Constitution of the Social: Making Persons and Things*, Cambridge: Cambridge University Press.
Tober, D.M., (2001), 'Semen as gift, semen as goods: reproductive workers and the market in altruism', *Body and Society*, 7(2–3): 137–160.
UK Data Archive, (2009), *Managing and Sharing Data: A Best Practice Guide for Researchers*, Colchester: University of Essex.
Waldby, C., (2000), *The Visible Human Project: Informatic Bodies and Posthuman Medicine*, London: Routledge.
Waldby, C., (2002), 'Stem cells, tissue cultures and the production of value', *Health*, 6: 305–323.
Waldby, C. and Mitchell, R., (2006), *Tissue Economies: Blood, Organs and Cell Lines in Late Capitalism*, Durham, NC: Duke University Press.
Zelizer, V.A., (1978), 'Human values and the market: the case of life insurance and death in 19th century America', *American Journal of Sociology*, 84 (3): 591–610.
Zelizer, V.A., (1985), *Pricing the Priceless Child*, Princeton, NJ: Princeton University Press.

# Measuring the value of sociology? Some notes on performative metricization in the contemporary academy

## Aidan Kelly and Roger Burrows

**Abstract:** The performative co-construction of academic life through myriad metrics is now a global phenomenon as indicated by the plethora of university research or journal ranking systems and the publication of 'league' tables based on them. If these metrics are seen as actively constituting the social world, can an analysis of this 'naturally occurring' data reveal how these new technologies of value and measure are recursively defining the practices and subjects of university life? In the UK higher education sector, the otherwise mundane realities of academic life have come to be recursively lived through a succession of research assessment exercises (RAEs). Lived through not only in the RAEs themselves, but also through the managed incremental changes to the academic and organizational practices linked to the institutional imaginings of planning for, and anticipating the consequences of, the actual exercises. In the 'planning for' mode an increasing proportion of formerly sociology submissions have shifted into 'social policy'. This is one instance of how institutional 'gameplaying' in relation to the RAE enacts the social in quite fundamental ways. Planning an RAE 2008 submission in Sociology required anticipation of how a panel of 16 peers would evaluate 39 institutions by weighted, relative worth of: aggregated data from 1,267 individuals who, between them cited a total of 3,729 'outputs'; the detailed narrative and statistical data on the research environment; and a narrative account of academic 'esteem'. This data provided such institutional variables as postgraduate student numbers, sources of student funding, and research income from various sources. To evaluate the 'quality' of outputs various measures of the 'impact' and/or 'influence' of journals, as developed from the Thomson-Reuters Journal Citation Reports, was linked to the data. An exploratory modelling exercise using these variables to predict RAE 2008 revealed that despite what we might like to think about the subtle nuances involved in peer review judgements, it turns out that a fairly astonishing 83 per cent of the variance in outcomes can be predicted by some fairly simple 'shadow metrics': quality of journals in the submission, research income per capita and scale of research activity. We conclude that measuring the value of sociology involves multiple mutual constructions of reality within which ever more nuanced data assemblages are increasingly implicated and that analysis of this data can make explicit some of the parameters of enactment within which we operate in the contemporary academy.

**Key words:** statistical co-construction, metrics, research assessment exercise (RAE), sociology, performativity, enactment, UK

## Introduction

Academic life, like so many other spheres of what we used to think of as the 'public sector', has become increasingly metricized (Hammer, 2011). The various technologies of the audit culture have reached ever deeper into the everyday fabric of university life (Strathern, 2000). In the UK, for example, the life-world of the university is increasingly enacted through complex data assemblages drawing upon all manner of emissions emanating from routine academic practices such as recruiting students, teaching, marking, giving feedback, applying for research funding, publishing and citing the work of others (De Angelis and Harvie, 2009). Some of these emissions are digital by-products of routine transactions (such as journal citations), others have to be collected by means of surveys or other formal data collection techniques (such as the National Student Survey[1] (NSS)) and others still require the formation of a whole expensive bureaucratic edifice designed to assess the quality of administrative, teaching and research work (such as – the focus of this paper – research assessment exercises). The performative mutual or co-construction (Saetnan *et al.*, 2011) of academic life through myriad metrics – such as the NSS, the Transparent Approach to Costing (TRAC)[2] data, data on average UCAS entry tariffs,[3] PhD completion rates, research income per capita, individual and group h-indices (Woeginger, 2008), journal impact factors, Quality Assurance Agency (QAA) subject and institutional reviews and so on – is ubiquitous. Increasingly, of course, such data is also being formally aggregated into any number of commercially driven ranking and 'league' table systems, such as those developed by various national newspapers and, now, at a global level, by Times Higher Education (THE).[4] Adopting a view of such data assemblages as not simply imprints or products of the social world, but as actively constituting that world, leads us to focus on the work that new technologies of value and measure do in constituting the university and recursively defining its practices and subjects. This, of course, is not just of analytic interest; as the post-Browne[5] reforms of British higher education begin to take hold, these various metrics will become instantiated in the 'prices' we are able to charge for our courses.

Our focus in this paper is on what has hitherto been one of the most important metrics –the various attempts that have been made to measure the value of the research that academics undertake in the UK in order to inform state funding allocation decisions.[6] The paper begins by briefly reviewing the various iterations of measuring the 'quality' of research that has been tried over the last few decades. It then takes a detailed descriptive case study of the manner in which our own discipline – sociology – has been evaluated, with a particular focus on the most recent exercise, the results of which were reported in 2008. This may appear to be a rather dull – if worthy – exercise, likely to be of little interest to an international readership and/or colleagues with a primary interest in more conceptual debates about measure and value in contemporary sociological analysis. We hope to demonstrate otherwise for three reasons – although readers unfamiliar with and/or intolerant of quantitative styles of work may need to bear with us a little.

First, the institutional arrangements we are about to describe for making judgements about the quality of research are fast becoming internationalized, and many colleagues outside of the UK are already subject to or are about to become subject to very similar regimes of research assessment. Similar schemes have been operationalized in Australia,[7] Hong Kong and New Zealand, for example. But, as already noted, even in those countries where state-sponsored measurement of research quality is not yet being used to determine the allocation of resources – such as the USA – the ongoing metrification of research performance to determine the supposed global standing of particular institutions and subjects within them by commercial providers of data, means that there is no escape from this particular manifestation of the relationship between measure and value (Hicks, 2009).

Second, the theoretical and methodological anxieties which currently permeate the social sciences – and perhaps sociology in particular (Savage and Burrows, 2007) – are thoroughly enmeshed with the processes we describe. The enactment of value and relative worth in academic work by formal processes of academic judgement, measurement and algorithmic resource allocation has become fundamental to survival. Both authors are old enough to remember a time when the quality of what one wrote was still a matter of the inherent characteristics of the piece rather than largely a function of where it was published, who funded it and how many times it was cited. As we shall show below, although we sometimes comfort ourselves that such inherent (almost aesthetic) judgements of the value of our work ('outputs') made by our 'peers' still provides the basis for our position in the academic 'league table', in actuality these judgements almost perfectly mirror a set of quite basic underlying statistical drivers of 'quality'. As we all quietly make decisions about what to write about, how to write it, where to send it for publication and the rest – sometimes as directed by our institutions, but more often than not under our own volition – many of us profoundly intuit that the metrics we are orientating towards are producing disciplinary knowledge that could, and perhaps should, be other than that which we end up with.[8]

Third, much of what we are about to describe – and, indeed, some of the methods we employ to do it – impinge more directly than one might initially suspect on many of the broader debates with which this monograph is concerned. We are perhaps a little more circumspect than are some of the other contributors here to the idea that conventional hegemonic methods of social research are dysfunctional 'for grasping the complex and generative character of reality' (Adkins, 2009a: 234). As we hope to demonstrate later on in this paper, even if one accepts as a domain assumption of sociological practice that statistical metrics and social and organizational processes are mutually constitutive (Law, 2004; Saetnan *et al.*, 2011), some quite simple statistical analyses of administrative and transactional data still have something to offer as a descriptive device, even when the object of our inquiry is something as supposedly complex, unstable, elusive, vague and multiple as the quality of sociological research in the UK.

## A brief history of the assessment of research quality

University research in the UK has long been subject to something called a 'dual support system' made up of two parts: block grants provided by the government in order to provide a general underpinning for research capacity; and, second, funds for specific research grants, made available by competition, administered by the research councils (for the social sciences this was mainly the Social Science Research Council (SSRC) until 1983 when (due to largely political motivations) it was transmogrified into the Economic and Social Research Council (ESRC)). These two sources of funding for research thus relied on very different administrative processes. Although it was clear on what basis specific research grants were awarded – peer-review and competition – the allocation of block grants was an altogether different matter. Up until the mid-1980s it would be fair to say that their allocation was, at best, opaque. At the time the University Grants Committee (UGC) was responsible for the allocation of block grants and it, along with many other public sector bodies, was encouraged by the Thatcher regime to begin to take measures of performance seriously in the allocation of funds between institutions (Johnes *et al.*, 1993). So, with the publication of *A Strategy for Higher Education into the 1990s* (UGC, 1984) began the long process of the development of ever more refined, precise and supposedly transparent mechanisms for measuring the quality of research in order to inform funding allocation decisions.

A first, at best half-hearted, attempt was made in 1985–86 to make some sort of judgements about the relative quality of university-based research. The criteria by which the quality of research was judged in this first Research Selectivity Exercise (RSE), as it came to be known, was hardly more transparent than had been the allocation of block grants. Each subject area within participating institutions was asked to produce a brief 'research profile', of no more than three sides of A4 paper, within which, it was suggested, might be information on: indices of any financial support for research; staff and research student numbers; any measures of research performance deemed significant; a statement of current and likely future research priorities; and the titles of no more than five books or articles produced since 1980 considered to be typical of the best research produced (Bence and Oppenheim, 2005). On 27 May 1986 the 'results' of this first RSE were published to some consternation within the academy. Each subject within each university had been judged as either 'outstanding', 'better than average', 'about average', or 'below average'. However, as Smith (1986: 247) noted at the time: 'No evidence or argument was provided in support of the ratings, and there was no statement of method or formula adopted'.

A more robust second attempt was made by, what by then had become, the University Funding Council (UFC) in 1989. This second RSE was taken far more seriously as it was becoming increasingly apparent that the results would significantly impact upon funding allocations. The 1989 RSE was based on 'informed peer review' from 70 advisory groups and panels, containing 300 individuals, and was estimated to have cost about one per cent of the total university research budget of around £500 million in 1989–90 (Johnes et al., 1993: 273). This time the panels were provided with far more structured data on research performance including: the number of publications (books, chapters in books, papers in journals and other identifiable outputs) in relation to the number of full-time academic staff; bibliographical details of up to two publications for each full-time member of academic staff; the number and value of research grants and research contracts; and the number of research studentships.

This information was used by each advisory group in order to rate each unit of assessment on a five-point scale using the rhetoric of 'national level' and 'international level' excellence. So, for example: the lowest rating was a '1' meaning that there existed national levels of excellence in none, or virtually none, of the sub-areas of activity; the mid-point was '3' meaning national levels of excellence in the majority of the sub-areas of activity; and the top-rating, '5', was defined as international levels of excellence in some sub-areas of activity and national level in virtually all others.

By the time of the third exercise in 1992 the university sector had been expanded to include the ex-polytechnics. Each institution was now invited to select 'research active' staff in post on 30 June 1992 for assessment. Each assessment was divided into 72 academic units of assessment (UoAs). The data collected became more extensive; in addition to each academic nominating two publications, quantitative information on all publications was also required. Each submission was then ranked on a five-point scale very similar to the one used in 1996. The allocation of resource by the UFC was then based upon not only a 'quality' measure using this scale, but also the 'volume' measure based upon the number of 'research active' staff submitted (Bence and Oppenheim, 2005: 145–146).

The fourth exercise in 1996 relied less upon quantitative measures of research output and more on the quality of publications. 'Research active' staff in 69 different UoAs had to provide details of up to four publications published during the period covered by the assessment and this was supplemented with details of 'indications of peer esteem' in the form of editorships of prestigious journal, papers given at key conferences and so on (Bence and Oppenheim, 2005). The rating scale was further finessed (to become, essentially, a seven-point scale) with the introduction of a new 'top' 5* rating and the former band 3 being subdivided into 3a and 3b. The 'measurement' of 'quality' was undertaken by peer review panels. Again resources were distributed based on the quality grade multiplied by the volume of research active staff.

Further recalibrations in the process were undertaken for the fifth exercise in 2001 in order to make it more transparent (Bence and Oppenheim, 2005: 147–151). However, the essence of the assessment remained intact even though the descriptions attached to the points on the rating scales were reworded somewhat. UoAs awarded a 5* in 2001 who had also received such a rating in 1996 were later awarded a new 6* rating to produce a new eight-point scale.

Throughout this period not only did the information gathering involved in the various exercises become ever more detailed and prescribed, there was also clearly an aspiration to shift the level of measurement used to assess the quality of research from an ever more differentiated ordinal scale towards one closer to a cardinal level of measure (which was almost completely realized in the 2008 exercise, about which more below). The combination of an ever more refined quality rating being traded off against a volume measure decided at an institutional level led, inevitably, to ever more 'game-playing' by universities. Anyone who has worked within the UK higher education sector during this period will attest to how much academic and organizational practices have been incrementally recalibrated in relation to the RAE. Increasingly many of the mundane realities of academic life have been recursively lived through not only the exercises themselves, but institutional imaginings of what such future exercises might bring. Indeed, orientating towards the RAE and scenario planning for possible outcomes has become central to the more routine discourse of futurism (Adkins, 2009b) that has come to permeate university life.

For the sixth and most recent exercise, the results of which were published in 2008, the process of research quality assessment was altered quite fundamentally in order to produce a rating system that could better approximate to an interval level of measurement. Rather than each submission being awarded an overall rating, each was given a 'quality profile'. This quality profile was constructed from three sub-profiles relating to 'outputs', 'research environment' and 'esteem'. The weightings attached to each of these sub-profiles varied between UoAs. In the case of sociology 'outputs' were weighted at 75 per cent, 'environment' at 20 per cent and 'esteem' at 5 per cent. A panel of 16 peers[9] examined – in the case of sociology – 39 detailed submissions containing information on: four publications for each member of staff submitted; a detailed narrative and statistical data on the research environment; and a narrative on various esteem measures. Each output was evaluated as follows[10]: 4* Quality that is world-leading in terms of originality, significance and rigour; 3* Quality that is internationally excellent in terms of originality, significance and rigour but which nonetheless falls short of the highest standards of excellence; 2* Quality that is recognized internationally in terms of originality, significance and rigour; 1* Quality that is recognized nationally in terms of originality, significance and rigour; and 'Unclassified Quality' that falls below the standard of nationally recognized work, or work which does not meet the published definition of research for the purposes of the assessment.

The same descriptions were then also applied to the information provided on the research environment and esteem in each submission (although exactly

**Table 1:** *Sub-profiles for sociology at Goldsmiths and York*

| Sub-profiles | Outputs | | | | | Environment | | | | Esteem | | | | Final profile | | | |
|---|---|---|---|---|---|---|---|---|---|---|---|---|---|---|---|---|---|
| UoAs | 4* | 3* | 2* | 1* | U/C | 4* | 3* | 2* | 1* | 4* | 3* | 2* | 1* | 4* | 3* | 2* | 1* |
| Goldsmiths | 20.6 | 26.2 | 40.5 | 11.1 | 1.6 | 80 | 20 | 0 | 0 | 80 | 20 | 0 | 0 | 35 | 25 | 30 | 10 |
| York | 18.3 | 32.4 | 30.3 | 8.5 | 0.0 | 70 | 30 | 0 | 0 | 70 | 10 | 20 | 0 | 30 | 30 | 35 | 5 |

how an ordinal scale was applied to the measurement of the quality of the narratives remains unclear). If we take our own two institutions (at the time of writing, Burrows subsequently moved to Goldsmiths) – Goldsmiths and York[11] – by way of example we can see how the overall quality profiles were derived (Table 1).

At Goldsmiths 20.6 per cent of published outputs were graded at 4*, whilst at York the figure was 18.3 per cent. At Goldsmiths 80 per cent of both the research environment and esteem were graded at 4* quality whilst at York the comparable figures were both 70 per cent. Once the weightings were applied to the three sub-profiles the overall research quality profiles is revealed as 35 : 25 : 30 : 10 for Goldsmiths and 30 : 30 : 35 : 5 for York. A summary measure of these profiles in the form of a grade point average (GPA) gives both institutions a similar score of 2.85. This GPA was widely used to construct the various 'league tables' that have inevitably followed each RAE.[12]

These research quality profiles, weighted by the number of staff submitted within each submission, were used to inform the allocation of over £12 million of funding to sociology per annum (known in the argot of the RAE as 'QR'). Initially this allocation was based on 2* being weighted at 1, 3* at 3 and 4* at 7. This resulted in highly disparate allocations of resource: Manchester, for example, gaining £23,776 per capita; Goldsmiths and Essex both £22,799 per capita; and York £21,822. Further down the rankings, however, allocations were substantially less; Liverpool gained just £9,445 per capita; Teesside £8,794 per capita; and Huddersfield just £6,514.[13] Subsequently these allocations were even more steeply ramped to favour 'excellence' in research to become 1 : 3 : 9, thus concentrating funding even further towards those UoAs with the highest proportion of 4* work.

Table 2 shows the consolidated results for the RAEs in 1992, 1996, 2001 and 2008 for the sociology UoA. It is a complex table that requires some deciphering. The first column shows the alphabetically ordered (current) names of all of the institutions who have ever submitted to the sociology UoA in any of the four RAEs (in England, Northern Ireland, Scotland and then in Wales). The results are shown for each of the assessments along with the number of 'research active' full-time equivalent (FTE) staff submitted. When sociologists were submitted under the auspices of the social policy UoA instead of sociology UoA, this is indicated. When no submission was made this is indicated by 'ns'. This means that either sociologists (if any) at the institution were not submitted to

**Table 2:** *The results of the RAEs in 1992, 1996, 2001 and 2008 for the sociology UoA*

|  | 1992 | | 1996 | | 2001 | | 2008 | |
|---|---|---|---|---|---|---|---|---|
| Institution | Grade | FTEs | Grade | FTEs | Grade | FTEs | Grade | FTEs |
| Anglia | 3 | 1.0 | 2 | 9.5 | Social Policy | | Social Policy | |
| Bath Spa | 1 | 5.0 | 2 | 3.0 | ns | ns | ns | ns |
| Bath | 3 | 14.5 | 3a | 13.1 | Social Policy | | Social Policy | |
| Birkbeck | ns | ns | ns | ns | 3a | 1.0 | 2.10 | 24.55 |
| Birmingham | 3 | 6.0 | ns | ns | ns | ns | 1.95 | 18.0 |
| Bradford | 2 | 13.0 | 3a | 12.3 | Social Policy | | Social Policy | |
| Bristol | 2 | 8.0 | 3a | 10.5 | 5 | 13.0 | 2.40 | 17.93 |
| Brunel | 3 | 10.4 | 4 | 10.7 | 5 | 16.5 | 2.45 | 11.0 |
| Bucks | 1 | 2.0 | ns | ns | ns | ns | ns | ns |
| Cambridge | 5 | 23.8 | 4 | 30.8 | 5 | 21.8 | 2.65 | 21.0 |
| Guildhall | 1 | 4.0 | 2 | 5.0 | 3a | 6.0 | Social Policy | |
| City University | 4 | 13.0 | 4 | 21.6 | 4 | 11.7 | 2.30 | 27.2 |
| Coventry | ns | ns | 1 | 2.0 | ns | ns | ns | ns |
| Crew and Alsager | 1 | 6.0 | ns | ns | ns | ns | ns | ns |
| Derby | 1 | 12.1 | 3b | 8.2 | 2 | 14.2 | ns | ns |
| Durham | 3 | 23.0 | 3a | 21.7 | 4 | 13.0 | Social Policy | |
| East Anglia | 3 | 4.9 | ns | ns | ns | ns | ns | ns |
| East London | 3 | 9.6 | 3a | 26.3 | 4 | 38.9 | 2.20 | 31.9 |
| Essex | 5 | 26.6 | 5* | 32.7 | 5*/6* | 41.1 | 2.85 | 43.7 |
| Exeter | 2 | 10.5 | 3a | 8.2 | 5 | 10.0 | 2.70 | 18.72 |
| Goldsmiths | 3 | 15.0 | 5 | 15.5 | 5* | 24.0 | 2.85 | 32.6 |
| Greenwich | 2 | 12.0 | 3a | 13.5 | 3a | 16.0 | ns | ns |
| Huddersfield | ns | ns | ns | ns | 2 | 5.0 | 1.70 | 9.0 |
| Hull | 3 | 9.0 | Social Policy | | Social Policy | | Social Policy | |
| Keele | 3 | 13.5 | 3b | 14.0 | Social Policy | | Social Policy | |
| Kent | 4 | 12.5 | 3a | 10.5 | Social Policy | | Social Policy | |
| Central Lancashire | 1 | 6.0 | 2 | 4.0 | 3b | 18.5 | Social Policy | |
| Lancaster | 5 | 23.5 | 5* | 28.5 | 5*/6* | 28.3 | 2.80 | 29.8 |
| Leeds | 4 | 12.0 | 4 | 21.6 | Social Policy | | Social Policy | |
| Leicester | 3 | 17.0 | 4 | 19.0 | 4 | 22.3 | 2.10 | 12.5 |
| Liverpool | 2 | 14.0 | 3b | 9.3 | Social Policy | | 1.95 | 21.0 |
| Liverpool Hope | ns | ns | 2 | 4.0 | 2 | 6.6 | ns | ns |
| Liverpool John Moores | 1 | 37.0 | ns | ns | ns | ns | ns | ns |
| LSE | 4 | 16.4 | 4 | 27.2 | 5 | 38.8 | 2.40 | 37.75 |
| Loughborough | 5 | 26.8 | 5 | 33.0 | 5* | 37.0 | 2.40 | 47.22 |
| Manchester | 4 | 17.0 | 5 | 33.2 | 5* | 39.3 | 2.85 | 49.2 |
| Manchester Metropolitan | 2 | 7.0 | 3b | 13.0 | 3a | 18.0 | 2.15 | 22.5 |
| Middlesex | 3 | 12.0 | Social Policy | | Social Policy | | Social Policy | |
| Newcastle upon Tyne | Social Policy | | Social Policy | | Social Policy | | 2.50 | 21.6 |
| Northampton | ns | ns | ns | ns | 3b | 10.4 | ns | ns |

Table 2: *Continued*

| Institution | 1992 Grade | 1992 FTEs | 1996 Grade | 1996 FTEs | 2001 Grade | 2001 FTEs | 2008 Grade | 2008 FTEs |
|---|---|---|---|---|---|---|---|---|
| North London | ns | ns | 4 | 2.5 | 3b | 4.5 | Social Policy | |
| Northumbria | 2 | 11.0 | 2 | 11.0 | Social Policy | | Social Policy | |
| Nottingham | Social Policy | | 3b | 24.8 | Social Policy | | 2.40 | 8.3 |
| Nottingham Trent | 2 | 8.5 | 3b | 7.0 | Social Policy | | Social Policy | |
| Open University | 4 | 11.5 | 4 | 14.0 | 4 | 14.0 | 2.60 | 42.3 |
| Oxford | 4 | 22.9 | 5 | 7.0 | 5 | 13.0 | 2.65 | 18.75 |
| Oxford Brookes | 2 | 3.5 | 3b | 6.0 | 4 | 10.5 | ns | ns |
| Plymouth | 3 | 14.0 | 3a | 25.4 | 4 | 13.2 | 2.15 | 23.0 |
| Portsmouth | 2 | 9.0 | 3a/3b | 10.0 | 3a | 27.5 | ns | ns |
| Reading | 2 | 11.0 | 3b | 9.0 | 3a | 12.8 | ns | ns |
| Roehampton | 2 | 14.7 | 3b | 22.0 | 3a | 12.0 | 2.05 | 16.25 |
| Royal Holloway | 3 | 8.0 | 3a | 9.0 | Social Policy | | Social Policy | |
| St Mary's College | ns | ns | 2 | 3.0 | ns | ns | ns | ns |
| Salford | 4 | 10.0 | 4 | 17.0 | 4 | 19.6 | Social Policy | |
| Southampton Institute | 1 | 5.0 | ns | ns | ns | ns | ns | ns |
| Southampton | 3 | 13.6 | 4 | 17.0 | Social Policy | | Social Policy | |
| Staffordshire | 2 | 16.0 | 3b | 16.4 | 3a | 7.2 | ns | ns |
| Surrey | 4 | 14.9 | 5 | 15.8 | 5* | 23.4 | 2.75 | 21.4 |
| Sussex | 4 | 10.0 | 4 | 25.3 | 4 | 22.6 | 2.55 | 14.0 |
| Teesside | 3 | 9.0 | 3a | 9.0 | 3a | 23.0 | 1.95 | 10.0 |
| Trinity and All Saints College | 1 | 4.0 | 1 | 2.0 | ns | ns | ns | ns |
| Warwick | 5 | 29.5 | 5 | 31.5 | 5 | 27.8 | 2.70 | 37.8 |
| UWE, Bristol | 2 | 7.0 | 3b | 22.0 | 3a | 15.7 | 1.65 | 12.0 |
| Worcester College of HE | 1 | 1.0 | 2 | 3.0 | 2 | 6.6 | ns | ns |
| York | 3 | 11.5 | 4 | 10.0 | 5 | 14.0 | 2.85 | 21.2 |
| Queens, Belfast | 4 | 12.0 | 4 | 14.0 | 5 | 22.8 | 2.60 | 23.0 |
| Ulster | 3 | 10.0 | 3b | 9.0 | 3b | 9.0 | Social Policy | |
| Aberdeen | 2 | 7.9 | 3a | 9.7 | 5 | 14.9 | 2.60 | 14.0 |
| Edinburgh | 5 | 26.5 | 5 | 23.4 | 5 | 22.9 | 2.75 | 46.3 |
| Glasgow Caledonian | 2 | 10.0 | ns | ns | 3a | 10.5 | 1.50 | 11.2 |
| Glasgow | 4 | 17.0 | 4 | 18.0 | 4 | 20.0 | 2.25 | 27.5 |
| Napier | ns | ns | ns | ns | ns | ns | 1.55 | 6.8 |
| Paisley | 1 | 13.0 | ns | ns | ns | ns | ns | ns |
| Robert Gordon | ns | ns | ns | ns | ns | ns | 1.40 | 6.0 |
| Strathclyde | 2 | 4.3 | 3a | 7.0 | 3a | 7.0 | 1.95 | 9.0 |
| Cardiff | 3 | 15.8 | 4 | 30.1 | 5 | 33.0 | 2.70 | 61.4 |
| Glamorgan | 1 | 6.0 | Social Policy | | Social Policy | | Social Policy | |
| Swansea | 3 | 14.4 | Social Policy | | Social Policy | | Social Policy | |
| **Totals** | **67** | **826.6** | **59** | **892.8** | **48** | **858.9** | **39** | **927.37** |

a particular RAE or they were submitted under the auspices of a different UoA (other than social policy).

So, to take a couple of illustrative examples, 12 sociologists were submitted by Leeds in 1992 and were graded '4'. In 1996, 21.6 were submitted and they obtained the same grade. However, in subsequent exercises Leeds did not submit under the auspices of the sociology UoA, choosing instead to submit to the social policy UoA. Lancaster, on the other hand, submitted to the sociology UoA on all four occasions: 23.5 staff were submitted in 1992 and were graded '5'; in 1996, 28.5 were submitted and were again awarded the top grade (now a 5*); in 2001 the 28.3 staff submitted again gained a 5*, subsequently raised to a 6* (having obtained a 5* on two occasions); and in 2008, 29.8 staff were submitted gaining a GPA of 2.80 (ranking them fifth out of 39 on this measure).[14]

The table reveals a secular decline in the number of submissions made to the sociology UoA, from 67 in 1992 to just 39 in 2008. Related to this, it also shows how, over time, an increasing proportion of submissions have shifted into social policy. Here is a prime example of how institutional 'game-playing' in relation to the RAE enacts the social in quite fundamental ways. Colleagues who otherwise self-identify as sociologists are now constituted as social policy analysts. However, despite this, it also reveals an increase in the number of research active staff submitted to the sociology UoA, from a total of 826.6 in 1992 to 927.37 in 2008. It also shows, and as Savage (2011) has recently observed, that sociology has fared relatively well in research intensive institutions but less so in those more orientated towards teaching. In 2008 the four top-rated departments had all displayed remarkable growth compared to 1992: Essex had grown by 64 per cent; York by 84 per cent; Goldsmiths by 117 per cent; and Manchester by 189 per cent. It is clear that the results of the RAE – as a fundamental element of the broader performative data assemblage within which UK higher education is now so enmeshed – has been integral to the restructuring of our discipline.

In a sense what follows is an attempt on our part to explore the performative character of the social processes that resulted in the 39 submissions being ordered and ranked in the manner in which they were. The 'raw' material for the exercise – the grants, the students supervised, the books, chapters and articles published, the activities that supposedly accrue 'esteem' (editing journals, giving a conference plenary, getting prizes and so on), the 'strategic hires', the new investment in research infrastructures and so on, are all (more or less) elegantly inscribed in (bespoke) software. Then data is collected, numbers are crunched, 'outputs' selected, narratives constructed, excuses made (illnesses, the birth of children, inexperience and other life-events), panels are selected, reading is completed, 'scorecards' are filled, trains, hotels and meals are booked, debates and disagreements ensue – and at the end of the process a set of 39 quality profiles are revealed to public scrutiny

Once released, the data takes on a reified form and also develops an autonomous 'public life'. It is not only used to inform funding allocation decisions. It is inserted in other secondary algorithms used to determine the eligibility to apply for certain types of research and postgraduate funding. It is used as a rhetorical device by institutions in their prospectuses, on their websites and in their funding bids. It feeds into myriad aggregate league tables manipulable via web 2.0 applications by students, industry, colleagues, government, the media and so on. Some of us celebrate the outcomes; others are forced to rethink their strategies; others still are closed down. But, in the end, we are all implicated and some come to realize that this is a performative 'game' from which it is almost impossible to escape. Hammer (2011: 79), for example, points to the brilliant HBO TV series *The Wire* (see Penfold-Mounce *et al.*, 2011, for a broader introduction to the sociological relevance of the show) to elaborate on this general point. Many of the episodes deal with issues of value and measure, and 'the strategies and problematizations that can be related to governing by numbers', in particular. Most of Series 3, for example, is concerned with the role of metrics and performance measures in neo-liberal governmentality, especially the co-constructive processes of institutional life. But it is perhaps the sagely pronouncements of one of the best-loved characters in the show, the gay stick-up artist Omar Little, that best encapsulates the dilemma we are trying to register here: 'the game's out there, and it's play or get played'. The scaling up of the RAE means that universities *must* act strategically in order to gain more QR and this, in turn, creates a new type of competition that is far more than just a battle over reputational capital; it becomes more and more about the 'bottom line'. Indeed, the constitutive power of this data increasingly functions via myriad processes of 'financialization'.

## The 'shadow metrics' of the 2008 RAE

We now want to move to more concrete analysis and focus on the results of the most recent RAE for sociology using the full submission data released in May 2009. We should begin by noting some major limitations with the data which means that coverage of *all* sociological research in the UK is partial. The National Student Survey (NSS)[15] suggests that in the year the RAE data was gathered sociology was taught in 89 higher education institutions in the UK (with 67 institutions offering single honours degrees through UCAS) whilst social policy was offered in only 33. However, as we have seen, only 39 RAE submissions were made to the sociology UoA, whilst 67 were made to the social policy UoA. Clearly institutions are involved in complex 'game playing' with many choosing to submit what is clearly mainstream sociological research to the social policy panel because their organizational arrangements make this a sensible thing to do in terms of the viability of the narratives they are able to construct about their research environments. At both of our own institutions – Goldsmiths and York – the existing departmental structures meant that separate submissions to both the Sociology *and* the Social Work and Social Policy and Administration panels was a viable option. However, in many institutions the departmental/school co-location of sociologists with social policy analysts and others meant that a submission to the social policy panel was a more tempting prospect (although, of course, RAE-related considerations often play a central role in institutional restructuring strategies in the first place). The consequence of this is that many sociologists working in some of the historically most important institutions for the subject (Savage, 2010) – Durham, Keele, Kent, Leeds, Nottingham,[16] Salford, Sheffield and Southampton amongst them – are excluded from the analysis which follows.

Although the data is 'partial', what we want to try and do is to see how easy it is to mimic the judgements made by peers on the panel, by trying to construct statistical models able to predict the GPAs of each submission. We recognize, of course, the playful irony in our attempt to do this in a paper about the metricization of academic life-worlds. Our point in so doing, however, is that despite what we might like to think about the subtle nuances involved in peer review judgements, it turns out that even they are explicable in terms of some fairly simple 'shadow metrics'. These shadow metrics could, of course, be thought of as simply those variables best able to statistically model the judgements of the panel. But if we take the 'performative turn' in social science research at all seriously (Law, 2004) we must recognize that there is more to it than that. It is almost certainly the case that these judgements are already shaped by the 'public life of data' – such as the increasingly well publicized impact factors of journals – and/or perhaps these very metrics are themselves simply the outcome of prior academic reputation (people read journals with a good historical reputation so they are the ones that get the citations and thus the high impact factors). Be this as it may, what we want to do here is to decipher the underlying statistical patterns that structure the data. What inferences about shadow metrics can we squeeze out of our 39 cases? What we want to model is the distribution of the overall quality profiles. A summary of this data is given in Table 3.

On average about 16 per cent of sociological research was graded as 4* – but with some submissions achieving as much as 40 per cent in this category. Over 2 per cent of research submitted was unclassified. The minimum GPA was 1.4

**Table 3:** *Summary of quality profiles for sociology submissions in the RAE 2008 (%)*

| Quality rating | N | Minimum | Maximum | Mean | Standard Deviation |
|---|---|---|---|---|---|
| 4* | 39 | 0.0 | 40.0 | 15.8 | 11.8 |
| 3* | 39 | 5.0 | 40.0 | 26.8 | 7.7 |
| 2* | 39 | 25.0 | 55.0 | 34.6 | 6.2 |
| 1* | 39 | 5.0 | 45.0 | 20.4 | 11.5 |
| Unclassified | 39 | 0.0 | 15.0 | 2.4 | 3.4 |
| GPA score | 39 | 1.4 | 2.85 | 2.33 | 0.4 |
| 9 : 3 : 1 Funding GPA | 39 | 0.7 | 4.45 | 2.6 | 1.1 |

and the maximum was 2.85 with a mean of 2.33. It turns out that the GPA weighted by the 9 : 3 : 1 weights for the initial round of funding allocations is the version of the variable that is the most susceptible to statistical modelling.[17] This runs from a minimum of 0.7 (Robert Gordon) to a maximum of 4.45 (Manchester) with a mean of 2.6 and a standard deviation of 1.1. It is variation in this weighted version of the GPA that we attempt to model.

The most powerful single predictor of how well a submission did in the RAE 2008 was how well it did in the RAE 2001. If one considers the 33 cases submitted to both assessments the degree of continuity is quite stark. Indeed, in statistical terms, variation in the results obtained in 2001 'explain' 76 per cent of the variation in 2008. However, even if we put past performance to one side we can still construct models that are highly predictive of variation in the weighted GPAs by using data contained within each of the submissions and linking this data to other publically available sources.

The 39 submissions contained information on 1,267[18] individuals who, between them produced a total of 3,729 'outputs'. For reasons that we will explain below, where these outputs were articles published in journals included in the Thomson-Reuters Social Science Citation Index (SSCI) we attached various measures of the 'impact' and/or 'influence' of the journal. We then aggregated the total number of outputs in the various formats and these measures of 'journal quality' (where available) to the institutional level. We then added additional institutional variables to the dataset derived from the submissions such as postgraduate student numbers, sources of student funding, research income from the various sources, and so on.

Given the small number of cases we have available relative to the number of possible predictor variables some method of summarizing multiple indicators was desirable. The method used was, first, to consider a range of indicators within each of a number of different categories of potential interest – *volume, research income, journal quality* and other factors[19] – and to decide which the most suitable single variable was to represent the range of possibilities. Once these variables had been selected we then entered them into an OLS regression model using forward selection stepwise procedures. Use of forward rather than backward selection avoids the problems of multicollinearity when regressing indicators of the same measure against a criterion variable. The results of this exercise is to produce either the single most important predictor of the GPA score or a weighted additive index of those indicators that have an impact on the GPA score.

*Size of submission*

We might consider that, *a priori*, the size of a submission would be positively associated with the GPA. Scale, of course, is in part a function of previous research performance, but it could also be important since leading figures in the field might be more likely to be attracted to larger UoAs that have practices and infrastructure supportive of high quality research activity. We examined a range of variables that would measure variations in the scale of the submission. The single variable that gave us most purchase for accounting for variation in the weighted GPA in this area was the $log_e$ of the total number of outputs submitted.[20]

## Research income

Variations in both total research income and research income per capita were highly correlated with variations in the weighted GPA. The mean level of research income per capita over the period covered by the assessment was £124,600; the minimum was £8,000 and the maximum £394,000. However, a better measure than this was the $log_e$ of research income per capita derived from the UK research councils. On average 43.1 per cent of research income came from this source (with a minimum of zero and a maximum of 91.6 per cent): mean research council income was £55,200; the minimum was zero and the maximum £309,000. Variation in research council income per capita over the period of the assessment explained some 46 per cent of the variation in weighted GPA.

## A citation-based metric?

We next considered how best we might incorporate some form of citations-based metrics into the analysis, especially given all of the recent controversy concerning their potential role in any future research quality assessments.[21] Although what follows is inevitably crude, following through the logic of what is possible has the advantage that, as a potentially incendiary analytic by-product, we are able to produce a journal ranking scheme for the discipline of sociology in the UK based upon the judgements made in the RAE 2008.

Of the 3,729 outputs submitted: 2,366 (63.4 per cent) were journal articles; 619 (16.6 per cent) were authored or co-authored books; 526 (14.1 per cent) were chapters in edited books; 96 (2.6 per cent) were edited books; with the other 122 (3.2 per cent) items were a mixture of Internet publications, research reports, conference contributions, digital or visual media, exhibitions or other forms of assessable output. Here we want to focus on the 2,366 journal articles. These articles were published in a total of 847 different journals (a huge range which speaks perhaps to the lack of a core to the discipline in the UK?). Of these 847 journals 309 (34 per cent) were included in the Thompson-Reuters Journal Citation Reports (JCR)®.[22] These claim to offer:

> a systematic, objective means to critically evaluate the world's leading journals, with quantifiable, statistical information based on citation data. By compiling articles' cited references, *JCR Web* helps to measure research influence and impact at the journal and category levels, and shows the relationship between citing and cited journals.[23]

For each journal output in the RAE 2008 with a JCR entry we attached a range of different citation-based measures of impact or influence.[24] An excellent discussion of the various metrics available can be found in Pringle (2008). Perhaps the best-known measure is the Journal *Impact Factor* (IF) which is a ratio of citations and recent citable items published.[25] Crudely, an IF of 1.0 means that, on average, an article published in the journal is currently cited once. An IF of 2.5 means that, on average, an article published is cited two and a half times. At the time of writing, the journal, to which this monograph is related, for example, currently has an IF of 1.019 which places it 40th out of the 98 sociology journals currently monitored within the JCR.

There are, however, at least another five different measures of journal impact or influence that can be constructed based upon citation practices: the 5-year mean impact; an Immediacy Index; the Cited Half Life; something called the JCR Eigenfactor; and a complex metric known as Article Influence Score (AIS). In our analysis we considered the utility of all six of these measures in accounting for variation in the weighted GPA for sociology. In the modelling it was the most complex of these metrics – the AIS – that was, and by some distance, the best predictor of RAE 2008 outcomes. So what is the AIS? It is based upon the Eigenfactor Score which, like the IF, is essentially a ratio of the number of citations to the total number of articles published, but it eliminates journal-level self-citations and weights each reference according to a stochastic measure of the amount of time researchers report reading the journal. Unlike the IF, the Eigenfactor is not scaled to journal size, so typically a larger journal (in terms of the number of articles published) will have a larger value than a smaller journal. A journal's AIS score is the journal's Eigenfactor Score divided by the fraction of articles published by the journal. It aims to measure the average influence of each article published by the journal for the first five years after publication. The mean AIS Score is 1.00; a score greater than 1.00 indicates that each article in the journal has an above-average influence; a score less than 1.00 indicates that each article in the journal has a below-average influence. That fraction is normalized so that the sum total of articles from all journals is 1.00. Within the discipline of sociology the journal with the highest AIS is the *American Sociological Review* (*ASR*) with a current AIS of 4.03. The *British Journal of Sociology* is the most highly ranked UK based sociology journal on this metric with an AIS of 1.33. On this metric the journal associated with this monograph ranks 38th globally with an AIS of 0.602. In general our analysis suggests that sociologists, in the UK at least – as evidenced by their submissions made to the 2008 RAE – publish in journals with less than average global influence when compared to non-sociology journals in the social sciences more generally (cf. Erikson, 2005; Payne, 2007).

In hindsight, it is perhaps not surprising that the AIS, although only an indirect measure of the quality of the research published in a journal, is a good predictor of the outcomes of RAE 2008. However, we also wished to confront one of the main problems of citation indices: their failure to recognize 'disciplinarity'. Academics publish to address audiences defined by discipline boundaries, and across these boundaries there are important variations in citation practices. A sociologist publishing in a medical journal would benefit from the higher rates of citation typical of that field of study; however, it might be thought that the article is of more limited value to the core concerns of sociology as a discipline. Global citation-based measures provide just one metric of journal quality. Clearly different disciplines within different national contexts will give different priorities to different journals. The *ASR* may be top of the pile in the JCR but within our own two institutions within the UK it is read only by the occasional 'socially minded' econometrician, whilst journals much further down the global rankings are much more highly valued – the *Sociological Review* included! So how can we best adjust the AIS to take account of such variation?

If we assume that the best papers, for example, those of paradigm-changing potential or otherwise addressing the core concerns of the discipline, are more likely to be published in the journals selected as 'suitable' by research active sociologists, then the authors of such papers are more likely to choose the 'core' sociology journals rather than those representing a more marginal area of the discipline. These arguments required us to weight the AIS by some measure of each journal's 'centrality' to the discipline. Our thinking is that, in one sense, data from the RAE 2008 gives us a clear indication of the journals most 'valued' by UK sociologists. This 'value' was measured by the number of times a journal was chosen for inclusion in the sociology submissions made for the 2008 RAE. When the AIS scores for each journal were weighted by the number of citations this did prove to be a far more effective predictor of RAE 2008 outcomes than the simple unweighted scores.

We experimented with various ways of operationalizing the centrality weighted AIS within our analysis. Given that our concern was to measure what might be thought of as the 'top' journals in the UK we ranked all of the journals in the submissions by their centrality weighted AIS scores, and then we calculated the proportion of each institution's journal articles that were in the highest quartile. Across the institutions, the average 'top quartile' proportion was 45 per cent of the articles submitted, the lowest proportion was just 18 per cent, and the highest was 64 per cent.[26] It was this final adjustment to the citation impact data that provided the most effective predictor of weighted GPA scores in RAE 2008. It was the percentage of journal articles included in a submission that were published in the 'top' quartile of journals (ranked by AIS adjusted for journal centrality in UK sociology) that proved to be the best citation based predictor of the outcomes of RAE 2008.

## Some implied journal rankings in UK sociology?

Although not central to what follows, readers may find the journal ranking that we used in the analysis of interest. However, perhaps we need to recognize that in producing this ranking we might concretize them and thus contribute to the very constitutive powers of the data that are the focus of the paper. With these 'dangers' in mind, Table 4 shows the 'top 20' journals based upon our measure of journal AIS weighted by centrality to the discipline in the UK.[27]

**Table 4:** *The 'top 20' journals in UK sociology*

| Journal title | Number of articles in submissions | Weighted AIS |
|---|---|---|
| 1 Sociology | 91 | 81.9 |
| 2 British Journal of Sociology | 58 | 70.8 |
| 3 Social Science and Medicine | 54 | 65.7 |
| 4 Sociological Review | 57 | 43.4 |
| 5 Sociology of Health and Illness | 40 | 39.9 |
| 6 American Journal of Sociology | 7 | 26.6 |
| 7 Journal of Ethnic and Racial Studies | 24 | 21.2 |
| 8 Social Studies of Science | 23 | 21.0 |
| 9 American Sociological Review | 5 | 19.5 |
| 10 Economy and Society | 18 | 17.7 |
| 11 Work, Employment and Society | 23 | 17.7 |
| 12 Environment and Planning A | 20 | 17.5 |
| 13 Theory, Culture and Society | 39 | 16.8 |
| 14 Child Development | 7 | 16.4 |
| 15 European Sociological Review | 24 | 16.4 |
| 16 British Journal of Criminology | 36 | 15.4 |
| 17 British Journal of Social Psychology | 13 | 13.9 |
| 18 Journal of the Royal Statistical Society Series A | 10 | 13.5 |
| 19 Journal of Social Policy | 18 | 11.5 |
| 20 Urban Studies | 13 | 9.6 |

This ranking throws up few surprises. The 'big 3' mainstream UK sociology journals – *Sociology*, the *British Journal of Sociology* and *Sociological Review* – feature highly, mainly due to the number of articles published in them submitted to the RAE. The strength and quality of UK work in medical sociology is also apparent with both *Social Science and Medicine* and *Sociology of Health and Illness* ranking highly (as a result of both a reasonably large number of submissions published in these journals combined with a relatively high – for sociology – AIS).

# The final model

Although we could have constructed a more complex model containing up to five different variables able to explain some 87 per cent of the variation in the weighted GPA scores a more parsimonious model containing just three variables does the job almost as well – explaining 83 per cent of the variation – but which is far more interpretable analytically (and remember we only have 39 cases from which to make any inferences about which 'shadow metrics' are implicitly operating here). The final model contains: *the $\log_e$ of the number of outputs*; *the per capita research income obtained from research councils*; and *the*

*Measuring the value of sociology?*

**Table 5:** *OLS model predicting (9 : 3 : 1) weighted GPA scores for sociology (RAE 2008)*

| Model explains 83% of the variance in the RAE 2008 weighted GPA | Beta coefficients | Sig. | Tolerance |
|---|---|---|---|
| Number of outputs ($\log_e$) in RAE submission | 0.53 | 0.00 | 0.72 |
| Research Council Research Income ($\log_e$) per Category A staff FTE | 0.37 | 0.00 | 0.68 |
| Percentage of articles in top quartile journals as defined by centrality-weighted AIS | 0.37 | 0.01 | 0.90 |

*percentage of articles published in the top quartile of the most influential journals in UK sociology.* This is shown in Table 5.

The biggest influence on the weighted GPA is the size of the submission (with a beta coefficient of 0.53); essentially, on average, the larger the scale of the submission the better the result obtained. The two other variables in the model – research income from UK research councils per capita, and the percentage of articles published in the top quartile of the highest quality journals – both have a similar impact on the weighted GPA (as indicated by beta coefficients of 0.37). So the model implies that use of these three 'shadow metrics' would have produced a very similar ranking of research quality to that actually produced by the more qualitative process of informed peer review actually undertaken.

How can we account for this 'agreement' between the long and complex qualitative deliberations of the peer review panel and predictions of a simple three-variable linear regression model? Are panels merely the means of reproducing established intellectual hierarchies dominated by traditional universities and conservative institutionalized judgements? Is peer-review 'high-trust' because it would always fail to propose radical shifts in funding? Certainly academics appear wedded to the notion that only the exhaustive, expensive qualitative processes of peer review are capable of delivering legitimate outcomes. Yet when we turn the 'naturally occurring' quantitative submission data (ignoring the narrative that sets the context for the data – known at the RA5) into a set of fairly simple measures, these allow us to explain a very high proportion of the variance in the GPA scores allocated. Here we have a series of decisions made by sociologists who inhabit an intellectual world generally dominated (in the UK at least) by subjectivism, anti-positivism and relativism that are themselves largely predicted by a set of quantitative indicators formed into a simple regression model embodying what some might view as an opposing ontology and epistemology. Or is another explanation possible? Could the outcomes of the RAE 2008 for sociology implied by our simple model be interpreted as little more than the product of the peer review of prior peer review? For example, both the awarding of ESRC grants and the acceptance of an article for publication in a 'good' journal both involve extensive processes of peer review. Is the model able to mimic the judgements of the panel as well as it does because the variables it uses are themselves originally derived from complex processes of qualitative peer review translated into quantitative metrics? Of course, we do not know the answer to these questions. But what we can surmise is that measuring the value of sociology (or rather, sociological research) – or any academic discipline for that matter – involves multiple mutual constructions of reality within which ever more nuanced data assemblages are increasingly implicated. What we hope we have shown here is that, on occasion, a playful and reflexive engagement with some of this data can still usefully make explicit some of the parameters of enactment within which we operate within the contemporary academy.

## Acknowledgements

Thanks are due to Dave Beer, Mike Savage and Paul Wakeling for comments on earlier drafts of this paper. Needless to say that none of them are responsible for what we have to say here.

## Notes

1 See http://www.thestudentsurvey.com/
2 See http://www.hefce.ac.uk/finance/fundinghe/trac/
3 See http://www.ucas.ac.uk/students/ucas_tariff/
4 See http://www.timeshighereducation.co.uk/world-university-rankings/
5 *The Independent Review of Higher Education Funding and Student Finance*, published on 12 October 2010, see http://hereview.independent.gov.uk/hereview/
6 Readers may find the recent thoughts of Nigel Thrift on these issues of interest. In a speech at a recent conference in Wellington, New Zealand (*Imagining Value, Running Hot 2010: Wonder and Widgets – Realising the Value of Research for NZ*, 1–3 November 2010, available at http://www.youtube.com/watch?v=S8KqDfapipI) he offers an analysis that tries to combine his role as Vice-Chancellor of a leading research intensive university with that of a social and cultural theorist.
7 The results of the first exercise in Australia – Excellence in Research for Australia (ERA) – were published as we were drafting this paper. Using a simple five-point scale each institutional outlet carrying out sociological research has been evaluated. Of the 34 outlets evaluated, only one – the University of Queensland – achieved the 'top' '5' ranking and only four achieved a '4'. The results can be found at http://www.arc.gov.au/era/outcomes_2010/FoR/SBE1608.
8 How could this be otherwise? We have been driven by organizational concerns about who and what is 'RAEable' (we will explain below what the RAE is for readers unfamiliar with the beast) for so long now that the fabric of the life-world of the academy is now largely woven using this particular pattern.
9 The details of panel membership can be found at http://www.rae.ac.uk/pubs/2007/03/.
10 Derived from http://www.rae.ac.uk/aboutus/quality.asp.
11 The original submissions for which are available at http://www.rae.ac.uk/submissions/submission.aspx?id=129&type=hei&subid=1354 and http://www.rae.ac.uk/submissions/submission.aspx?id=174&type=hei&subid=1024.

*Measuring the value of sociology?*

12 See the *Guardian* league tables for sociology at http://www.guardian.co.uk/education/table/2008/dec/18/rae-2008-sociology for example.
13 This data can be found at http://www.hefce.ac.uk/pubs/hefce/2009/09_08/.
14 See the *Guardian* league table rankings using this measure already referred to under note 12.
15 Available at http://unistats.direct.gov.uk/.
16 Nottingham is a complex case because it does appear in the dataset but, in fact, the majority of the sociologists working in the School of Sociology and Social Policy were submitted under the auspices of social policy. The Nottingham sociology submission is wholly made up of staff working in their Institute for Science and Society (ISS).
17 So, by way of illustration, using our two examples of Goldsmiths and York, the (9 : 3 : 1) weighted GPA for Goldsmiths is given by $(0.35 \times 9) + (0.25 \times 3) + (0.3 \times 1) = 4.2$ and for York is given by $(0.30 \times 9) + (0.30 \times 3) + (0.35 \times 1) = 3.95$.
18 This figure differs from the total of 927.37 FTEs shown in Table 2 because it is based on a simple count (eg a 0.5 FTE counts as 1 here) of all people submitted even if they were not eligible to be included in the volume measure (eg 'Category C' staff).
19 We also examined data in relation to *postgraduate students* and *types of submitted outputs*. The proportion of postgraduate students funded by the UK research councils correlates positively and the proportion funded by the institution itself correlates negatively with the weighted GPA. However, neither correlation is particularly strong and other variables have much greater explanatory strength so we do not consider this factor any further here. Variations in the types of output submitted do not seem to have much influence on the weighted GPA, other than if a large proportion of outputs are 'other forms of output' – that is, not a journal article, authored book, edited book or chapter in a book. Although having a high proportion of journal articles does not in itself correlate highly with the GPA, as we will see below, the proportion of such articles published in 'good quality' journals' does have a significant impact on the weighted GPA.
20 It was a better measure than the number of staff submitted. In most cases four outputs per member of staff submitted was expected. However, for 'early-career' researchers a minimum of one or two outputs was acceptable. For staff working less than full time a reduced number of outputs was also acceptable. A reduced number of outputs was also acceptable if a staff member had special circumstances such as periods of maternity leave or periods of illness during the assessment period. So this means that there is not a perfect correlation between the numbers of FTEs submitted for assessment and the number of outputs.
21 See, for example, the June 2009 HEFCE Report on the matter http://www.hefce.ac.uk/pubs/rdreports/2009/rd13_09/.
22 Some 38 per cent of journal articles submitted were in journals in the JCR.
23 From http://thomsonreuters.com/products_services/science/science_products/a-z/journal_citation_reports (accessed on 23 July 2010).
24 Note that our analysis is based upon the impact or influence of the journal within which the article was published and *not upon* any measure of the impact or influence of the individual article itself.
25 As Pringle (2008: 87) explains 'It is calculated as follows: A = total cites in 2006. B = 2006 cites to articles published in 2004–5 (a subset of A). C = number of articles. . .published in 2004–5. D = B/C = 2006 impact factor'.
26 We also examined a measure based upon the proportion of all outputs submitted that were journal articles of this type, but it was not as powerful. As we have already noted, the overall proportion of outputs that were journal articles was 63.4 per cent. However, this figure varied between a minimum of 23.8 per cent and a maximum of 92.1 per cent. The measure we are using here is based upon the proportion of journal articles in each submission (which itself varies) that are published in the 'top' quartile of journals (based upon our ranking).
27 So, to take a couple of examples, the AIS for Sociology is just 0.9 whilst that for Behavioural and Brain Science (BBS) is 8.5. However *Sociology* articles appear 91 times whilst there is only one instance of an article from BBS. So we have weighted journals by how many times they appear in the RAE 2008 submission to get an estimate of their 'centrality' to the discipline in the UK.

# References

Adkins, L., (2009a), 'Feminism after measure', *Feminist Theory*, 10(3): 323–339.
Adkins, L., (2009b), 'Sociological futures: from clock time to event time', *Sociological Research Online*, 14(4), available at: http://www.socresonline.org.uk/14/4/8.html
Bence, V. and Oppenheim, C., (2005), 'The evolution of the UK's Research Assessment Exercise: publications, performance and perceptions', *Journal of Educational Administration and History*, 37(2): 137–155.
De Angelis, M. and Harvie, D., (2009), ' "Cognitive capitalism" and the rat-race: how capital measures immaterial labour in British universities', *Historical Materialism*, 17(3): 3–30.
Erikson, R., (2005), 'A view from Sweden', in A. Halsey and G. Runciman (eds), *British Sociology Seen from Without and Within*, Oxford: Oxford University Press.
Hammer, S., (2011), 'Governing by indicators and outcomes: a neoliberal governmentality?' in A. R. Saetnan, H. M. Lomell and S. Hammer (eds), *The Mutual Construction of Statistics and Society*, London: Routledge.
Hicks, D., (2009), 'Evolving regimes of multi-university research evaluation', *Higher Education*, 57: 393–404.
Johnes, J., Taylor, J. and Francis, B., (1993), 'The research performance of UK universities: a statistical analysis of the results of the 1989 Research Selectivity Exercise', *Journal of the Royal Statistical Society. Series A (Statistics in Society)*, 156(2): 271–286.
Law, J., (2004), *After Method: Mess in Social Science Research*, London: Routledge.
Payne, G., (2007), 'Social divisions, social mobilities and social research: methodological issues after 40 years', *Sociology*, 41(5): 901–915.
Penfold-Mounce, R., Beer, D. and Burrows, R., (2011), '*The Wire* as social science fiction', *Sociology*, 45(1): 152–167.
Pringle, J., (2008), 'Trends in the use of ISI citation databases for evaluation', *Learned Publishing*, 21(2): 85–91.
Saetnan, A., Lomell, H. and Hammer, S. (eds), (2011), *The Mutual Construction of Statistics and Society*, London: Routledge.
Savage, M., (2010), *Identities and Social Change in Britain since 1940: The Politics of Method*, Oxford: Oxford University Press.
Savage, M., (2011), 'Unpicking sociology's misfortunes', *British Journal of Sociology*, 61(4): 659–665.
Savage, M. and Burrows, R., (2007), 'The coming crisis of empirical sociology', *Sociology*, 41(5): 885–899.
Smith, D., (1986), 'UGC research ratings: pass or fail?' *Area*, 18(3): 247–250.
Strathern, M., (ed.), (2000), *Audit Cultures: Anthropological Studies in Accountability, Ethics and the Academy*, London: Routledge.
University Grants Committee, (1984), *A Strategy for Higher Education into the 1990s: The University Grants Committee's Advice*, London: HMSO.
Woeginger, G., (2008), 'An axiomatic characterization of the Hirsch-index', *Mathematical Social Sciences*, 56(2): 224–232.

# Measure, value and the current crises of sociology

*Nicholas Gane*

**Abstract:** This paper returns to C. Wright Mills' *The Sociological Imagination* to make an argument about the crisis of sociological method and theory today. Mills' famous text opens with a stinging critique of abstracted empiricism and grand theory on the grounds that they fetishize either methods or concepts. It is argued that Mills' critique can be applied to current sociological practices and thinking. The first part of this paper centres on questions of method, and reads between Mills' critique of abstracted empiricism and a recent debate over what Mike Savage and Roger Burrows call the 'coming crisis of empirical sociology'. In the light of this, it is argued that two crises currently haunt empirical sociology: a crisis of *imagination* and *measurement*. The second part of the paper then moves to the analysis of what Mills calls 'grand theory'. Here, two parallel crises are identified: a *generational* crisis within social theory that is tied in turn to what might be called a crisis of the *concept*. The conclusion of the paper returns to Mills in order to rethink his vision of the promise or *value* of sociology. It is argued that innovative conceptual work must lie at the heart of future sociological thinking if it is to move beyond the parallel traps of what Mills calls abstracted empiricism and grand theory.

**Keywords:** concepts, crisis, empiricism, measure, method, Mills, theory, value

## Introduction

It has been said many times before that sociology is in a state of crisis, and indeed it might be argued that sociology has been in crisis as a discipline since its formal inception at the turn of the 20th century. However, whereas previous 'crises' have tended to centre on the displacement of one theoretical trend by another, or the shift from one set of epistemological or methodological commitments to a new agenda or style of working, the current crisis of sociology appears to be something different, for today there appear to be no clear theoretical or methodological grounds or procedures upon or through which unity or, perhaps more importantly, a common sense of *value* can be restored to the discipline. The excitement and invention of theoretical sociology, for example, has, with a few notable exceptions, long disappeared, and quantitative and qualitative methodological work that was once unique to sociology is now performed equally well, if not better, outside the discipline or even the academy (see Savage and Burrows, 2007). Sociology seems to have lost its identity and to some extent lost its way. And if this is not worrying enough, the discipline is facing a range of new institutional pressures, particularly in the United Kingdom, where the future of state funding for the social sciences in general, and sociology in particular, is looking increasingly precarious. In the face of these developments, not to mention the unprecedented de-centring and specialization of the discipline, sociology genuinely seems to be in, or at least threatened by, a condition of crisis.

The present paper examines some of the key aspects of this situation. It does so by arguing that a number of these seemingly new developments are anticipated by C. Wright Mills in his now classic work, *The Sociological Imagination* (1959). This book is famous for its opening argument that the promise of sociology lies in its ability to connect private troubles and public issues, or more broadly questions of biography and history. The present paper, however, is concerned with the presentation of the discipline that underpins the core arguments of this text. For Mills' claim that sociology should attend to questions of biography and history, while interesting and important in itself, is a provocative response to a discipline that was in a deepening state of crisis. Mills' characterization of the sociology of his day is now famous, for he argues that it was torn between, on one hand, 'grand theory', exemplified by the dense writings of Talcott Parsons, and on the other, the 'abstracted empiricism' of 'specialists in method' such as Paul Lazarsfeld. What unites these seemingly unconnected strands of sociology is a common tendency to fetishize either theory or method. Mills argues that on one hand, grand theory fetishizes its concepts, and as a consequence works at such a high level of abstraction that it 'outruns any specific and empirical problem' (1959: 58), while on the other, abstracted empiricism loses its grip on the problems of the empirical world by confusing 'whatever is to be studied with the set of methods suggested for its study' (1959: 61). The argument of the present paper is that while Parsons and Lazarsfeld barely feature in contemporary sociology, this double impasse of theory and method remains with us today, and for this reason, among others (see Back, 2007; Fraser, 2009; Kemple and Mawani, 2009), there is a strong case for returning to Mills' work. The aim of this paper is to re-read Mills' *Sociological Imagination* to consider current crises of theory and method, and to pose again the question of the 'promise' or *value* of the discipline. The paper has two main parts that together question the continuing role of imagination in the discipline. The first part addresses questions of methodology by returning to Mills' arguments about the pitfalls of abstracted empiricism in the light of a recent exchange over the 'coming crisis of empirical sociology' (Savage and Burrows, 2007). It will be argued that mainstream empirical sociology today faces a crisis of methodological invention, particularly where qualitative and quantitative techniques are adopted as *a priori* commitments, and also a crisis of measurement as the academy loses the relative sovereignty it previously held over quantitative research techniques. The second part of this paper returns to Mills' arguments about grand theory to outline a parallel but not identical set of problems in the world of theoretical sociology. It will be argued that social theory is currently suffering from a lack of conceptual renewal, innovation and excitement, and that this, at least in part, is because theoretical sociology is today passing through a state of generational crisis. In returning to Mills to make these arguments about invention and imagination in the discipline, particular attention will be paid to sociological concepts of measure and value; concepts which, historically, have been central to thinking about sociological method and theory respectively.

## Abstracted empiricism

A key but neglected text for thinking about the value of measurement in sociology, and the value of quantitative approaches to methodology more generally, is C. Wright Mills' *The Sociological Imagination*. This book, which was first published in 1959, tends to be read today for its opening account of the 'promise' of sociology (something we will return to in the concluding section of this paper), and its appendix on 'intellectual craftsmanship'. However, other parts of this text, while sadly neglected, are equally as important. In the third chapter of this book, for example, Mills launches a stinging attack on what he calls abstracted empiricism: the practice of applying an established set of methodological techniques or conventions to the study of any empirical problem. Mills argues that the mistake of such an approach is that it elevates a prior commitment to specific research techniques (commonly called 'methods') over the challenges presented to us by the empirical world: 'Methodology, in short, seems to determine the problems' (1959: 67). Mills terms this an 'inhibition' which blocks rather than exercises the sociological imagination, for in his eyes a truly empirical methodology has to be flexible and innovative as it is formed in response to questions arising from the worlds we are attempting to study. In this view, the empirical is both a source of creativity and inspiration as well as being something that is to be explained (see Gane, 2009), and because of this should never be subordinated to a prior methodological commitment. Mills insists: 'no method . . . should be used to delimit the problems that we take up, if for no other reason that the most interesting and difficult issues of *method* usually begin where established techniques do not apply' (1959: 83). The challenge then is to think creatively about sociological methods in the face of the complexities of the empirical worlds with which we are engaged. To do so, Mills advises us not to move from an initial selection of a method to the analysis of a particular problem but the reverse: the problem, including its scale, should be used to determine the method. This means that method is tied to context, and is not something that can be assumed to have a universal application. Hence, Mills declares: 'Every man his own methodologist! Methodologists! Get to work!' (1959: 137).

Mills' critique of the tendency to fetishize methods within 'empirical' sociology (if it can truly be called this) can potentially be applied to qualitative and quantitative methodologies alike, but, his primary target in *The Sociological Imagination* is the statistical bias of applied social research, and in particular the work of Paul Lazarsfeld. Mills states that this type of sociology tends to fall into 'a more or less standard pattern' for it 'takes as the basic source of its "data" the more or less set interview with a series of individuals selected by a sampling procedure'. He continues: 'Their answers are classified and . . . used to make statistical runs by means of which relations are sought. Undoubtedly this fact, and the consequent ease with which the procedure is learned by any fairly intelligent person, accounts for much of its appeal' (1959: 60). Mills' objection to this type of quantitative research is that it subjects any potential problem – such as 'public opinion' or 'voting behaviour' – to standardized forms of statistical investigation. His argument is that such research starts with a concern for numbers or measurement, which it then elevates over the specific qualities of the empirical world it is attempting to analyse. The problem with this practice, as stated above, is that it works by moving from method to the empirical rather than vice versa, and this means that the challenges of the empirical are not always heard. For Mills, it is not the case that quantitative methodology per se is the problem (for depending on the empirical question this might be fitting), but rather the stamping of quantitative techniques upon all aspects of the social world regardless of the specific contexts and demands of this world. Such work, which makes an *a priori* methodological commitment in advance of whatever it seeks to study, can only frame and deal with empirical problems in narrow and repetitive ways, or in the words of Mills: 'within the curiously self-imposed limitations of [an] arbitrary epistemology' (1959: 65). It is through the exercise of such an epistemology that empirical sociology becomes what Mills calls 'abstracted empiricism'. For when research techniques determine the scope, range and focal points of investigation, sociology becomes abstracted from the empirical data that should be posing the questions, and as a consequence is destined to produce a 'thinness of result' (Mills, 1959: 76).

Mills, however, pushes this position further, for he is concerned not just with the epistemological limitations of abstracted empiricism, but also with its institutional dynamics, many of which can still be observed today. He proposes, for example, that the cost of large-scale statistical research cannot but direct its scope and focus. He states: 'as such studies are usually quite expensive, they have had to be shaped by some concern for the problems of the interests that have paid for them' (Mills, 1959: 75). Mills' point is a sensitive one: that the reliance of quantitative sociological work on sources of external funding means that the research problems addressed by such work are not always dictated by the academy but by agencies (commercial, state or even military; 1959: 115) that provide the cash. For Mills, this brings a potential conflict between the 'economics of truth', by which he means 'the costs of the research', and the 'politics of truth' or 'the use of research to clarify significant issues and to bring political controversy closer to realities' (1959: 75). Abstracted empiricism subordinates the latter to the former as increasingly it relies on money that influences the agenda of its proposed research. This development is accompanied by the emergence of a new breed of administrative intellectuals within the discipline, and a new businesslike ethos within the academy more generally. Mills explains: 'As the costs of research increase . . . there comes about a corporate control over the division of labour. The idea of a university as a circle of professorial peers . . . tends to be replaced by the idea of a university as a set of research bureaucracies . . .' (1959: 116). This situation, which was identified by Mills only in its nascent state, has led many since to trace and question the corporate ethos of universities today. One notable statement on this question is by Bill Readings, who in his book *The University in Ruins* argues that we are witnessing the 're-conception of the University as a corporation, one of whose functions (products?) is the granting of degrees with a cultural cachet, but whose overall nature is corporate rather than cultural' (1996: 11).

Mills himself addresses the new capitalistic and bureaucratic ethos of the university in the fifth chapter of *The Sociological Imagination*. His position is uncompromising. He argues that abstracted empiricism is accompanied by a new conservatism of 'a managerial and manipulative sort' (1959: 113), for increasingly universities are populated by 'intellectual administrators and research promoters' and by 'younger recruits, better described as research technicians than as social scientists' (1959: 117). The former are, in the words of Mills, 'members of The Committee; they are on The Board of Directors; they can get you the job, the trip, the research grant. They are the executives of the mind . . .' (1959: 117). The latter are the new recruits of abstracted empiricism who are trained solely in 'this one perspective, this one vocabulary, this one set of techniques' and who know nothing else but to work with a specific set of 'explicitly coded' methods (1959: 119). For Mills, this new generation of 'research technicians', who at best offer a 'formal and empty ingenuity', are largely immune to other ways of thinking and working as they do little more than apply their methodological techniques in routine and blinkered ways. He complains: 'I have seldom seen one of these young men . . . in a condition of genuine intellectual puzzlement. And I have never seen any passionate curiosity about a great problem, the sort of curiosity that compels the mind to travel anywhere in any means, to remake itself if necessary, in order to find out' (Mills, 1959: 118). Again, the problem for Mills is that this fetishization or 'ritual following' of methodological techniques narrows or even blocks our capacity to listen to and learn from the empirical world, as for this to happen method must not be pre-conceived but secondary to the questions or problems in hand. Mills here treats abstracted empiricism as a bureaucracy of intellect that mirrors that of the academy; one that is slowly starving sociology of its creativity and imagination and which therefore is to be opposed at all costs.

These fierce comments by Mills are all too often bypassed by contemporary readers of *The Sociological Imagination*, but interestingly a number of Mills' broader statements on method and methodology frame a recent exchange over what Savage and Burrows (2007) call 'the coming crisis of empirical sociology'.

This exchange, while taking its lead from the work of Gouldner (1970), centres on a further but connected argument made by Mills: that the sociological imagination is not confined to the discipline of sociology or even the academy. Mills makes this argument in at least two places in the opening chapter of *The Sociological Imagination*. The first is in his observation that the sociological imagination can be found routinely in 'factual and moral concerns, in literary work and in political analysis', and because of this it is becoming 'the major common denominator of our cultural life and its signal feature' (1959: 21). The second is in a footnote in which Mills argues that much of what the sociological imagination means 'is not at all expressed by sociologists. In England, for example, sociology as an abstract discipline is still somewhat marginal, yet in much English journalism, fiction, and above all history, the sociological imagination is very well developed indeed' (1959: 26).

These statements are more telling than they might at first appear. They propose, first, that within the academy, some of the most important sociological thinking takes place not just outside of abstracted empiricism, but outside of the discipline. Mills sees the working of a sociological imagination, for example, within some forms of political and literary analysis. Today, we might add the social is being theorized in a range of other disciplines, including women's studies, media theory, cultural studies and geography (see below, and Gane, 2004), that often seem better at doing this than sociology itself (Rustin, 2010: 48). Second, the above quotes from Mills suggest that sociology is becoming, in the words of Gouldner (see 1970: 4–7), a form of popular culture (see also Beer and Burrows, 2010), for the sociological imagination can now be found in media industries that seek to understand 'the intimate realities of ourselves in connexion with larger social realities' (Mills, 1959: 22). Savage and Burrows develop this line of argument in their paper on 'The Coming Crisis of Empirical Sociology' by proposing that qualitative methods such as the interview that were once distinctive to the discipline of sociology can now be found almost everywhere. They reflect: 'although it was sociologists who pioneered the use of these methods in allowing popular narratives to be made "public", the routine use of such methods in all forms of contemporary journalism, from the colour magazine to the Oprah Winfrey show, marks a clear shift of expertise away from the academy' (Savage and Burrows, 2007: 893; for a more detailed analysis of this development and other connected trends, see Savage, 2010: 237–249). This shift of expertise also applies to quantitative methodologies, which are now often deployed in commercial settings in ways that are more powerful and innovative than anything found within academic sociology. One example of this new breed of commercial sociology is the geodemographics industry (see Burrows and Gane, 2006), which produces spatial mappings of social class by working with transactional datasets that are unprecedented in terms of their scale and complexity. In the face of such developments, quantitative sociology stands on the brink of a crisis, for it can no longer compete with the methodologies and datasets that are used routinely by commercial agencies. For Savage and Burrows, this is one instance of a wider process whereby the academy is losing its sovereignty over the methods it once pioneered (for an earlier expression of this argument, see Law, 2004: 3). Indeed, they argue that the days when sociologists could lay claim to 'a series of distinctive methodological tools' (2007: 886) are now firmly in the past.

Savage and Burrows give a number of examples that support this position, some of which are striking. Savage recalls a conversation at an ESRC methods festival with someone with an attachment to a leading telecoms company who had 'the entire records of every phone call made on his system over several years, amounting to several billion ties' (Savage and Burrows, 2007: 886–887). Savage reflects that this data 'dwarves anything that an academic social scientist could garner. Crucially, it was data that did not require a special effort to collect, but was the digital by-product of the routine operations of a large capitalist institution. It is also private data to which most academics have no access' (2007: 887). The data available to quantitative sociologists is, then, a key issue (see Abbott, 2006: 57), as is the continuing value of their core methodologies. Savage and Burrows pick the sample survey as their primary example. They argue that the 'glory years' (roughly 1950–90) of this method are over for the following reasons: first, the response rates of such surveys are falling; second, their sampling frames tend to be restricted to national spaces; and third, large-scale survey research now takes place almost routinely throughout the commercial world. On this latter development, they suggest that a 'telling issue is the proliferation of survey research in private companies, especially in areas of market research. Such survey research now has very limited reference to academic expertise' (Savage and Burrows, 2007: 890). More tellingly: 'contemporary capitalist organizations now simply don't need the empirical expertise of quantitative social scientists as they go about their business . . . Most powerful institutional agents now have more effective research tools than sample surveys' (2007: 891). The argument here is two-fold: the sample survey is now outdated in the face of advanced quantitative techniques developed in the commercial sector, and for this reason, among others, this sector is less reliant on the academy for its methodological prowess and innovation than in the past. In the face of this situation, Savage and Burrows issue a stark warning: 'those sociologists who stake the expertise of their discipline to this method might want to reflect on whether this might leave them exposed to marginalization or even redundancy' (2007: 892).

Rosemary Crompton (2008) has responded to this paper by Savage and Burrows in a paper entitled 'Forty Years of *Sociology*'. She makes two main arguments. The first is that Savage and Burrows downplay the continuing importance of quantitative methodologies such as the sample survey by privileging classification over causality as the primary concern of current forms of empirical sociology. This objection has been contested by Savage and Burrows (2009: 769; see also Webber, 2009), but is interesting nonetheless for it raises the question of whether classification and causality can be treated as two separate things. One of the most important features of emergent geodemographic classifications is that they have causal and even normative effects. This is not just because of their symbolic meanings (see Burrows and Gane, 2006: 806), but because increasingly they are used to make decisions about the distribution of material resources on the ground. This means that even if such classifications are fictional they are at the same time very 'real'. Given this, one task of empirical sociology might be to reconsider the interplay between classification and causality, or epistemology and ontology more broadly, by addressing the lives of such classificatory systems and the effects they produce.

Second, Crompton argues that the main problem facing quantitative sociology today is not that its methodological tools are outdated, but that there is a lack of 'expertise' in this area (2008: 1223; see also the recent ESRC International Benchmarking Review[1]). At the same time, Crompton is sceptical of the value of what might be called commercial sociology: sociology that takes place outside the academy in commercial settings. For while she concedes that geodemographic analyses of social class 'can generate precise contemporary social mappings', she argues that they are also problematic for 'as with any multiple measure deriving from consumption patterns, the measure is likely to be unstable, and to consume considerable resources in its maintenance' (2008: 1221). It is not altogether clear on what grounds geodemographic classifications such as Mosaic might be termed unstable. Indeed, it might be argued in reply that such classifications are more flexible, fast-moving and therefore more robust than any comparable classification produced either by the academy or the state. Moreover, there is perhaps a connection between what Crompton calls the lack of 'quantitative expertise' in the discipline and her observation that such large-scale yet intricate geodemographic work requires serious financial backing. For increasingly such work can only take place in the commercial sector: in companies that not only have the resources to develop innovative, large-scale quantitative methodologies, but also the financial power to attract and keep the requisite sociological talent (the geodemographic package Mosaic, for example, is produced by the FTSE 100 company Experian).

So where does this take us? By revisiting Mills' critique of abstracted empiricism it is possible to argue that empirical sociology is facing a crisis along two interrelated fronts. First, is a crisis of *imagination*. The fetishization of ready-made quantitative and qualitative methods is more apparent now than it was when Mills wrote *The Sociological Imagination* in the late 1950s. John Law, one of the few commentators to have addressed this situation, identifies an emergent 'methodological hegemony' that threatens to impose 'a set of constraining normative blinkers' on sociological research (Law, 2004: 4). It is still common, for example, for mainstream sociological research and teaching to display an *a priori* commitment to the value of standardized quantitative or qualitative methods. For Law, the common dictum here is: 'If you want to understand reality properly then you need to follow the methodological rules' (2004: 5). This means, in Mills' terms, that empirical problems are commonly determined by prior methodological commitments. Law responds by questioning the ways in which such 'methods *produce* the reality they understand' (2004: 5). Equally, one might ask about the empirical 'realities' that such methodological practices leave untouched. It is noticeable, for example, that many of the urgent and pressing events of our times barely feature within mainstream sociology: the wars in Iraq and Afghanistan, the terrorist attacks in New York, Madrid, London and Mumbai, the ongoing financial crisis, to name but a few. This may be because of the complex relationship of history and sociology, and a sociological aversion to the analysis of events (see Gane, 2006), but it could also be because of a 'fetishism' of method that, in Mills' words, subsequently 'determines the problems'. This 'methodological inhibition' is today deeply engrained within the institutional structures of the academy. In the UK, it is drilled into future academics at an early stage, for postgraduate students are expected to be trained in 'methodology' before they embark on doctoral study. This training involves the learning of core quantitative and qualitative methods, not to mention 'ethics', which are then supposed to frame any subsequent empirical research. This takes us back to the very heart of Mills' *Sociological Imagination*, which warns against such 'training' in the strongest possible terms:

> 'crash programmes' in methodology are not likely to help social science develop. Really useful accounts of method cannot be forced in that way, if they are not very firmly related to the actual working of social study, a sense of significant problem and the passion to solve it – nowadays so often lost – cannot be allowed full play in the mind of the working social scientist. (1959: 136)

In line with his earlier position, such 'training', for Mills, should be reversed so that it starts with problems in the empirical world which challenge us to think creatively about the means for their study. Method is never ready-made, and, to use the words of Becker, is 'too important to be left to methodologists' (cited in Burrows, 1993: 46). The challenge of conceiving methods out of the empirical is, for Mills, one of the great endeavours of sociological thought, and is one that cannot proceed without creativity and imagination. For in Millsian terms, a discipline dominated by stock quantitative and qualitative methods is a discipline not only lacking in imagination, but also one that in spite of its claims can never be empirical in any meaningful sense.

Second, is a crisis of *measurement*, or more specifically a crisis in the value of quantitative sociologies that centre on the production of data through techniques of measurement. In the third chapter of *The Sociological Imagination*, Mills is critical of Lazarsfeld's quasi-Comtean view that the sociologist is to become 'the methodologist of all the social sciences' (1959: 70). Mills' rejection of this statement is multifaceted: it rests partly on a critique of Lazarsfeld's method and partly on the belief that sociology might learn from the ways in which other academic disciplines exercise a sociological imagination. Further to this, Mills raises the key but neglected question of the connection of academic sociology to its commercial other. This connection is central to the recent exchange over the coming crisis of empirical sociology, which asks of the continuing value (economic or otherwise) of quantitative research within the academy now that commercial organizations are able to conduct such research with greater resources, and arguably greater imagination and accuracy. What is the future of quantitative forms of sociology that in the past have been valued for their capacity for measurement but today have lost their sovereignty over quantitative research techniques, and with this some of their previous methodological prowess? This concern lies at the heart of Savage and Burrows' warning that quantitative sociology within the academy is threatened by marginalization and redundancy. For in an economic competition for the production of quantitative 'truths' (see Lyotard, 1984: 46–47), quantitative sociology is unlikely to win, especially given the precarious state of higher education funding in the UK.[2] Against this backdrop, Mills' comments regarding the costs of large-scale empirical work, and more generally the connection between the politics and economics of truth, seem more pertinent than ever. For how can the academic forms of quantitative research possibly compete with the vast transactional datasets and technical powers of the private sector? Savage and Burrows address precisely this question, and respond with the following declaration:

> Welcome to the world of 'knowing capitalism': a world inundated with complex processes of social and cultural digitization; a world in which commercial forces predominate; a world in which we, as sociologists, are losing whatever jurisdiction we had over the study of the 'social' as the generation, mobilization and analysis of social data become ubiquitous. (2009: 763)

This might sound bleak for the future of the discipline, or at least for the future of quantitative sociological research, but perhaps Mills offers us some ways out of this situation? One might be to revisit complex questions regarding the value of measurement, and of the value of a sociology that is not tied to the latter. Another, more concretely, might be to acknowledge that the academy cannot compete in terms of access to and processing of data, and to think instead more creatively about what method is and what it might help us to achieve. To do this it might be useful to follow Mills' assertion that a sociological imagination exists outside of the academy, for one might then ask what academic sociology might learn, methodologically or otherwise, from the study of the operation of this imagination in commercial settings (see Burrows and Gane, 2006). For those interested in descriptive sociology, this might provide insight into new techniques for studying large-scale and complex social phenomena, while for those with more analytical or critical leanings, it might enhance our understanding of the methodological and technical practices that lie at the heart of contemporary 'knowing' capitalism.

## Grand theory

A crisis of method, however, is only half of the problem, for Mills argues that a number of parallel but not identical crises are to be found in the world of theory. In similar fashion to the above, this section will draw upon Mills' arguments in order to address the crisis of imagination that lies at the heart of theoretical sociology today. To do so, it is first necessary to revisit Mills' account of the theoretical work that was characteristic of his time, and more specifically his attack on the ascendency of what he called 'grand theory'. Mills' position will be re-read alongside more recent interventions on the status of grand theory by Quentin Skinner and William Outhwaite. This will lead in turn to a questioning of the role of concepts in social theory and, finally, if only in brief, to a reflection on the continuing value or 'promise' of sociology more generally.

For Mills, the problems of grand theory run parallel to those of abstracted empiricism (see 1959: 60), for whereas the latter proceeds through a fetishization of methodological techniques in place of a genuine engagement with empirical problems, grand theory fetishizes abstract concepts and systems to the extent that all contact with both empirical reality and history is lost. Mills states: 'The basic cause of grand theory is the initial choice of a level of thinking so general that its practitioners cannot logically get down to observation' (1959: 42). The main advocate of such theory, for Mills, is Talcott Parsons. Throughout the course of Chapter 2 of *The Sociological Imagination*, Mills takes a series of quotes from Parsons' *The Social System* and translates them 'into English'. This ridicule of Parsons' work comes as little surprise as there was a history of animosity between the two thinkers dating back to the mid-1940s (see Mills, 2000: 74). In *The Sociological Imagination*, Mills gives the following reason for his attack: 'My purpose in all this is to help grand theorists get down from their useless heights' (1959: 42). Beyond this playful sparring with Parsons, there is a serious point to Mills' argument. His starting point is the observation that grand theory proceeds through the 'associating and dissociating of concepts' (1959: 34). Such theory, he argues, connects together concepts to form an abstract and general system instead of addressing their potential use and meaning in connection to pressing empirical problems. For Mills, 'Grand theory is drunk on syntax, blind to semantics' (1959: 42). The parallels between abstracted empiricism and grand theory are clear, for whereas in the former, techniques of research take priority over questions raised by the empirical world, in the latter analysis of empirical problems is displaced by 'an arid game of Concepts' (1959: 43). Mills stands against this 'formalist withdrawal' of theory at all costs. He argues that the key to the development of an imaginative yet systematic and effective sociology lies in our ability to control the level of abstraction at which we work. This means that there can be no universal scheme or system through which problems arising in the empirical world can be understood, for what is needed instead is a 'variety of . . . working models' (1959: 57) as well as a detailed understanding of the historical contexts and complexities of the phenomena under study. Mills returns to this point in a later chapter of *The Sociological Imagination* – 'The Use of History' – where he argues that 'To fulfil their tasks, or even to state them well, social scientists must use the full materials of history . . . All sociology worthy of the name is "historical sociology"' (1959: 162). He adds that this attention to history is missing from grand theory and abstracted empiricism alike, for the tendency is to retreat into the 'undue formality' of either abstract concepts or research techniques, and in both cases this blocks the possibility of truly comparative work (for a recent statement on the complex connection of history and sociology, see Savage, 2010).

Mills' critique of grand theory may at first sight seem less far-reaching than his critique of abstracted empiricism. Echoes of Mills' objections to the abstractions of Parsonian thinking, however, can still be detected today in debates over the status and future of theory within sociology. A key point of orientation is Quentin Skinner's *The Return of Grand Theory in the Human Sciences* (1985), which examines the fate of grand theory after Parsons. Skinner opens this book with a brief summary of the argument of *The Sociological Imagination*. He states:

> Mills isolated and castigated two major theoretical traditions which he saw as inimical to the effective development of . . . *The Sociological Imagination*. The first was the tendency – one that he associated in particular with the philosophies of Comte and Marx, Spencer and Weber – to manipulate the evidence of history in such a way as to manufacture 'a trans-historical strait jacket'. But the other and even larger impediment to the progress of the human sciences he labelled Grand Theory, by which he meant the belief that the primary goal of the social disciplines should be that of seeking to construct 'a systematic theory of "the nature of man and society"'. (1985: 3)

Close readers of Mills' work will notice two peculiarities in this reading of *The Sociological Imagination*. The first is that Mills objects to grand theory because it works at too high a level of generality because it fetishizes its concepts (1959: 44). This is *the* basic argument of the second chapter of *The Sociological Imagination*, and one that is strangely absent from Skinner's reading. Skinner's only mention of concepts comes in a brief observation on the relationship between philosophy and 'other cultural disciplines' that characterized postwar scepticism to grand theory: 'A philosopher was taken to be someone whose basic concern is to explicate general concepts by way of analysing the meanings of the terms used to express them' (Skinner, 1985: 4). This argument that concepts belong to the realm of philosophy is a common one and can be found in thinkers as far removed as Isaiah Berlin and Gilles Deleuze (see Gane, 2009). However, in the context of the current paper it is important for it raises the question of the role of concepts within sociological thought, and this is something I will return to below. The second peculiarity of Skinner's reading lies in its separation of trans-historical theoretical work from grand theory. Mills argues that grand theory is problematic because it privileges conceptual formalism over the empirical richness of historical analysis. This is a charge he levels at both grand theorists and abstracted empiricists. He argues: 'Social scientists may – in fact many do – attempt to retreat from history by means of undue formality of Concept and technique. But these attempts require them to make assumptions about the nature of history and of society that are neither fruitful nor true' (Mills, 1959: 174). Contrary to Skinner, this is not a charge that Mills levels at either Weber or Marx, as, quite rightly, he argues that their 'conceptions about society were closely joined with historical exposition' (Mills, 1959: 58). The problem, for Mills at the time of writing *The Sociological Imagination*, was a quite different one, namely 'the amnesia of the American scholar' and the 'formalist withdrawal' from history of Parsonian sociology in particular.

Skinner's separation of trans-historical sociology from systematic theories of the 'nature of man and society' is not without consequence, for it enables him to define the detailed historical work of Michel Foucault or the *Annales* school as 'grand theory'. This is a little strange given Foucault's attention to local, subversive forms of historical knowledge, along with his call for specific rather than general intellectual work. A similar objection might be made to terming the philosophy of Jacques Derrida (who also appears in this book) grand theory in the Millsian sense. Skinner himself concedes that:

> If there is one feature to all the thinkers I have singled out, it is a willingness to emphasise the importance of the local and the contingent, a desire to underline the extent to which our own concepts and attitudes have been shaped by particular historical circumstances, and a correspondingly strong dislike . . . of all overarching theories and schemes of explanation. (1985:12)

It is not altogether clear that the figures discussed in *The Return of Grand Theory* – including Jürgen Habermas, Thomas Kuhn, Hans-Georg Gadamer and Claude Lévi-Strauss – do indeed share a comparable commitment to 'the local and the contingent'. In any case, how could such commitment be reconciled with theory that is at the same time systematic and grand? For Skinner, the answer is two-fold. First, he argues that these thinkers 'almost in spite of themselves . . . have proved to be among the grandest theorists of common practice throughout a wide range of the social disciplines' (1985: 13). Second, he adds that 'there has been an unashamed return to the deliberate construction of precisely those grand theories of human nature and conduct which Wright Mills and his generation had hoped to outlaw from any central place in the human sciences' (1985: 13). Skinner cites Habermas as an example, for he takes rationality as his central theme – in Millsian terms this is presumably the concept he fetishizes – by developing 'abstract theories of social structure' via Parsons on one hand, and reconstructing historical materialism via Marx on the other (1985: 17). For Skinner, this places Habermas very much within the tradition of grand theory outlined by Mills. This judgement seems well founded, but whether the same can be said of thinkers such as Foucault who do not deal with abstract theories of social structure in any sense is, to say the least, questionable.

This question of whether the thinkers discussed by Skinner are in fact 'grand theorists' in the Millsian sense cannot be pursued at further length here. It is worth noting, however, that this text on the return of grand theory remains influential today. William Outhwaite – who contributed a chapter on Gadamer to Skinner's collection (1985: 21–39) – has recently considered the position of such theory within British sociology. Outhwaite traces the emergence of a new canon of social theory made up of four thinkers who have been 'ascribed a comparably prominent superstar role' (2009: 1030): Zygmunt Bauman, Ulrich Beck, Pierre Bourdieu and Anthony Giddens. One might ask why none of the figures previously addressed by Skinner – in particular Foucault and Habermas – have entered into this canon of British sociology. This is a complex question that concerns the historical influence of different types of continental thought on British sociology (see, for example, Rex, 1983), and which cannot be addressed here. Outhwaite touches upon this question only in brief in a footnote (2009: 1039), for his main task instead is to trace the biographical and intellectual trajectories of the above four thinkers by arguing that 'for practical purposes' they 'can be assigned to the same generational cohort' (2009: 130). This idea of a 'generational cohort' is a key point of interest. For Outhwaite, a 'period of 33–35 years' is 'the crucial accounting unit in the history of thought' (2009: 1029). He draws this observation from the work of Randall Collins, who in his *Sociology of Philosophies* argues that 'A 33-year period is the approximate length of an individual's creative work. By the end of that time, a cohort of thinkers will be virtually replaced by a new adult generation' (Collins, 1998: xix). Outhwaite identifies 1971 as the year 'to start the Collins clock' for the formation of the new canon. He explains: 'Bauman has just arrived in Leeds; Bourdieu is well established in Paris and Giddens at Cambridge; Beck is completing his doctorate' (Outhwaite, 2009: 1030). Outhwaite proceeds to give an overview of each thinker's life and works, before asking what appears to be the central evaluative question of this paper: 'Is the return of "grand theory" likely to be permanent?' (2009: 1037). His answer, in the very last line of the conclusion and which is given without any accompanying justification, is yes: 'the style of theorizing' which has been introduced by these four thinkers 'seems to be here to stay' (2009: 1038).

For the purposes of the present paper, the above arguments of Skinner and Outhwaite are useful in at least two respects. First, they place into question the generational shifts that underpin the canonization of social theory; and second, they return us to Mills' question of the fate of conceptual fetishism, or what he called 'grand theory'. First, I will address the former: what might be termed the current *generational* crisis of social theory. It is not altogether clear why, for Outhwaite, 1971 is the key year for the formation of his canon, for at this time Beck, Bauman, Giddens and Bourdieu were not only at different stages in their careers but were also far removed from each other in terms of their theoretical interests and positions (one might add that these four thinkers are 'theorists' in quite different senses of the word). But if we do start the clock at this seemingly arbitrary date, and we accept Collins' view of the lifespan of generational cohorts, then where did things stand in 2004, 33 years on? For if Collins and Outhwaite are right, this should have been the point at which the creative work of these theorists started to fade and was displaced by a younger generation of thinkers. But why did this not happen and why is this canon still so dominant within British sociology? To use Outhwaite's words, why is the grand theory of Bauman, Beck, Bourdieu and Giddens seemingly 'here to stay'?

This question of generational change within sociology, which Mills only touches upon in his remarks on the new methodological recruits to the discipline, and which Outhwaite raises rather than answers, is explored by Andrew Abbott. In a paper on knowledge accumulation within sociology, Abbott (2006) collects data from five leading North American journals in order to determine the age of materials that are still influential within the discipline. In so doing, he raises questions that are not simply confined to the analysis of North American sociology. For Abbott disputes the idea that increasingly 'the old stuff' in sociology is simply forgotten, for his findings are 'inconsistent with the claim that contemporary scholars pay less attention to earlier work than their predecessors. That is . . . I think the glass is half full, not half empty, and that it is getting fuller' (Abbott, 2006: 59). This judgement is questionable, for surely the key point is not simply the extent to which previous sociological resources are drawn upon today, but how such materials are cited and in what context. Transposed into a British setting, for example, is it a sign of the health of the discipline that the four canonical theorists named by Outhwaite are cited so commonly within mainstream contemporary sociological work? Or might this indicate the absence of a new generation of theoretical sociologists that should by now have displaced the existing canon? Abbott, like Collins, has his own vision of generational change, and argues that the lifespan of most sociological literatures or careers is roughly 25 years. He states that this:

> . . . is about the length of time it takes a single group of individuals to make up some new ideas, seize the soap-boxes, train a generation or two of students, and finally settle into late career exhaustion. Their students may keep things going, but their students' students tend to be fairly mechanical appliers of the original insights. The really creative people don't make their careers by hitching themselves to other people's wagons. (2006: 61)

Setting aside questions of whether Outhwaite, Collins and Abbott are right to tie generational cohorts and generational change to rigid time-spans (which in itself is highly debatable), the following question might be posed to Abbott by way of response: where are the 'really creative people' who are thinking beyond the canon outlined by Outhwaite or even Skinner before him? To put this bluntly, and to paraphrase Rosemary Crompton's complaint regarding the current absence of methodological expertise: what has happened to the next generation of theoretical talent within the discipline?

One answer is offered by Steve Fuller, who in many ways echoes Mills in arguing that the scope for creativity and imagination in sociology is today constrained by audit measures such as the Research Assessment Exercise (RAE) that alienate 'ideas from the thinker' by reducing them to 'outputs' that are judged by their market value. Such measures, at least in the UK, centre increasingly on the 'impact' of published work, and promote the assumption that there is a direct correlation between the mass citation and intrinsic worth of sociological research. For Fuller, what is disturbing about this development is that it tends to bolster the existing canon at the expense of risk-taking – what he calls 'bullshit' (see Fuller, 2009: 143–163) – and more broadly the production of anything qualitatively new:

the problem with this practice is not what it says about the relatively few who receive the lion's share of citations – but the many more who prop up these market leaders by citing them so much. It fosters a dependency culture whereby academics are rewarded for feats of ventriloquism, that is, an ability to speak through the authority of others. The result is institutionalized cowardice. (Fuller, 2009: 86)

This might, at least in part, explain the citation of what Abbott calls 'old stuff' in his survey of North American journals, along with the continued stability of Outhwaite's canon. For increasingly the social sciences are dominated in these settings (the global picture is undoubtedly more complex) by an institutional culture that privileges the repetition of the same, both in terms of citation practices and the content of outputs, over work that genuinely changes the rules of the game and with this the game itself (what Lyotard might once have called parology). Hence, Abbott's 'really creative people' that refuse to hitch themselves 'to other people's wagons' are increasingly difficult to find. To understand exactly why this is the case, further sociological work is needed on the audit measures and inscription practices that underpin this new bureaucracy of the intellect. Such work might ask the following: are particular academic journals and publishing houses privileged within these audit measures, and if so, why? Is it a sign of the health of the discipline when the volume of published outputs of individual scholars is rewarded regardless of their thematic and analytic repetition? Can the value of sociological work legitimately be measured in terms of its 'impact'? And what is the future of the research monograph (historically the primary medium for theoretical work)? Such questions, which will find different answers in different national contexts, force us to think further about both the institutional underpinnings of the discipline, as well as the presentational forms of sociology and the media of its transmission. These latter questions are particularly important if it remains an aspiration of the discipline to have any kind of 'public' presence or audience (see Back, 2007: 160–161).

Such questions cannot be addressed at any length here, but nonetheless they point to an underlying politics of publishing and citation that is neglected by Abbott. This politics is tied to broader questions concerning the continuing promise or value of social theory, and of what *value* itself is or potentially can be outside of institutional or quantitative notions of measurement. One might ask, for example, of the underlying politics of audit measures such as the RAE/REF in the UK, and the impact of such measures upon the ambition, imagination and scope of sociological research over the past 20 years. Fuller is forceful on this point, for he declares that such measures encourage a narrowness of mind because they reward scholars not for taking risks but for publishing repeatedly in specialist research areas. For Fuller, the consequence of this development is alarming: 'Ask even a distinguished professor something related to but slightly off his official topic and you might as well have flashed your headlights at an innocent deer' (2009: 84). What is surprising, given that classification is a major point of critical interest within sociology, is that the politics and consequences of audit measures such as the RAE have so rarely been questioned from within the discipline (exceptions are Fraser, 2009; Burrows and Kelly in the present volume). Les Back (2010) rightly observes that 'there is a timidity and cynicism that hangs over the anxiety ridden sociological habitus preoccupied as it is with the ever changing measure of intellectual value and audit'. This is perhaps set to change in the face of the crisis of funding that presently looms over social science and the humanities in the UK, for questions regarding the distribution of resources within the academy, or what Mills called the politics and economics of truth, are increasingly taking centre-stage.[3] With this, theoretical questions regarding the underlying politics of knowledge production and the commodification of intellectual work are likely to make a return, including those identified by Lyotard over 30 years ago: 'who decides what knowledge is, and who knows what needs to be decided?' (1984: 9).

A further pressing question concerns the relation of sociology to its fellow disciplines – again something that Mills touches upon in his *Sociological Imagination*. As stated above, the year 2004, according to Outhwaite's clock, should have seen the existing canon of social theory come to an end. This does not seem to have happened, but at the same time it depends on where one looks, and on what is to count as 'social' theory, for some of the most powerful exercises of a sociological imagination are to be found at the institutional margins or even outside of the discipline as it is commonly recognized (equally, it might be argued there are academics who work in sociology departments who would not consider themselves to be 'sociologists' in any conventional sense). A key consideration is of the status of the discipline in relation to its others, for sociology has been characterized variously as an 'exporter discipline' (Holmwood, 2010) and as a 'parasite' (Urry, 2002). There are also important questions to be addressed about whether the boundaries of social theory should be relaxed, or whether the discipline should look inwards to ask of its own core aims, grounds and objectives in a bid to (re-)define its future. Against the backdrop of such questions, the early 2000s are perhaps more interesting than they might at first seem, for while they did not bring the collapse of the paradigm outlined by Outhwaite, they did see the publication of three very different works that questioned the future prospects for theoretical work: Eagleton's *After Theory* (2004), Butler, Guillory and Thomas's *What's Left of Theory?* (2000) and my own *The Future of Social Theory* (Gane, 2004). The first of these texts questions the ambitions of cultural theory after its 'golden age'; the second reflects on the status of literary theory following the apparent demise of the Left; and the third draws together key thinkers from sociology, cultural studies and philosophy to think again about what the concept of 'the social' might mean today (for a more historical reading of this concept, see also Joyce, 2002). These three texts are quite different in terms of their aims and scope, but are united by their questioning of the social and the cultural through the exercise of a conceptual vocabulary and theoretical imagination that cannot be found exclusively within sociology (a related and pressing question is of what counts as 'theory' across different disciplinary domains; see Hunter, 2006). This is nothing new, for some of the most important works of social theory of the late 20th century were forged out of disenchantment with the disciplinary and institutional limitations of sociology: in women's studies, cultural studies and (new) media studies. Mills rightly reminds us that the sociological imagination is routinely at work outside of both sociology and the academy. Given this, it would perhaps be worth returning to these disciplinary and institutional boundaries to ask what type of theoretical work it is possible to produce within the discipline today, and why mainstream sociology, despite its stated intentions, often remains unwilling to listen to its disciplinary others?

In an oblique way, Outhwaite's recent paper, while focusing on a predominantly British canon, leaves us with the question of what is left of theory within sociology. By way of response, it might be argued that social theory, at least as it is found in the mainstream, is passing through something of a generational crisis. Outhwaite's canon is living on beyond its expected, and some might argue useful, lifespan. It is, to borrow Beck's own phrase, a *zombie* canon. Increasingly, theoretical ideas, and more specifically sociological concepts, are drawn in a ready-made fashion from the writings of a select body of thinkers rather than being re-forged or invented anew. This fetishism of the concept – be it risk, reflexivity or liquidity – lies at the heart of Mills' critique of grand theory, and is the key part of his argument missed by Skinner. Such work blocks rather than exercises the sociological imagination because it starts with a meta-concept or process that is then stamped on every aspect of the so-called 'empirical' worlds under study. A common practice is to invent a new type of 'society' or 'modernity' under which all empirical details and complexities can be subsumed: 'risk' society (Beck), 'network' or 'information' society (Castells), 'liquid' modernity (Bauman), 'high' or 'late' modernity (Giddens), to name but a few. In each case, these leading concepts are fetishized in the Millsian sense.[4] Castells (who I would add to Outhwaite's canon) talks, for example, of network or information society but says little about the empirical complexities of either networks or information (see Gane and Beer, 2008: 15–33). A similar charge might be levelled at Beck or Bauman's theory of individualization, which sees a shift of powers and responsibilities down from the state to the individual, but says little about the emergence of new authoritarian state (bio-)powers over territories or populations post-9/11, or the intricate connections between the state and market capitalism that have emerged through the recent financial crisis (see Gane, 2012). Others, meanwhile, have taken issue with the thin concept of reflexivity that underpins such thinking as well as the structural constraints of class that these meta-theories tend to downplay (see Atkinson, 2007, 2008). In each of these cases, such grand theoretical work starts with a meta-concept or process – be it risk or liquidity – that frames all subsequent analysis and understanding of 'empirical' events or examples. In the writings of Bauman, for example, there is little attention to basic questions concerning the when, where and who of 'liquid modernity'. This a-historicism or trans-historicism, contra Skinner, is a central feature of what Mills calls grand theory, and for this reason Mills' critique of Parsons is still of contemporary significance even if interest in Parsons' work per se has long since faded. This leaves us in turn with Outhwaite's question of whether grand theory is here to stay. This question is impossible to answer, but by way of response one might instead ask the following: what would it take for this (grand) theoretical canon to be displaced? One answer, in part inspired by Mills, is that sociology needs to renew its theoretical imagination. For this to happen, flexible and inventive conceptual work is needed that addresses the pressing empirical demands of the day while at the same time retaining a sense of historicity and scale (which Howard Becker has long-argued that British sociology in particular lacks, see Becker in Mullan, 1987: 140). Such work would give the discipline new tools for thinking, and would enable the 'zombie' concepts of existing cannons to be refined, reinvented or finally laid to rest, depending on the problem in hand. This, I would argue, is a key step in re-animating the sociological imagination, even if it is not one that is core to Mills' own concerns. Indeed, it is perhaps here, with the intricacies of concepts, in particular their formation and displacement, that we reach the limits of Mills' text.

## Concluding remarks

The paper has attempted to draw into question some of the problems of contemporary sociology through a re-reading of a classic but in many ways neglected text: Mills' *Sociological Imagination*. One of the appealing features of this text is not simply its attention to the connections between biography and history, as commonly stated, but also its ability to work beyond an apparent impasse between sociological method and theory: between abstracted empiricism, on the one hand, and grand theory on the other. For Mills, parallel problems run through these approaches, as the former proceeds through the reduction of methods to a set of preconceived techniques, and the latter through trans-historical abstraction and the fetishism of concepts. The argument of the present paper is that Mills' double-pronged attack against the then prevalent forms of method and theory is instructive today, for it suggests how we might move beyond some of the current limitations of the discipline. One such limitation is the widespread stand-off between theoreticians and methodologists, some of whom go as far as blaming each other for the demise of sociology. Goldthorpe, for example, writes: 'there is a manifest lack of integration of research and theory . . . Here, I believe, chief responsibility has to lie with theorists . . .' (2000: 2). Mills offers his own provocation, for he argues that the fetishization of either theory or method is equally mistaken. In so doing, he returns us to primary questions of what is meant by 'the empirical', and what sociology is or can be as an empirical discipline. These issues, which have been the subject of renewed interest (see Adkins and Lury, 2009), arise primarily because Mills treats theory and method as second-order questions that only come into play following an initial encounter with an empirical problem. This takes him close to the radical empiricism of more fashionable thinkers such as Deleuze (see Fraser, 2009; Gane, 2009), who not only draws on Hume to think about 'the flux of the sensible', but also asserts the role of imagination and mind in forging a 'collection of impressions and images, or a set of perceptions' out of raw empirical data (Deleuze, 1991: 87). It is precisely at this point, for both Deleuze and Mills, that the work of philosophy and sociology respectively – through the subsequent forging of concepts and methods – begins.

Working in the spirit of Mills, Les Back argues that for sociology to be attentive to the empirical it must develop an art of listening that takes us beyond existing methodological and theoretical dogmas. Furthermore, he suggests that literary practices of inscription are needed to bring sociology alive, for too often sociologists 'swim unnoticed at the shallow end of the literary pond' (Back, 2007: 177). This idea of a 'literary sociology' (see Back, 2007: 164) is intriguing in the light of Abbott's (2007) recent call for a 'lyrical' sociology, which itself is far removed from poetic forms of sociology that reside at the limits of the discipline (see, for example, Baudrillard, 1990). I would add to this, however, that concept formation must also lie at the heart of empirical sociology. At first sight, Mills and Deleuze appear to depart on this point, for whereas Mills is reticent to see sociology reduced to 'an arid game of Concepts' (1959: 43), Deleuze argues that concepts are indispensible bridges between empirical reality and its presentation in thought. But to be clear: Mills' objection is to work that 'sets forth a realm of concepts' (1959: 44) that are then elevated to such a level that they then outrun 'any specific and empirical problem' (1959: 58). This means that concepts, like methods, should be developed out of, and in connection to, the complexities of the empirical world (the recent attempt to formulate 'mobile methods' is interesting in this respect, see Büscher *et al.*, 2010). Concepts should not be static, abstract devices that are devised and deployed in any general or universal way. This, for Mills, is exactly the problem of grand theory, where they become little more than 'sponge-words' (1959: 53): weak analytic descriptors or tools that do little more than absorb the energy of the worlds they are attempting to study. This crisis of concepts lies at the heart of grand theory, and runs parallel to the crisis of measurement that today haunts abstracted forms of empiricism. Mills responds by reminding us that the task in both cases is not to festishize the ready-made, but rather to invent or re-forge useful analytical devices and practical techniques out of the empirical problems that we face. This is an ongoing and difficult challenge. It may involve breathing new life into concepts that currently lie neglected, including, for example, the concept of 'value': a concept that was once central to Marxist and Weberian sociologies. For in the face of renewed institutional pressures for sociology to justify itself, one might ask again what value is outside of quantitative notions of measurement? In asking such questions, we return to where Mills begins: with the promise of sociological work. For in the face of the crises outlined in this paper, this question of the promise or *value* of the discipline requires renewed attention.

## Acknowledgements

I would like to thank Lisa Adkins, Les Back, David Beer, Roger Burrows, Thomas Kemple, Celia Lury, and Mike Savage for commenting on early drafts of this paper.

## Notes

1 ESRC International Benchmarking Review, available at: http://www.esrcsocietytoday.ac.uk/ESRCInfoCentre/Images/Sociology%20IBR%20Report_tcm6-36279.pdf
2 See http://hereview.independent.gov.uk/hereview/report/
3 This is especially the case in the UK following the release of the recent Higher Education White Paper, see http://www.bis.gov.uk/assets/biscore/higher-education/docs/h/11-944-higher-education-students-at-heart-of-system.pdf
4 A figure not dealt with in the course of this paper is Bruno Latour. Latour's work, while deeply influential in the sphere of science and technology studies, is not part of the current canon of mainstream sociology, in part because it has been concerned predominantly with the pursuit of an anthropology of science, but perhaps also because it has refused, on the one hand, the Durkheimian formulation of the social as society, on the other Marxist conceptions of the commodity, fetishism and reification (see Latour in Gane, 2004: 77–81). Instead, like Deleuze and Guattari (1987: 218–219), Latour turns to the work of Gabriel Tarde in an attempt to explore the social as a form and practice of association. This may be read as an attempt by Latour to resist the fetishization of concepts by calling into question their continued empirical purchase (see Gane and Beer, 2008: 27–31). The most famous instance of this is where Latour questions the canon of actor-network theory that his own work helped to found: 'there are four things that do not work with actor-network theory: the word actor, the word network, the word theory and the hyphen!' (Latour, 1999: 15). Two observations might be made here. First, Latour's disavowal of actor-network theory by no means signalled the end of this type of work, which in many ways continues to be fetishized by its followers. Second, Latour's subsequent writings have had, at least to date, comparatively little impact on the discipline (see, for example, Latour 2004, 2011). One might draw an unlikely comparison here with the work of Jean Baudrillard, which beyond its attention to hyperreality, simulation and war has barely been read (see, for example, Baudrillard, 2001, 2002, 2003). In both cases, what appealed to the sociological mainstream was a ready-made theoretical or methodological framework with related concepts that could be deployed to a range of empirical situations: in the case of Latour this is actor-network theory and an anthropology of the modern, and in Baudrillard it is symbolic exchange and four orders of simulacra. As soon as both thinkers moved on to think respectively about the politics of nature (Latour) and singularity and alternative forms of exchange (Baudrillard) their mainstream sociological popularity and circulation faded. This situation can perhaps be read as an example of the continuing methodological and theoretical timidity of the discipline.

## References

Abbott, A., (2006), 'Reconceptualizing knowledge accumulation in sociology', *The American Sociologist*, 37(2): 57–66.
Abbott, A., (2007), 'Against narrative: a preface to lyrical sociology', *Sociological Theory*, 25(1): 67–99.
Adkins, L. and Lury, C., (2009), 'Introduction: what is the empirical?' *European Journal of Social Theory*, 12(1): 5–20.

Atkinson, W., (2007), 'Beck, individualization and the death of class: a critique', *British Journal of Sociology*, 58(3): 349–366.
Atkinson, W., (2008), 'Not all that was solid has melted into air (or liquid): a critique of Bauman on individualization and class in liquid modernity', *Sociological Review*, 56(1): 1–16.
Back, L., (2007), *The Art of Listening*, Oxford: Berg.
Back, L., (2010), 'Sociology's promise', unpublished paper.
Baudrillard, J., (1990), *Cool Memories*, London: Verso.
Baudrillard, J., (2001), *Impossible Exchange*, London: Verso.
Baudrillard, J., (2002), *Screened Out*, London: Verso.
Baudrillard, J., (2003), *Passwords*, London: Verso.
Beer, D. and Burrows, R., (2010), 'The sociological imagination as popular culture', in J. Burnett, S. Jeffers and G. Thomas (eds), *New Social Connections*, Basingstoke: Palgrave.
Burrows, R., (1993), 'Some notes towards a realistic realism: the practical implications of realist philosophies of science for social science research methods', *International Journal of Sociology and Social Policy*, 9(4): 46–63.
Burrows, R. and Gane, N., (2006), 'Geodemographics, software and class', *Sociology*, 40(5): 793–812.
Büscher, M., Urry, J. and Witchger, K., (eds), (2010), *Mobile Methods*, London: Routledge.
Butler, J., Guillory, J. and Thomas, K., (eds), (2000), *What's Left of Theory?: New Work on the State and Politics of Literary Theory*, London: Routledge.
Collins, R., (1998), *The Sociology of Philosophies: A Global Theory of Intellectual Change*, Cambridge, MA: Harvard University Press.
Crompton, R., (2008), 'Forty years of *Sociology*: some comments', *Sociology*, 42(6): 1218–1227.
Deleuze, G., (1991), *Empiricism and Subjectivity: An Essay on Hume's Theory of Human Nature*, New York: Columbia University Press.
Deleuze, G. and Guattari, F., (1987), *A Thousand Plateaus*, London: Athlone.
Eagleton, T., (2004), *After Theory*, Hardmondsworth: Penguin.
Fraser, M., (2009), 'Experiencing sociology', *European Journal of Social Theory*, 12(1): 63–81.
Fuller, S., (2009), *The Sociology of Intellectual Life: The Career of the Mind In and Around the Academy*, London: Sage.
Gane, N., (2004), *The Future of Social Theory*, London: Continuum.
Gane, N., (2006), 'Speed-up or slow down? Social theory in the information age', *Information, Communication and Society*, 9(1): 20–38.
Gane, N., (2009), 'Concepts and the "new" empiricism', *European Journal of Social Theory*, 12(1): 83–97.
Gane, N., (2012), *Max Weber and Contemporary Capitalism*, Basingstoke: Palgrave.
Gane, N. and Beer, D., (2008), *New Media: The Key Concepts*, Oxford: Berg.
Goldthorpe, J., (2000), *On Sociology: Numbers, Narratives, and the Integration of Theory and Research*, Oxford: Oxford University Press.
Gouldner, A., (1970), *The Coming Crisis of Western Sociology*, New York: Basic Books.
Holmwood, J., (2010), 'Sociology's misfortune: disciplines, interdisciplinarity and the impact of audit culture', *British Journal of Sociology*, 61(4): 639–658.
Hunter, I., (2006), 'The history of theory', *Critical Inquiry*, 33(1): 78–112.
Joyce, P., (2002), *The Social in Question: New Bearings*, London: Routledge.
Kemple, T. and Mawani, R., (2009), 'The sociological imagination and its imperial shadows', *Theory, Culture and Society*, 26(7–8): 228–249.
Latour, B., (1999), 'On recalling ANT', in J. Law and J. Hassard (eds), *Actor Network Theory and After*, Oxford: Blackwell.
Latour, B., (2004), *The Politics of Nature*, Cambridge: Cambridge University Press.
Latour, B., (2011), *On the Modern Cult of the Factish Gods*, Durham: Duke University Press.
Law, J., (2004), *After Method: Mess in Social Science Research*, London: Routledge.
Lyotard, J.-F., (1984), *The Postmodern Condition*, Manchester: Manchester University Press.
Mills, C.W., (1959), *The Sociological Imagination*, Harmondsworth: Penguin.

Mills, C.W., (2000), *Letters and Autobiographical Writings*, Berkeley: University of California Press.
Mullan, B., (1987), *Sociologists on Sociology*, London: Croom Helm.
Outhwaite, W., (2009), 'Canon formation in late 20th-century British sociology', *Sociology*, 43(6): 1029–1045.
Readings, B., (1996), *The University in Ruins*, Cambridge, MA: Harvard University Press.
Rex, J., (1983), 'British sociology 1960–80: an essay', *Social Forces*, 61(4): 999–1009.
Rustin, M., (2010), 'Nouns and verbs: old and new strategies for sociology', in J. Burnett, S. Jeffers and G. Thomas (eds), *New Social Connections*, Basingstoke: Palgrave.
Savage, M., (2010), *Identities and Social Change in Britain since 1940: The Politics of Method*, Oxford: Oxford University Press.
Savage, M. and Burrows, R., (2007), 'The coming crisis of empirical sociology', *Sociology*, 41(5): 885–899.
Savage, M. and Burrows, R., (2009), 'Some further reflections on the coming crisis of empirical sociology', *Sociology*, 43(4): 762–772.
Skinner, Q. (ed.), (1985), *The Return of Grand Theory in the Human Sciences*, Cambridge: Cambridge University Press.
Urry, J., (2002), *Consuming Places*, London: Routledge.
Webber, R., (2009), 'Response to "The Coming Crisis of Empirical Sociology": an outline of the research potential of administrative and transactional data', *Sociology*, 43(1): 169–178.

# Notes on contributors

**Lisa Adkins** is Professor of Sociology at the University of Newcastle, Australia. She has written widely in the areas of economic sociology, social and cultural theory and the sociology of gender. Publications include *Revisions: Gender and Sexuality in Later Modernity* (2002) and *Feminism after Bourdieu* (2005) as well as recent journal special issues on the themes of *'What is the Empirical?'* (2009, with C. Lury) and *'Restless Capitalism'* (2008, with E. Jokinen). She is currently writing a manuscript bringing together her recent work on changing temporalities of value and labour in contemporary capitalism. e-mail: lisa.adkins@newcastle.edu.au

**Adam Arvidsson** teaches sociology at the University of Milano and does research on new media and reputation economies at the Copenhagen Business School. He is the author of *Brands: Meaning and Value in Media Culture* (London: Routledge, 2006). His new book, *The Ethical Economy: An Argument for the Democratization of Value* (co-authored with Nicolai Peitersen) is forthcoming with Columbia University Press in 2012. e-mail: adam.arvidsson@unimi.it

**Roger Burrows** is Professor of Sociology at Goldsmiths, University of London, UK. Prior to this he was Professor of Sociology at the University of York. His current research is in the areas of urban studies and social informatics. e-mail: r.burrows@gold.ac.uk

**Nicholas Gane** is Reader in Sociology at the University of York, UK. His research interests lie broadly in the fields of social and cultural theory. His publications include *Max Weber and Postmodern Theory* (Palgrave, 2002); *The Future of Social Theory* (Continuum, 2004); and *New Media: The Key Concepts* (with David Beer, Berg, 2008). He is currently working on a book entitled *Max Weber Today* to be published in 2012 with Palgrave. e-mail: nicholas.gane@york.ac.uk

**Ana Gross** is a Sociology PhD student at Goldsmiths College, University of London. Her current research investigates contemporary data forms and focuses on the qualification processes and devices which enable the emergence of data units as differentiated entities. Her thesis draws on Science and Technology Studies, Actor Network Theory and Economic Sociology while empirically engaging with data regulations and data manipulation and visualization technologies. Her project is currently funded by the Economic and Social Research Council. e-mail: anagross@gmail.com

**Aidan Kelly** is Senior Lecturer in social research methods in the Department of Sociology at Goldsmiths, University of London. His recent research has been on the modelling of RAE 2008 outcomes in Business and Management Studies and the use of citation metrics to evaluate research quality (see http://www.the-abs.org.uk/files//RAE2008_ABS2009_final.pdf). He is an editor of the *ABS Guide to Journal Quality in Business and Management Studies*. e-mail: a.kelly@gold.ac.uk

**Celia Lury** is a Professor of Sociology and Director of the Centre for Interdisciplinary Methodologies, Warwick University. She has written widely on the culture industry, branding and consumer culture. Publications include *Global Culture Industry: The Mediation of Things* (Polity, 2007, with Scott Lash), *Branding: The Logos of the Global Economy* (Routledge, 2004), and *Consumer Culture* (2nd edn, Polity and Rutgers, 2010). She is currently researching issues of method, measurement and value in the context of a topological rationality. e-mail: c.lury@gold.ac.uk

**Fabian Muniesa** is a Senior Researcher at the Centre de Sociologie de l'Innovation (CSI) in the Ecole des Mines de Paris (now Mines ParisTech), France. His research contributions are mostly located in the fields of science and technology studies and economic sociology. His work primarily aims at developing a pragmatist, materialist approach to the study of calculation, valuation and organization. His past and current research interests include the automation of financial markets, the practice of economics, the implementation of performance indicators, the pedagogy of business and the anthropology of experiments in the social sciences. He is currently working on a research project titled 'Performativity in Business Education, Management Consulting and Entrepreneurial Finance' (PERFORMABUSINESS) which benefits from an ERC Starting Grant (project number 263529). e-mail: fabian.muniesa@mines-paristech.fr

**Evelyn Ruppert** is an Open University Research Associate with the Centre for Research on Socio-cultural Change (CRESC), a major ESRC-funded Open University/Manchester University research centre (http://www.cresc.ac.uk/people/dr-evelyn-ruppert). She co-convenes the *Social Life of Methods* (SLOM) theme together with John Law. Her work is in the sociology of governance and explores how methods of enumeration such as censuses and transactional registers enact different kinds of subjects and populations and make different forms of power and intervention possible. More generally, her work is concerned with how the circulation and mobilization of government digital transactional data is connected to a changing relation to data and quantification. e-mail: e.ruppert@open.ac.uk

*Notes on contributors*

**Mike Savage** is Professor of Sociology at the University of York, where he is also Director of the York European Centre for Cultural Exploration. His recent books include the co-authored *Culture, Class, Distinction* (Routledge, 2009) and *Identities and Social Change in Britain since 1940: The Politics of Method* (Oxford University Press, 2010). e-mail: mike.savage@york.ac.uk

**Emma Uprichard** is a Senior Lecturer in the Department of Sociology at Goldsmiths, University of London. She has a particular interest in the methodological challenge of applying complexity theory as a way of studying social change through time and space. She is currently PI on the ESRC grant, 'Food Matters: A Sociological Case Study of Food and Eating across the Life Course in York c. 1945–2010'. Her substantive research interests include complexity theory, children and childhood, cities and urban change, time, and food. e-mail: e.uprichard@gold.ac.uk

**Helen Verran** is a Reader in History and Philosophy of Science in the School of Historical and Philosophical Studies at the University of Melbourne, Australia. Her prize winning *Science and an African Logic* focuses on Yoruba (West African) numbers, measures and values. She is currently working on a book manuscript with the working title *Nature as Singular and in General: Infrastructure, Numbers and Politics*. e-mail: hrv@unimelb.edu.au

# Index

Abbott, A. 94, 95, 110, 165, 166, 170
academic research (*see also* Research Assessment Exercise) 131–2; assessment of quality 133–40
adequacy 17
Adler, P. 43–4
advertising, power of 49–50
affect 40, 47, 50; and brand valuation 46' economic value and 47, 48, 50; measurability of 41, 47, 52; objectification of 53; remediation of 8, 47–9; value and 41–6
affective proximity 49–52, 53, 54
affective relations 49–50
Ambler, T. 46
*American Sociological Review* 144
anonymity 120
anonymization 14–15, 115, 119–23
anthropology of finance 33
Article Influence Score (AIS) 144–5, 146
Arvidsson, A. 8–9
assets, intangible 8, 40, 43–4
audience segmentation 50
audit culture 131, 166, 167
audit measures 167–8
Australia *see* Snowy River
autonomy of the individual 116, 117, 118

Back, L. 167, 170
Badiou, A. 20
Baudrillard, J. 171n
Bauman, Z. 89, 164, 168
Beck, U. 164, 168
Bhaskar, R. 96, 106, 107, 109–10
biopolitics 114
Bourdieu, P. 16
Bowker, G. 96, 109
Brake, Tom 88

*Brand Asset Valuator* 46
*BrandZ* 46
brand valuation 8, 45–6, 47, 52
brands 44, 54
*British Journal of Sociology* 144, 146
British Sociological Association, *Statement of Ethical Practice* 116, 117, 118, 128
Brooke, H. 75
Burrows, R. 3, 6, 15–16, 17, 114, 123, 124, 155, 156–7, 160
business education, pedagogy of 29–32
business enterprises (*see also* corporation finance) 28
Butler, J. 167
Byrne, D. 94, 105, 110

Callon, M. 115, 127
capitalization of earnings 30, 32
case-based pedagogy 29–30
Castells, M. 168
change, measurement of 13, 94–5, 108, 109, 110
Cicourel, A. 108
Cilliers, P. 106
citation-based measures 143–5
classification/s 13, 96, 109, 114, 166; analysis of 94; category changes 94–5, 108, 109; descriptions of 94, 95, 96, 107–8; fuzzy 108
classification systems, changes in 94, 96, 110
Collins, R. 164, 165
commercial organizations, production of social data 5–6, 15, 17, 94, 156, 158
concepts 17, 161, 162, 168, 170
conceptual invention 18
confidentiality 120

*Index*

consumer culture 45, 48, 50
control society 9, 63, 71
Cooper, M. 14
copyright 122, 128
corporation finance 28–9, 30–1, 31–2, 32–4; performativity and 32
crisis of sociology 3, 6, 15, 16–17, 151–2, 158–60
Crompton, R. 157, 158
Crowdsourcing 84, 89n

*Daily Telegraph* 76–7, 78, 84
data (*see also* digital data; dirty data; social data) 5, 6; aggregation of 6, 78; from directories 97, 104, 105; government access to 73, 83–4, 85, 86; mobilization of 77–84; transactional 11, 77–84
data analysis 87–8
data assemblages 131
data economy 115–26
data processing 122–3
Data Protection Act 1998 117, 118, 120, 121, 122, 127
Data.gov 86, 87
databases 6, 114; commercial 73–4
Deleuze, G. 33, 47, 63, 170
Dennis, K. 90n
Derrida, J. 163
descriptions of classifications 94, 95, 96, 107–8
design 68, 69, 71
Desorisières, A. 9, 10, 12, 19, 107
Dewey, J. 24, 25–6, 27, 32–3
Dewing, A.S. 28–9, 30–1
digital data 6, 73, 84, 114, 123–4, 157; analysis of 87–8; political mobilization of 74, 76–7, 86
dirty data 13, 94, 103, 104–5, 107, 110
disciplinary society 63

Eagleton, T. 167
Economic and Social Research Council (ESRC), *Ethics Framework* 116, 117, 118, 128
economic value 40, 42, 47, 49; and affect 47, 48, 50; brands 45–6
Eigenfactor Score 144

empiricism: abstracted 152, 153–60, 170; parochial 17
enactment of value 132, 141
endurance 12, 21
enumerated entities 60, 65–6, 68, 71
ESRC (Economic and Social Research Council) 116, 117, 118, 128
ethics 14–15, 115, 125; and value creation in social research 115–16
event analysis 17
Every Child Matters 83–4
existence, knowledge and 106–7, 107–8, 110
expertise 6, 67–8; move away from the academy 156–7; scientific 9; threat to 2, 3, 6, 89

Facebook 49, 51, 52, 84
facts 65, 67
Filloux, F. 88
financial capitalism 32–4
financial valuation 7–8, 27–32
flank movement 8, 25–6, 323–3
food retail outlets, category changes 97–105
Fordism 40, 42–3
Foucault, M. 63, 163
Fraser, M. 125
Fuller, M. 6
Fuller, S. 165–6
funding: for social science research 3, 152, 167; for universities 136

Gadamer, H.-G. 163
Gane, N. 16–18, 167
general equivalent 52–4
general intellect 44
general sentiment 41, 46–54
geodemographics 156, 157–8
Giddens. A. 3, 164, 168
Goldthorpe, J. 169
Gouldner, A. 2, 156
government 64, 67; access to data 73, 83–4, 85, 86; knowledge and 63, 69–70, 71
governmentality 63
grand theory 17, 160–9, 170
Gross, A. 14–15

Guérois, M. 107
Guyer, J. 18

Habermas, J. 163
Hacking, I. 71–2, 96, 109
Hammer, S. 140
Harvard Business School 29
Heckscher, C. 43–4
Hirst, T. 90
history, sociology and 161–2, 162–3
human agency 15, 115, 117
Hume, D. 170

icons 20, 21, 66, 68, 70
imagination 18, 152, 153, 155, 156, 158
incommensurability 126
indices 19, 20, 66, 67–8, 70, 71; numbers as 10, 65–6
individual 125; autonomy of 116, 117, 118; relationship with aggregate 115, 116, 122, 124, 126
informed consent 14, 115, 116–19, 123
intangible assets 8, 40, 43–4
Interbrand 45–6
investment banking 33

Journal Impact Factor 144
journalists, and MPs expenses 75–6, 87–8
journals 166; articles in 143–5; ranking 145–6
judgments 132

Karpik, L. 126
Kelly, A. 15–16
Kelly's Directories, data from 97, 104, 105
Kittler, F. 48
knowledge 65, 67, 69; existence and 106–7, 107–8, 109; government policy and 63, 69–70, 71
Kundra, Vivek 86

labour time 8, 40, 42
Latour, B. 10, 21, 123, 124, 125, 126, 171n
Law, J. 158

Lazarsfeld, P. 152, 154, 159
life, value of 114–15
Lippmann, W. 28
Liu, A. 40
longitudinal quantitative analysis 13–14, 93–7, 107–10
Lyotard, J. 167

Mackenzie, A. 6
Marsh, C. 108
Marx, K. 54, 162
material production 43–4
measurement 6–7, 106, 132, 159; literal/by fiat 108–9; performativity of 3, 16; politics of 12–13, 13–14, 187, 189; scientific 10–11; of the social 5, 108–9, 124; spaces of 9
measures 8, 21; and control society 60–1, 63, 69; as representations 106
media, and digital data analysis 87–8
mental communion 48, 54
method/s 1, 3, 153, 159, 170; theory and 152, 170
methodology: quantitative 154, 156–8, 159–60; sociological 1, 2, 153–4, 156, 157, 158–9; statistical 154
metrics, in academic life 131, 134–6; 'shadow' 140–5
Mills, C.W. 2, 17, 94; *The Sociological Imagination* 152, 153–6, 158–62, 167, 168–9, 170
mobilization: of data 77–84, 86; of the public 84–6, 87
model of river-reach 64–5, 68
modernity 168
more-than-representational spaces 18–19, 21
Morris, C.W. 27
MPs expenses scandal 11, 74, 75–7, 87; transactional data 77–84
multivariate cluster analysis 50, 51
Muniesa, F. 7–8
Murphy, John 45

natural sciences, social science and 70
network analysis 51, 52
Nowotny, H. 20
number systems 108

*Index*

numbers 9, 20, 21, 65; changes in 20; as indices 10, 65–6; as measurements of value 66, 67; in political deliberation 9, 10; as symbols 10
Nuremberg Code 116

opinion formation 48
Outhwaite, W. 163–4, 165, 168, 169

Parisi, L. 20
Parsons, T. 152, 161
partiality 21–2, 67, 68, 70, 71
participation 21–2, 70
Paulus, F. 107
peer review 16, 134, 147; construction of statistical model to mimic 141–8
Peirce, C.S. 66
performativity 3, 16; in corporate finance 32; in social science research 131, 139–40, 141; of valuation 33
personal data 118–19, 121
Polanyi, K. 31
political mobilization 84–6, 87
politics of measurement 12–13, 13–14, 87, 89
Poovey, M. 65
post-representation 18–19
pragmatism, and valuation 7, 25–7, 29, 32, 33
prediction 94
Pringle, J. 143
privacy 118
productive time 40, 41
productivity 8, 42–3
property rights, over data 14, 119
psychographics 50–1, 53
public affect 47–9, 51
public engagement 84–6
public/private boundaries 11, 12, 84
public sphere, remediation of 47–9
publishing, politics of 166

qualitative research 50, 156, 158; cost of 154–5
quantitative analysis 13–14, 93–7, 107–10
quantitative change 95, 105–6

quantitative data 95, 108
quantitative methodology 13, 156–8, 159–60

Rayner. G. 76
Readings, B. 155
representations, measures as 106
reputation 52
Research Assessment Exercise 15, 16, 130, 135, 139, 165; 2008 140–5
research grants 143; allocation of 133, 136
research quality profiles 15, 135–6
Research Selectivity Exercise 133
research technicians 155
resemblance 68
Rheinberger, H.-J 19
Rose, N. 113–14
Ruppert, E. 11–13, 20–1, 122

Salinas, G. 46
Savage, M. 3, 6, 11–13, 17, 20–1, 114, 123, 124, 155, 156–7, 160
science 9, 10, 66–7, 69, 70
Scott, W.D. 49
sentiment analysis 51–2
shareholder value 33
signification 26–7, 32–3
signs 66
Skinner, Q. 162, 163
Smith, D. 133–4
Smith, Jackie 75, 76
Snowy River, Australia 9, 10, 61; proposed rehabilitation 62–4, 67–70
social change 95–6, 107
social data 5–6, 15, 17, 94, 121–2
social media 41, 48–9, 51–2, 53, 55
social policy units of assessment 139, 140
Social Research Association, *Ethical Guidelines* 116, 118, 120–1, 128
social sciences 10, 114, 132; ethics 14–15, value creation 14
social theory 17, 163–4, 166–7, 167–8; generational crisis 164–8

*The Sociological Imagination* (Mills) 152, 153–6, 158–62, 167, 168–9, 170
*Sociological Review* 145, 146

sociology 1; crisis of 3, 6, 15, 16–17, 151–2, 158–60; generational change 164–5; journal rankings in UK 145–6; methodology 1, 2, 153–4, 156, 157, 158–9; RAE results 136–9 (2008 140–5); units of assessment 139, 140; value of 132, 151–2, 159–60, 170
*Sociology* 146
Star, S.L. 109
Stark, D. 40
statistical co-construction 131, 141–8
statistics 9 10, 12, 154
Strathern, M. 119, 125
surveys 50, 51, 85, 131, 157
symbols 19–20, 21, 66, 67

Tarde, G. 47–8, 545
Taylorism 42, 43
theory (*see also* grand theory; social theory): methods and 152, 170; sociological 152, 161–9
TheyWorkForYou website 77, 88
Thrift, N. 18, 148n
traceability 10, 83, 123, 124, 126
traces, variables as 105–6
trajectories 93–4, 110, 126
transactional data 11, 77–84
transactional politics 11–12, 20, 74, 77
Twitter 55, 84

universities 154–5, 160; audit culture 131, 166–7; bureaucratic ethos 155, 166; metricization of 131, 132
Uprichard, E. 13–14
US VISIT programme 83

valuation 8, 16, 24, 29, 30–1; as an action 32; Dewey and 26, 33; financial 27–32; pragmatism and 7, 25–7, 29, 32, 33
value 8, 122; and affect 8, 41–6; of life 114–15; enactment of 132, 135–6, 141; measures of 8, 16, 19, 40, 66–7; method and 2; of social theory 166–7; of sociology 132, 151–2, 159–60, 170; and values 40, 41
value creation 3, 8, 14, 115–16, 126; brands 44–6, 47–9; intangible assets 42, 44; role of public affect 48–9
values 1–2, 40, 67, 69, 70; and control society 60–1; value and 40, 41
variables 106, 107; changing 94–5; as traces 105–6
Verran, H. 9–11
Virno, P. 44
visualizations of transactional data 12, 78, 80–3, 86
vital emissions 120, 122; conversion into data 115, 121, 123
vitality 14, 113

Waldby, C. 113
Web 2.0 devices 74, 77, 84–6, 87, 88
Weber, M. 2, 162
Winnert, R. 76

Yellow Pages, data from 97, 104, 105
York, food outlets, changing classifications of 95, 97–107

zombie canon 17, 18, 168, 169